The Athenian Empire
Fifth Edition

LACTOR Sourcebooks in Ancient History

For more than half a century, *LACTOR Sourcebooks in Ancient History* have been providing for the needs of students at schools and universities who are studying ancient history in English translation. Each volume focuses on a particular period or topic and offers a generous and judicious selection of primary texts in new translations. The texts selected include not only extracts from important literary sources but also numerous inscriptions, coin legends and extracts from legal and other texts, which are not otherwise easy for students to access. Many volumes include annotation as well as a glossary, maps and other relevant illustrations, and sometimes a short Introduction. The volumes are written and reviewed by experienced teachers of ancient history at both schools and universities. The series is now being published in print and digital form by Cambridge University Press, with plans for both new editions and completely new volumes.

Osborne	*The Athenian Empire*
Osborne	*The Old Oligarch*
Cooley	*Cicero's Consulship Campaign*
Grocock	*Inscriptions of Roman Britain*
Osborne	*Athenian Democracy*
Santangelo	*Late Republican Rome, 88-31 BC*
Warmington/Miller	*Inscriptions of the Roman Empire, AD 14-117*
Treggiari	*Cicero's Cilician Letters*
Rathbone/Rathbone	*Literary Sources for Roman Britain*
Sabben-Clare/Warman	*The Culture of Athens*
Stockton	*From the Gracchi to Sulla*
Edmondson	*Dio: the Julio-Claudians*
Brosius	*The Persian Empire from Cyrus II to Artaxerxes I*
Cooley/Wilson	*The Age of Augustus*
Levick	*The High Tide of Empire*
Cooley	*Tiberius to Nero*
Cooley	*The Flavians*
Cooley	*Sparta*

The Athenian Empire

Fifth Edition

——

Translated and edited with notes by
ROBIN OSBORNE
University of Cambridge

CAMBRIDGE
UNIVERSITY PRESS

Shaftesbury Road, Cambridge CB2 8EA, United Kingdom

One Liberty Plaza, 20th Floor, New York, NY 10006, USA

477 Williamstown Road, Port Melbourne, VIC 3207, Australia

314–321, 3rd Floor, Plot 3, Splendor Forum, Jasola District Centre, New Delhi – 110025, India

103 Penang Road, #05–06/07, Visioncrest Commercial, Singapore 238467

Cambridge University Press is part of Cambridge University Press & Assessment,
a department of the University of Cambridge.

We share the University's mission to contribute to society through the pursuit of
education, learning and research at the highest international levels of excellence.

www.cambridge.org
Information on this title: www.cambridge.org/9781009383646
DOI: 10.1017/9781009383622

Fourth edition ©The London Association of Classical Teachers 2000.

Fifth edition published by Cambridge University Press and Assessment, © The London Association of Classical
Teachers 2023.

First published 2023

A catalogue record for this publication is available from the British Library.

A Cataloging-in-Publication data record for this book is available from the Library of Congress.

ISBN 978-1-009-38364-6 Paperback

PREFACE TO THE FOURTH EDITION

LACTOR No.1 *The Athenian Empire* has in its previous 3 editions been the most widely used of LACTORs, and the London Association of Classical Teachers Publications Sub-committee was keen that it should be kept up to date. Simon Hornblower, who was primarily responsible for the last revision, preferred to leave the task to another, and at the request of the LACTOR Committee I undertook it. I expected that I should do little except bring the epigraphy and the bibliography up to date. In the event, however, this has been a radical revision, and since this will render using the fourth edition side by side with the third difficult, the user is owed an explanation.

LACTOR No. 1 started life in 1968 as a translation of the passages listed in 'Index III. The Athenian Empire' of Hill's *Sources for Greek History, B.C. 478-431* (second edition edited by R. Meiggs and A. Andrewes, Oxford, 1951). Although much material was subsequently added, not least in the way of notes and comment, the third edition continued to reflect that origin, being much fuller on material from before 431 B.C. than on later material. But many quite fundamental questions about Athens' Empire which texts relating to events down to 431 illuminate only fitfully are cast into a far more searching, even lurid, light by material related to later events. Not least among these are the fundamental questions about whether, and, if so, why and when the character of Athenian imperialism changed, and about the popularity of the Athenian empire.

I decided, therefore, that it would be appropriate substantially to supplement the material relating to the years between 431 and the end of the Peloponnesian War. One further consequence of this is that some material relating to those years which previously featured as illustrating institutions has now found a place in the expanded chronological section. Although some may see my decision to include more material in the chronological section as retrograde, I make no apology for it: only if one is aware of the chronological context of material, is it possible to make a sensible decision about whether it particularly reflects the conditions of its time or rather attitudes and behaviour that prevailed more generally.

In order the more closely to juxtapose Thucydides' account of the years between the Persian and Peloponnesian Wars (478–432, the Pentekontaetia) with the often divergent information derived from other ancient sources I have split up the Pentekontaetia, which was previously presented as a unit.

I have re-translated all the material presented here, although I have made frequent use of earlier translations, as also of suggestions from commentators (most notably Simon Hornblower's revision of Jowett's translation of Thucydides).

For all that I have made extensive changes, the body of the older editions survives under the new clothing. The bulk of the material collected in the earlier editions is present here, often in precisely the same order, and I have incorporated much editorial material wholesale. I am therefore greatly in the debt of earlier editors, and particularly of John Davies and Simon Hornblower. Simon Hornblower has placed me further in his debt by reading and commenting extensively on an earlier draft; among other things Note G on Religious aspects of Athenian Imperialism is here as a direct result of his intervention. I am also very grateful to John Roberts, John Murrell and Mark

Greenstock for reading the first draft and improving it in all sorts of ways, to Ken Hughes for his careful copy-editing, to Charles Crowther who helped produce the images of inscriptions, and to Henry Kim who kindly supplied the maps.

Robin Osborne

Corpus Christi College, Oxford

TABLE OF CONTENTS
(Numbers in bold print refer to passages)   *Page*

PART I. The Story of Empire

List of Maps, Tables and Figures

Maps

Table

Figures

Notes and Abbreviations

All dates are B.C. unless otherwise stated.

'Archaic period' is used to refer to the years 700-500; 'Classical period' is used to refer to the years 500-300; 'Hellenistic period' is used to refer to the years 300-100. Square brackets have been used to enclose editorial material inserted into texts. This material includes chapter and section numbers, explanatory glosses, and more or less conjectural supplements to fragmentary epigraphic texts e.g. [23.1] *or* The city [of Athens] *or* Peri[kles proposed]. In epigraphic texts, although I have sometimes put a square bracket part way through a proper name, in the case of words other than proper names that cannot be completely read on a stone I have decided whether or not there is serious doubt about the restoration, putting the English translation into square brackets only when such doubt exists.

Inscriptions are given by reference to ML if in that selection, by reference to *IG* or relevant corpus if not. See Concordance for references to Fornara. I give the most recent SEG reference for inscriptions on which comments have appeared in SEG since the last SEG index volume (Index to Vols. 26-35). Earlier SEG appearances can be traced back from the most recent.

AE	R. Meiggs *The Athenian Empire* (Oxford, 1972)
B	Section B of G. Hill (revised R. Meiggs and A. Andrewes) *Sources for Greek History B.C. 478-431*(Oxford, 1951)
CAH	*Cambridge Ancient History* 2nd edition
FGH	F. Jacoby ed. *Die Fragmente der griechischer Historiker* (1923-)
GD	P. Bruneau, J. Ducat *Guide de Délos* (ed.3) (Paris, 1983)
IG	*Inscriptiones Graecae*
ML	R. Meiggs and D.M. Lewis *A Selection of Greek Historical Inscriptions to the end of the Peloponnesian War* (revised edition, Oxford, 1988)
SEG	*Supplementum Epigraphicum Graecum*
Tod	M.N. Tod *Greek Historical Inscriptions.* Vol.2 (Oxford, 1947)

6 obols = 1 drachma (dr.)
100 drachmas = 1 mina or mna
60 minas = 1 talent (T)
1 Kyzikene stater $\simeq$ 25 dr.
1 medimnos = 52.5 litres $\simeq$ 35kg wheat, 30kg barley

Alphabetical List of Authors

Table of Concordance for Inscriptions

LACTOR 1⁴	LACTOR 1³	Hill²	*IG* i³	ML	Fornara	Subject
41	41	B9	1144			Casualty list
42		B14		33.1-4	78	Casualty list
43				34	77	Epitaph
44	44	B16	1150			Casualty list
45		B18		35.1-2		Argive casualties
46				36.1-4	80	Spartan victory dedication
62			227	70	138	Herakleides
67	140	B60		48		Casualty list
72			1164			Lemnian casualties
76	118	B54	41.90-109			Hestiaia
78	119	B53	40	52	103	Khalkis
90		B61	363	55	113	Athenian expenditure
91	107	B62	48	56.15-23	115	Samos
95			1180			Casualty list
120			65.7-24			Apollophanes
121	159	B82	61	65	128	Methone
122	160	B83	62			Aphytis and Poteidaia
123	161	B84	63			Aphytis
134			66.10-27			Mytilene
136	87	B86	68	68	133	Tribute collection
137C			1468bis			Athenian dedication on Delos
138	76	B87	71	69	136	425/4 Tribute Reassessment
172			96			Samos
174				82	152	Hegelokhos
179	98	B89	101	89	156	Neapolis
182	171	B90	118	87	162	Selymbria
183	99	B92	127	94	166	Samos
190	85	B46	34	46	98	Tribute payment
195	69	B43.36-8	439	59	120	Parthenon accounts
196	70	B65	465	60.11-13	118B	Propylaia accounts
197	71	B69	49.14-16		117	Water-supply
198	157	B39	1453	45	97	Coinage
205			78	73	140	Eleusis Firstfruits
207			130			Apollo Delios
208			1468			Theoroi to Delos
210			1460			Amphiktions at Delos
216	106	B26	14-15	40	71	Erythrai
217	129	B116				Erythrai magistrates
218	130	B30	21		92	Miletos
219	131	B49	37	47	99	Kolophon
220			1454			Karpathos
232	135	B55	46	49	100	Brea
234	172	B10	10	31	68	Phaselis
235	147	B33	19			Akheloion
236			27			Delphians

237	149	B80	156			Leonidas
238	150	B91	110	90	160	Oiniades
239	174		422.217-8, 375-8	(79)	(147D)	Property of Hermokopids
240	174		424.15-23	(79)	(147D)	Property of Hermokopids
241	174		426.43-51, 144-6, 161-2	(79)	(147D)	Property of Hermokopids
242	174		427.77-8	(79)	(147D)	Property of Hermokopids
243	174		430.11-13	(79)	(147D)	Property of Hermokopids
246	60	B93	(ii² 43. 15-46)	(Tod II 123)	(Harding 35)	Second Athenian Confederacy

Glossary

Agora	The city-centre, where people gathered to talk both for political purposes and to buy and sell. At Athens it contained the Council Chamber and lawcourts.
Akropolis	The citadel of a city, usually the site of the temple of the patron deity. At Athens the site of the Parthenon and Erekhtheion and the place where most stelai were erected.
Archon (*arkhōn*, pl. *arkhontes*)	A general word for a magistrate or official, but particularly used in Athens of the nine archons who had once been the principal or only Athenian magistrates. In the classical period they were chosen by lot and had mainly religious and judicial functions. One archon, the so-called Eponymous Archon, gave his name to the year at Athens: 'when Euthynos was archon...'. See also below on Polemarch.
Assembly (*ekklēsia*)	The meeting of the Athenian people some 40 times a year, usually on the Pnyx hill, at which all major public decisions were taken.
Cleruchy (*klēroukhia*)	See p.118.
Council (*boulē*)	Body of 500 Athenians over the age of 30 selected by lot, 50 from each of the ten Athenian tribes, to serve for a year as the committee which prepared business for the Assembly and saw that the Assembly's decisions were carried out.
Dikasts	The men who manned an Athenian lawcourt. The dikasts for any particular case were selected by lot from a panel of 6,000, had to be over 30 years old and voted by secret ballot without prior discussion and without a judge to direct them.
Eisphora (paying-in)	Rich Athenians had the capital value of their assets assessed, and they were then required, as frequently as the city's finances demanded it, to pay some small percentage of this assessed value as a tax.
Eleven	The Eleven were the officials responsible for the prison and the administration of punishment to condemned criminals.
Ephors	The chief magistrates at Sparta, five in number and elected annually. They were the main executive officers responsible for carrying out the Spartan Assembly's decisions, and one or more of them might accompany a King on campaign.
Generals (*stratēgoi*)	From the end of the sixth century the Athenians elected 10 Generals each year, normally one from each of the ten tribes. Individually or in groups they commanded Athenian troops in war.
Heliaia	Perhaps more properly 'Eliaia'. The chief and largest of the Athenian lawcourts, which was used for trials over which the Thesmothetai presided.

Hellēnotamiai	A board of 10 Athenian officials who received, recorded and made payments from the tribute of the allies. In 411 their number was increased to 20 and they seem to have taken on the functions of the *kolakretai*.
Inspectors (*episkopoi*)	Officials sent out by Athens to the allies, apparently with a roving commission to see that the allies were behaving properly.
Kōlakretai	Treasurers, whose terms of appointment are not properly understood, but who are called upon to provide money for various expenses. See further on *Hellenotamiai*.
Polemarch	One of the nine archons. Once the man who commanded the Athenian army, the Polemarch in the classical period had a particular role dealing with court cases involving non-Athenians.
President (*epistatēs*)	The man chosen by lot to chair the prytaneis for one day.
Proxenoi	Men who represented the interests of another city while living in their own community. The title was an honorific one, but *proxenoi* could expect good treatment from the city whose interests they served, and Athens came to be particularly protective of its *proxenoi*, who were not always popular with their own communities.
Prytaneis/prytany/ Prytaneion	The 50 Council Members from each tribe took it in turns to serve for a tenth of the year as prytaneis, that is as a standing committee of the Council, dealing with day-to-day emergencies and preparing Council business. The period of 35-36 days for which each tribe served was known as a 'prytany'. The building in which public hospitality was given was known as the Prytaneion.
Scrutiny (*euthynai*)	At the end of their term of office all public officials were subjected to an official scrutiny of their conduct while in office.
Sellers (*Pōlētai*)	Magistrates responsible for selling confiscated property, the rights to farm taxes, etc. to the highest bidder.
Stēlē (pl. stēlai)	A slab (of stone) on which inscriptions were carved.
Thesmothetai	The collective name for the six 'junior' archons, i.e. not the Eponymous Archon, Polemarch or King Archon. They were responsible for arranging trials.
Tribes (*phylai*)	In the reforms which were the basis of the classical democracy Kleisthenes divided the Athenians into 10 groups on the basis of their village or ward of residence. These 10 groups took their names from old Athenian heroes: Erekhtheus gave his name to the tribe Erekhtheis, Kekrops to the tribe Kekropis, Aias of Salamis to the tribe Aiantis and so on.

Notes on Authors and Works Quoted

Aelian (*c*.A.D.170-235). Part of the movement known as the 'Second Sophistic', which emulated the intellectual style of the fifth- and fourth-century Sophists. His *Varia Historia* excerpts sources which are often now lost, but even when those sources were themselves good, Aelian seems capable of introducing confusion and distortion, sometimes for moralising purposes.

Andokides (*c*.440-390). Athenian orator and politician who was involved in and informed upon the plot to mutilate the Herms in 415. Speech 3 was delivered in 392/1 after Andokides had been an ambassador to a peace conference at Sparta; in it Andokides tried unsuccessfully to persuade the Athenians to sign a peace treaty, and his claims in that speech, some of which are flagrantly false, have to be read in the light of his aims. See especially A. Missiou *The Subversive Oratory of Andocides* (Cambridge, 1992).

[Andokides] 4 *Against Alkibiades*. Preserved among the works of Andokides, this seems rather to be a well-informed literary exercise, perhaps dating to the 360s.

Antiphon (flourished 420-411). The first Athenian to write speeches for others to deliver and almost certainly himself prominent in the oligarchic coup of 411. Six speeches substantially survive (see M. Gagarin *Antiphon: Speeches* (Cambridge, 1996)), along with a collection of model speeches (*The Tetralogies*).

Aristophanes (*c*.445-after 375?). Comic dramatist whose earliest recorded work is the *Babylonians* of 427 and latest the *Wealth* of 389. The earlier of the eleven surviving plays all choose political targets.

Scholia on Aristophanes: line-by-line commentaries, sometimes deriving their information entirely from the text but on other occasions conveying the fruits of impressive Alexandrian critical scholarship.

Aristotle (384-322). His *Politics* seems to derive from lectures given by the philosopher in the 330s and is rich in allusions to particular political incidents as well as generalised claims about political behaviour.

[Aristotle] *Constitution of the Athenians* (*Athenaion Politeia* or *Ath. Pol.*). This work, largely known from a papyrus purchased by the British Museum in 1888-9 and published in 1891, is the only one of the 158 Constitutions of Greek states compiled under Aristotle's direction substantially surviving. Written in the 320s, it consists of a history of the Athenian constitution down to the end of the fifth century, followed by a description of how the Athenian constitution worked in the later fourth century. The historical section is compiled from earlier written accounts, particularly those by the local historians of Athens known as Atthidographers. There is a magisterial commentary on the whole work by P.J. Rhodes (Oxford, 1981, with addenda 1993).

Demosthenes (384-322). The most famous of all Athenian orators and an influential fourth-century politician. From the late 350s until the battle of Khaironeia in 337 Demosthenes urged the Athenians to resist Philip II of Macedon's expansionism. One of Demosthenes' chief persuasive gambits was comparing the Athenians of the fourth-century with (a rose-tinted view of) their fifth-century ancestors.

Diodoros (active 60-36 B.C.). A native of Sicily, Diodoros wrote a *Universal History* in 40 books, which attempted to give a year-by-year account of both Greek and Roman history. For much of his account of fifth-century Greece he seems to have followed the fourth-century historian Ephoros of Kyme. Ephoros organised his history by topic rather than by year, and Diodoros is inclined to include under a single year events that spread across several (he covers almost a decade as a single year at 11.60-61). At his best he conveys the virtues as well as the vices of his sources, at his worst he garbles even the accounts he has before him.

Dionysios of Halikarnassos (active 30-8 B.C.). Antiquarian and writer on rhetoric whose *Roman Antiquities* were published in 7 B.C. as an encomium of Roman virtues.

Eupolis (active 429-412). Comic dramatist, older contemporary and rival of Aristophanes. His plays include one ridiculing the wealthy Kallias son of Hipponikos and the sophists, one attacking Hyperbolos, and one bringing great Athenians of the past back from the Underworld. His *Cities* seems to date to *c.*420.

Harpokration (late second century A.D.). Alexandrian lexicographer, whose *Lexicon of the Ten Orators* is designed as an aid to reading Attic Greek. He draws his information both from scholars of the imperial age and from direct acquaintance with Classical and Hellenistic works of history and scholarship, as well as from the orators themselves.

Herodotos (*c.*480-410). Born at Halikarnassos but from its foundation resident at Thourioi, Herodotos (Hdt.) seems to have been writing his *Histories* during the Peloponnesian War, but his allusions to events after the defeat of the Persians in 479 are few, perhaps for political reasons.

Hesykhios (C5 A.D.). Lexicographer, whose work is preserved only in an abridged version. He based his work on earlier lexica.

Isokrates (436-338). Although not himself active as a speaker in the Athenian assembly, Isokrates' written orations provide an important commentary on Athenian politics in the fourth century, and he was important enough as a teacher of rhetoric to be attacked by Plato in his *Phaidros*. Isokrates thought that Greek cities should work together, and he urged Philip to lead the Greek states in a campaign against Persia.

Ktesias (late C5). Greek doctor from Knidos, who worked at the court of Artaxerxes II and wrote a history of Persia in 23 books, which preserves much entertaining gossip and perhaps some accurate history.

Lysias (459/8 or later-*c.*380). For the tradition about his early life, see **83**, where his residence in Thourioi is fact, but the date at which he moved there may be false. Lysias returned to Athens in 412/11. As a resident alien (metic), Lysias could take no part in the Athenian Assembly, but many of his forensic speeches have a political slant. In his Funeral Oration he turns his skill at glossing over inconvenient facts to the service of the encomium of Athens. He too is attacked in Plato's *Phaidros*.

Pausanias (fl. *c.*A.D. 150). Author of a *Guide to Greece*, whose 9 books cover the southern and central parts of the Greek mainland. In describing classical remains, he includes, as well as archaeological and topographical information, much accurate historical material drawn from both oral and written sources.

Plato (*c.*429-347). The works of the Athenian philosopher are frequently given a more or less specific historical setting, but other historical allusions in the Dialogues are rare. The *Seventh Letter*, whose genuineness is uncertain, is autobiographical.

Plutarch (before A.D. 50 - after A.D.120). Philosopher and biographer from Khaironeia in Boiotia, who also became a priest at Delphi. He himself insists that his *Parallel Lives*, of which we have 23 pairs, are not history, and he is interested in character rather than the analysis of events. He was extremely well read, although given to anachronistic assumptions and not consistently critical of his own sources.

Strabo (64-after A.D. 21). Author of a *Geography* in 17 books. This is a rich source of information about the world of his own day, but only occasionally sheds light on classical Greece.

Theophrastos of Eresos (*c*.371-287). Successor to Aristotle as head of the Lyceum. Several works (*On Plants, On Stones* etc.) survive, but the work that would be most useful to historians, *On Laws*, survives only in later quotations.

Theopompos of Khios (378/7-*c*.320). Historian whose epitome of Herodotos, continuation of Thucydides, and history of Philip of Macedon survive only in later quotations. His work displayed wide interests and frequent digressions, was laudatory of Philip and critical of Athens. Both his erudition and his strong invectives were famous in antiquity.

Thucydides (*c*.455-*c*.400). Athenian of aristocratic background with Thracian connections whose *History of the Peloponnesian War* in 8 books, with its account in Book 1 of the years between the Persian and Peloponnesian Wars, forms the backbone of all subsequent histories of Greece during this period. See further Note B (p.3).

Xenophon (*c*.430-*c*.350). Athenian who wrote *Memoirs of Sokrates*, an account of a mercenary expedition into the heart of Persia (the *Anabasis*), a continuation of Thucydides down to 362 (the *Hellenika*), and a number of pamphlets. Exiled from Athens for fighting against her at Koroneia in 394, he spent some time in Sparta and on an estate in Elis before retiring to Corinth. His historical works combine accurate detail and some perceptive analysis with a certain economy with the truth. His *Poroi*, written in the 350s, advises Athens on how to improve her economy.

[Xenophon] *Constitution of the Athenians*. This short work included among the pamphlets of Xenophon is distinct from them in style. From its historical allusions it has been thought to date to the late 420s, and it is thus the earliest surviving work of Attic prose. The author, who is often referred to as the 'Old Oligarch', explains, as if to oligarchs outside Athens, how it is that democracy sustains itself in Athens and cannot easily be overthrown. Although it offers little detailed historical analysis, it mentions in passing much that we are not told by other literary sources.

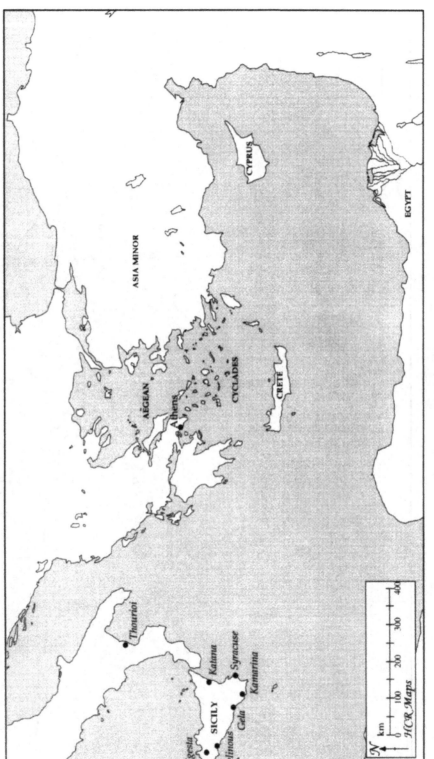

The Central and Eastern Mediterranean.

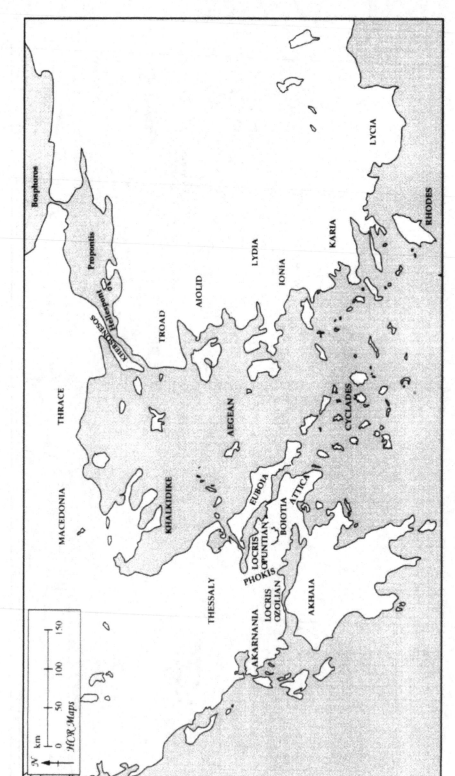

Greece and the Aegean and Asia Minor, indicating countries and regions.

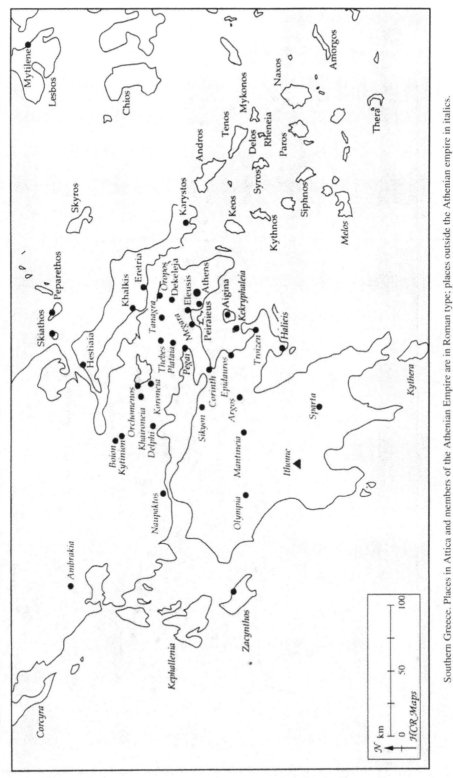

Southern Greece. Places in Attica and members of the Athenian Empire are in Roman type: places outside the Athenian empire in italics.

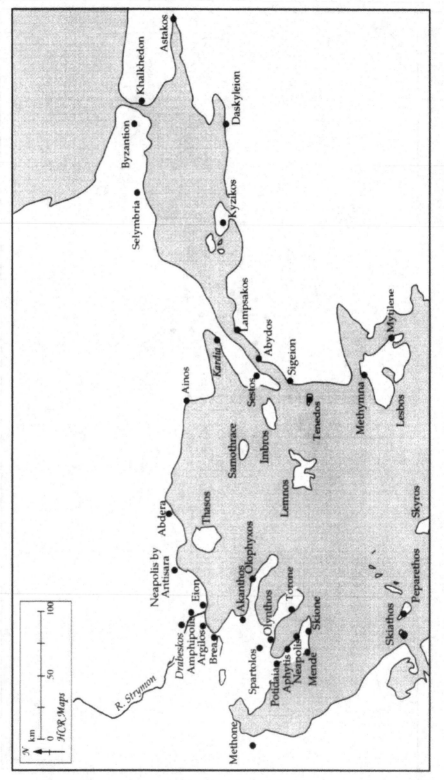

Northern Greece. Members of the Athenian Empire are in Roman type; places outside the Athenian empire in italics.

Greek Asia Minor. Members of the Athenian Empire in Roman type; places outside the Athenian empire in italics.

Part I The Story of Empire

Note A   When did Athenian imperialism begin?

Athens was one of few settlements in southern Greece continuously occupied from the Bronze Age through into the archaic period. The territory of Attica, which Athens came to dominate, seems to have served as a temporary refuge for those who, in the upheavals surrounding the destruction of the Mycenaean palaces, made their way east. Graves in the cemetery at Perati, belonging to the very last phase of the Bronze Age (known as L(ate) H(elladic) IIIC), seem to give evidence of transitory settlement in Attica of men moving east across the Aegean. In particular the artefactual assemblages at Perati can be closely paralleled with those found at Ialysos on Rhodes. Two centuries or so later close archaeological links can once more be found between Athens and the new foundation at Miletos. These archaeological similarities do not justify our believing the details of later stories of an 'Ionian Migration' from Athens to the coast of Asia Minor, but they do make it clear that close links between Athens and the eastern Aegean and its coasts go back to, and were to some extent maintained during, the Dark Age (c.1200-700).

Athens was certainly one of the best connected of Greek settlements during much of the Dark Age, receiving exotic goods from outside as well as within the Greek world, and exporting both her pottery and its innovative styles. In the eighth century Athens stands out in the Greek world for the quantity and quality of material recovered from her extensive cemeteries, and figurative art is pioneered by the painters of Athenian pottery. But in the eighth century Athens was increasingly isolated from the rest of the Greek world: little Athenian pottery of the second half of the eighth century was exported and Athens did not play any leading role in the establishment of settlements abroad that other cities pioneered during this period. At the end of the eighth century both the nature and the quantity of archaeological material recovered from Attica change markedly. The reasons for these peculiar developments are not certain, but some sort of social, and perhaps political, crisis seems highly likely.

It is only in the later seventh and early sixth century that Athens rejoins the mainstream of Greek cities, adopting a style of pot painting that borrows from Corinthian pottery and then eclipses it in the international market, establishing a settlement abroad at Sigeion at the mouth of the Hellespont, setting up a major festival involving competitive games (the Great Panathenaia, 566) and acquiring a 'tyrant' (a man who ruled by virtue of popularity and/or force, not constitutional position). Athenian families were prominent members of the international aristocracy of the sixth century (both the favourite and the eventual winner of the competition for the hand of the daughter of Kleisthenes, tyrant of Sikyon, were Athenians, Herodotos 6.126-131), but Athens as a state remained minor, having to fight repeatedly to remove the island of Salamis, just off her coast, from the control of her small neighbour Megara (finally sending settlers there in the last decade of the century, ML14), and even at the end of the century engaging inconclusively in warfare with the small Saronic island of Aigina.

Why was Athens not a more important power in the Greek world before the Persian Wars? and why did she become so important in the early fifth century? The answer to the first question may lie in part in the size of Attica. At about 2,400 square km., Athens' territory surpassed that of any other single city, except Sparta, in size. Archaeological evidence suggests that until the classical period even the agricultural potential of this territory was not fully exploited: Athenians had less reason than many to look elsewhere. Another part of the answer may lie in population size. Although the increase during the eighth century in the number of graves known from Attica has sometimes been taken to indicate a population explosion, changes in burial practice seem rather more likely. It may be only in the late sixth century that Athens began to have manpower at her disposal sufficient to encourage and sustain military activity on a large scale. Peter Garnsey has estimated that it was only in the fifth century that Athens began to need to import grain every year, rather than just in bad years, in order to feed her population.

Having manpower does not make a state powerful if it cannot organise that manpower. Whether or not Kleisthenes advertised to the Athenians that his reforms which established democracy would give them a more powerful army, there is little doubt that a more powerful army was indeed what they produced. The ten new 'tribes' that Kleisthenes created, which cut across regional loyalties within Attica and ensured that the Athenian Council always represented all local interest groups, were also used as the basis for an Athenian army. The effectiveness of the new army was immediately demonstrated by a victory over the Boiotians and Khalkidians together, which was used to establish an Athenian settlement at Khalkis, and the subsequent creation of 10 Generals and weakening of the military role of the Polemarch further strengthened the force.

If Athens' emergence as a major power has something to do with organised manpower, it also has something to do with monetary resources. The silver mines in the Laureion area of southern Attica were exploited as early as the Bronze Age, but systematic exploitation on a large scale seems to have been a feature only of the later sixth century, by which time, at least, the silver resources were treated as public property. Athens' earliest silver coinage, minted in the middle of the century, was not made of Laureion silver, but the 'owl' series, first struck probably in the 520s, was. Herodotos and the Aristotelian *Constitution of the Athenians* tell us that Themistokles persuaded the Athenians in the early fifth century to divert the considerable profits from the mines to the construction of the 170-oared warships known as triremes, and so create the naval power that ended up largely responsible for the defeat of the Persians at Salamis.

Some Athenian families had enjoyed close relations with the rulers of Lydia in the first half of the sixth century, and at the end of that century some were prepared to contemplate equally close relations with Persia. But by the time that an appeal came from the Ionians for help in throwing out their Persian-backed tyrants and revolting from Persia, Athens was prepared to send twenty ships, perhaps half her fleet, when the only other Greek mainland city to send help was Eretria which sent five ships, and then only, Herodotos says, to please the Milesians (Hdt. 5.99.1). The short-lived Athenian involvement in the Ionian Revolt showed that Athenians saw themselves as actors on more than just the local stage. By encouraging the Persian expeditions of 490 and 480-79, the Revolt ensured that Athens had to continue to embrace wider interests in order to protect her own.

Herodotos calls the Ionian Revolt 'the beginning of evils for the Greeks'; it might also be called the beginning of Athenian imperialism, for it set in chain the events that put empire within the Athenian grasp. So why did Athens send those twenty ships? Herodotos views the fact that Kleomenes king of Sparta responded negatively to the

Ionian request for help while Athens responded positively as a sign that it was easier to deceive 30,000 men than one man (Hdt. 5.97.2). That an Assembly meeting was involved at Athens, as apparently not at Sparta, may indeed have been decisive: emotional appeals may be hard for a group to resist, and it is relatively easy to ridicule speculation about possible future consequences when addressing a crowd. Later in the century Athenians seem to have had little trouble looking at difficult decisions exclusively from the viewpoint of their own interests, narrowly defined, but in 499 neither the young democracy nor its leaders were used to weighing up conflicting priorities. In any case, with Athenians by now settled not just at Sigeion but in the Khersonesos and on Lemnos (see **72**), Athens did have interests which Persian expansionism directly threatened.

Athens' lack of a history of leadership over other states explains how she found it easy to allow Sparta (already head of the so-called Peloponnesian League) to take the lead in the Hellenic League against Persia; her involvement in the Ionian Revolt, defeat of the Persians at Marathon, massive attack on Paros in *c.*487, and crucial contribution to Greek naval successes against Xerxes' invasion explain why Ionian Greeks might quickly turn to her to spearhead the ongoing campaign against Persia when Sparta showed reluctance to continue the struggle and Spartan leaders showed dubious attitudes towards those who had been fighting on the Persian side. If Athenian intentions in the 470s are open to debate, that is perhaps not least because Athenians were new to international power and there was no popular consensus at Athens about the right way to use the opportunity that presented itself. Both later writers of an apologist persuasion, and those who believe that she had only her own interests at heart from the beginning of the so-called Delian League, may correctly identify views held by different groups within the Athenian citizen body.

Note B Handling Thucydides on the formation and growth of the Athenian Empire

Any account of the growth and (changing) character of the Athenian empire between its foundation in 478 and the outbreak of the Peloponnesian War must rest heavily upon the account which Thucydides gives of the events of these years in the chapters known as the Pentekontaetia (the 'Fifty Years') (1.89-117). No other source offers a continuous independent account of these years; many later sources are probably or demonstrably inaccurate; contemporary inscriptions are few in number for this whole period, and particularly so for the period before 450, and when inscriptions survive they are often difficult to date or ill-preserved, and never give us adequate information about their context or causes, let alone their consequences.

But Thucydides' Pentekontaetia is not, and was never intended to be, a history of the Athenian Empire. Thucydides expressly gives an account of these years in order to explain Spartan fear of Athens' growing power, and he has manifestly selected the events he mentions to this end. As a result he omits events important in the internal history of the empire but without direct bearing on Sparta (most notably Athenian diplomatic relations with Persia, but also such matters as the movement of the League Treasury from Delos to Athens and the disciplining of allies of no great military strength), just as he omits events which were crucial in Athenian constitutional history and had important indirect effects on Athenian imperialism, but which were not in his view of great moment for relations with Sparta (note especially the absence of mention of the shadowy Ephialtic reforms, although he does mention subversive activities by desperate Athenian oligarchs a little later).

Two further features of the Pentekontaetia must be borne in mind: that Thucydides' account is also an interpretation, and that it is part of a larger work (whether that work was written as a unit or in parts which were more or less thoroughly revised in the light of what was written later). To take the second point first. Thucydides stops his account of the fifty years with the suppression of the Samian revolt, but that does not mean that he thought nothing relevant happened in the period 438-432. But he had already related incidents arising from disputes involving Poteidaia and Corcyra and would have occasion later to refer to Athenian activities in Akarnania and the north Aegean. The Pentekontaetia highlights a theme and sketches the case for its importance, but the reader is left to add in further relevant data when they are revealed: these later pieces of information are part of writing persuasive history, for the reader is made to feel that they independently confirm the interpretation that the historian has offered.

To confirm his hypothesis that the war which began in 431 was a result of Spartan fear of Athens' growing power, Thucydides needs to show not only that Athenian power grew and that Sparta was afraid, but also that the power and the fear were such as to cause war in 431 when they had not caused the two powers to come into continuous hostile contact at any earlier date. (The so-called 'First' Peloponnesian War from 460-445 involved only one battle between a Spartan and an Athenian army; most of the conflict was between Athens and Sparta's allies.) Thucydides has, therefore, to offer an interpretation of earlier events which shows both how they contributed to increasing Spartan fear in the long term and how it was that they did not lead Sparta to declare war immediately. Thus it is that he adopts the story that the Spartans were content to allow the Athenians to take over the leadership of the group of largely Ionian cities keen to continue the fight against Persia; the alliance formed by this group has come to be known as the Delian League because it initially established its Treasury on the sacred island of Delos; other contemporary observers were almost certainly telling a different story (**16, 28**). Similarly, Thucydides tells of the Spartans campaigning with a large army in central Greece in 458/7 because of a desire to help two tiny places to which they were linked by Dorian descent, and fighting a battle at Tanagra because they were unable otherwise to return through the Isthmus; but the size of the army and the position of Tanagra on the Aegean side of Boiotia, and close to the border with Attica at its easiest point of entry, strongly suggest that invading Attica, or threatening its invasion, were on the Spartan agenda from the beginning.

In reading the Pentekontaetia it is worth keeping an eye on how Thucydides constructs his account. If Thucydides' criticism of Hellanikos for inaccurate chronology (**29** 1.97.2) implies anything for his own account (in which he gives no precise dates), it should be that he narrates events in the order in which he believes they occurred. But if he denies himself manipulation of order as a way of drawing attention to, or from, particular events, he still can choose to discuss those events he selects at greater or lesser length. The sense that the Athenians were doing the Ionians a good deed in taking over the Delian League is strengthened by the amount of space devoted to problems with Pausanias (**7**). The impression of Athenian innocence is reinforced by the even longer account preceding this (**4**) of the ruse by which Themistokles succeeds in preventing Sparta stopping Athens rebuilding her walls, which suggests that in the years immediately after the Persian invasion Athens was primarily concerned with protecting herself, rather than with aggrandisement. By contrast, Thucydides runs rapidly through the capture of Eion and Skyros and the war with Karystos before pausing for general reflection on the suppression of the Naxian revolt, and this, together with the glance forward contained in describing Naxos as 'the first allied city deprived of its freedom', leads the reader to see Athens' relations with her allies as changing at this point (**29** 1.98-9). Interpretation is embedded in all these decisions about brevity or dilation, and readers must keep their eyes on the way they are constantly manipulated.

As a contemporary, almost certainly born during the 450s, Thucydides was in a much better position than we are to gather information about the events of these years. But not all sorts of information were equally easy to come by, and we may suspect that it was much easier to produce narrative of military events in their correct chronological order than to recover whose arguments prevailed in a political debate which occurred before Thucydides' entry to the Assembly – even a debate at Athens, let alone one in Sparta. In having to infer intentions from results, Thucydides was in a position not so dissimilar from that in which we find ourselves, and just occasionally our knowledge of material unknown to Thucydides or different perspective on material with which he was familiar (e.g. Herodotos' *Histories*) may enable us to question his conclusions.

The uniqueness of Thucydides' account, and his (rightful) status as an outstandingly perceptive historian, have meant that modern scholars of very different interests have been reluctant to question his interpretation. Critical engagement with Thucydides' Pentekontaetia is indeed essential for any history of these crucial central years of the fifth century, but that engagement should lead not to blind copying but to a sympathetic understanding of what Thucydides is doing and to a realisation that, in some circumstances, it is wise not to treat his account as the last word.

Note C   Using literary sources other than Thucydides

Literary sources other than Thucydides (and Herodotos) fall into three broad categories. There is contemporary drama, which for our purposes effectively means comedy (there is much to be said about tragedy and empire, but little can be revealed by short quotations); there is a little fifth-century and much fourth-century oratory; and there are the compilations of later writers of histories and lives. Each of these categories of source presents different sorts of difficulties.

Comedy

Both the extant plays of Aristophanes and surviving quotations from lost plays by Aristophanes and other comic dramatists offer a window onto Athenian attitudes to empire which is at once direct and oblique. It is direct because comedy latches on to current issues, and the very choice of subject matter for jokes gives an indication of the Athenian political agenda at the time of the play. It is oblique because the issues are presented in a way designed to cause laughter, and it is not always easy to detect how that laughter is being produced. Basic comic techniques include exaggeration (as over the length of absence of the ambassadors to Persia in **58**), defeating expectation (adding a fictitious and ridiculous element to an otherwise 'straight' description; as in **203**), allegory (turning Kleon's activities into those of a dog in the kitchen in *Wasps* 891-1008), and incongruity (a familiar fact put into unfamiliar company). These techniques can be combined. The historian has to be alive both to the possibility that genuine information is part of a joke, and that an audience may laugh at practices and attitudes which they themselves continue to support and promote outside the theatre. Kleon prosecuted Aristophanes for bringing Athens into disrepute before an audience that included allies in his play *Babylonians* of 426, which suggests that it is not only we who find it difficult to draw the line between fact and fiction.

The Orators

If comic dramatists select the features that they ridicule with an eye to laughter rather than to making a political point, the distortions of the orator (as of the writer of a pamphlet such as [Xenophon]'s *Constitution of the Athenians*) tend in a rather more consistent direction. The orator's aim is to persuade, and orators select ruthlessly with an eye to the favour of the court or Assembly which they are addressing (the same applies to speeches in Thucydides, which seem to reflect partly the arguments Thucydides knew to have been used by the speakers, and partly the arguments he thought *should* have been used). Scholars often suggest that the knowledge and memory of the audience addressed must have acted as a control upon the orator's fictions, but neither court nor Assembly gave its participants much chance to talk among themselves, and the orator could certainly get away with statements which some of those addressed would know to be untrue. We rarely know the results of the debates of which surviving speeches were part, and even when we do, we are more or less entirely ignorant as to why the court or Assembly supported or did not support the speaker. Orators' words cannot, therefore, be taken to indicate either the truth or what Athenians at large thought, and the overall intention of the speaker must always be taken into account in assessing the significance of what is said.

Later Historians

Herodotos and Thucydides work on the basis of what they observe themselves and are told by others. Those who later compiled historical accounts or wrote lives depended upon what had been written earlier. They were essentially in the same position as we are, albeit with considerably more fifth-century (and later) literature surviving for them to use. Often it is possible for us to see, in broad terms at least, what sources they are using and how they are using them. The Aristotelian *Constitution of the Athenians* manifestly derives some of its information, sometimes even phraseology, from Herodotos and Thucydides; Diodoros shows that one of his most important sources, the fourth-century historian Ephoros of Kyme, produced an account of the origins of the Peloponnesian War by supplementing information drawn from Thucydides with suggestions made by Aristophanes in *Peace* in order to give an internal political motivation to Athens' entry into war that Thucydides never even hints at. When in this way we can detect the sort of source being employed, we can also observe whether or not the writer has exercised good historical judgement. But in many cases the source of information remains obscure, and we can only decide the value of the information on the basis of the nature of the story told (is it an anecdote also told of another? is it internally consistent? is its chronology possible? and so on).

Major events of modern history are written up by numerous different individuals in different contexts, and the modern historian is always in a position to weigh one source against another. Often the ancient historian is faced with an event attested by a single source. In these circumstances it is important to go beyond the single sentence in which the information is given, assess the wider context and look at the way in which the writer in question deals with events about which we are better informed. It is for this reason that passages appear in this volume which do little more than paraphrase Thucydides as well as passages which contradict Thucydides or give quite different information. Before basing an argument on any single passage the wise historian will also look at what else the author in question is prepared to claim.

Note D Chronology

In Athens years were named after one of the nine archons (who was therefore called
the Eponymous Archon) and ran from midsummer to midsummer (hence such modern
datings as 424/3); in Sparta years were named after one of the five ephors. In Argos it
was the priestess of Hera who was the eponymous figure, and since she held office for
more than one year, dates were recorded according to the number of years a particular priestess had been in office. Thucydides uses all these three cities' dating systems
to fix the start of the war (2.2.1, see also 4.133.2-3 and 5.19.1) but expresses the view
that they are not adequate for the historian's task (5.20). He himself, having fixed the
beginning of the war, dates the events of the war according to the year of the war and
whether the event occurred in 'summer' (= spring and summer, March to early
November) or 'winter'.

Archon dates are but rarely referred to in other Athenian literature, and, except when
fixing a date is important to the argument, orators are mostly vague about when things
happened. Some later historians took over Thucydides' dating system, others attempted
to work by archon year. Diodoros, who does arrange his history year by year, dates his
years by Roman consuls, Athenian archons, and the year of the Olympiad; but he is at
best only as accurate as his sources allowed him to be, and, since he worked with
sources which did not always indicate dates precisely, he not infrequently can be shown
to record events under the wrong year, group events that lasted more than a year under
a single year's entry, or record the same event twice under different years (he even
records the death of King Arkhidamos of Sparta under the year 434 and then has him
lead invasions of Boiotia in 429 and Attica in 426 (the year he really died) (12.35.4,
47.1, 52.1)). Plutarch, not writing history (as he insists at *Alexander* 1.2), has little
interest in chronology and groups events as they illuminate his subject with little regard
for whether they happened at similar times (compare **51** with **53** or **231** with **68**)

Athenian public inscriptions often, although not always, gave a date by name of
archon and by the tribe which was providing the prytaneis (see **238**). When this information survives on a stone we can be sure of the year, but because which tribe provided
the prytaneis at which stage of the year was not fixed, we often cannot pinpoint the
time of the year. Most frequently, however, inscriptions survive in so damaged a condition that even if there was once an archon's name, it can no longer be read.

In the absence of an archon's name there are three ways of dating an inscription.

a) We may be able to identify the events to which the inscription relates with events
preserved in the historical record. How securely such an identification can be made
will vary: there is little dispute that **134** relates to the Athenian settlement after the
revolt of Mytilene, a little more dispute as to whether **78** relates to the Euboian revolt
of 445 (rather than an Athenian expedition to Euboia in 424/3 not recorded in
Thucydides but alluded to by a scholiast on Aristophanes *Wasps* 718), and a very open
question as to whether it is right to associate **190** with irregular tribute payment in the
early 440s as revealed by the Tribute Quota Lists.

b) A second way of dating an inscription is from the individuals mentioned.
Kleonymos is known to have moved one decree (**121**.32-56) in 426/5 (in this case we
know because the Secretary's name appears in an inscription dated by archon name);
when Kleonymos appears proposing another decree (**136**) the possibilities that he
proposed both in the same year, and did so as a member of the Council for that year,
must be good. A more difficult case is offered by **190**. This decree was proposed by

one Kleinias. Kleinias is not a common Athenian name but was used in the family of Alkibiades. More particularly it was the name of Alkibiades' father, who is known to have been killed in the battle of Koroneia in 446. If Alkibiades' father was the proposer of the decree, then we have a firm date before which the decree must have been moved. But we cannot be absolutely confident that the same man was involved.

c) A third means of dating is on the basis of the way the inscription is carved. Certain styles of writing and certain arrangements of the script on the stone are fashionable at one period rather than another. More particularly, the forms of letters change over time: even slight acquaintance with inscriptions well dated by other means reveals how very different sixth-century inscriptions from Attica are from those from the same area written in the fourth century. Those who have made a detailed study of inscriptions acquire some confidence that they can date letter-forms rather more closely than just to a century. But how much more closely? That scholars can sometimes detect the individual idiosyncrasies of a single mason and ascribe a number of different inscriptions to his hand may be held to reduce rather than increase our confidence that it is the date alone that determines the letter-forms of inscriptions. It is reasonable to expect that an individual mason may change his writing style only slightly over a working life that may last 30 years or more, and that masons trained at different periods may produce very different work at the same time.

Much has been made in the scholarship of the changing shape of one letter in particular: sigma written with three strokes rather than four. Some scholars have suggested that the form written with just three strokes was not employed after the middle of the 440s, and that the presence of a 'three-bar sigma' therefore indicates that an inscription dates pre-445. This has long been a controversial claim, and recently the case against it has been strengthened. Laser photography has been used to detect distortions of the crystalline structure in a marble stele whose surface is abraded, and these distortions have been interpreted to suggest that a previously unreadable letter in an archon's name in an inscription (ML37) that includes a three-bar sigma indicates that the archon was Antiphon, who was in office in 418/7, almost thirty years after the three-bar sigma is supposed to have died out. Although scholars continue to debate the validity of the technique and the interpretation of the laser image, confidence in the validity of dating on the basis of the letter-forms has rightly been further undermined by this recent work: as well as the three-bar sigma this inscription includes the letter rho in a form that has in the past been reckoned not to have been used after the early 430s.

Where all three of these dating techniques point in the same direction, we may have some confidence in that conclusion. In some cases, however, the different forms of evidence conflict. Thus one fragment of **198** (from Kos, but inscribed in the Attic alphabet and thus perhaps by an Athenian mason) has a three-bar sigma, although the parody in Aristophanes *Birds* (**199**) suggests a context of the years immediately before 414. Identification of individuals involved, what is known as prosopographical information, is hardly conclusive here: the decree mentions a Klearkhos as proposer of a decree, and the only Klearkhos known to have been politically active in fifth-century Athens is a man who was on the Council in 408/7 (*IGi*[3] 515.25 cf. 112.2); but other evidence (see notes on **198**) does seem to favour a later rather than an earlier date.

It is important therefore to be aware of whether the dating of epigraphic evidence is secure and of what its basis is. Inscriptions can provide solid independent pegs on which to hang floating literary data, but when it is the literary data which are the basis for the dating of an inscription, that inscription cannot then be deployed to support the interpretation of the literary data upon which its own date depends.

1.1. THE FORMATION OF THE DELIAN LEAGUE

None of the stories about the formation of the Delian League (see above p.4) that have come down to us date from earlier than the last quarter of the fifth century. Even the earliest writers had the benefit of hindsight, and are important as evidence not merely for what happened in 479-7 but for what were the issues argued about later in the century.

To carry the struggle against Persia into Ionia and the Hellespont? Differences between Athens and Sparta

1 [87.6] This decision of the [Spartan] assembly that the truce had been broken was taken in the fourteenth year [432] of the Thirty Years' Peace which was made after the Euboian affair [445]. [88] The Spartans voted that the Peace had been broken and that war should be declared, not so much because they were persuaded by the speeches of their allies as because they feared that the Athenians might become still more powerful, seeing that the greater part of Greece was already in their hands.

[89.1] To explain, the Athenians came to the situation in which they rose to greatness in the following way. [89.2] When the Persians retreated from Europe, defeated by the Greeks both at sea and on land, and after those Persians who fled with their ships to Mykale for refuge were destroyed, Leotykhidas the Spartan king, who was the leader of the Greeks at Mykale, went back home with the allies from the Peloponnese. But the Athenians and the allies from Ionia and the Hellespont who had now revolted from the Persian King stayed behind and besieged Sestos [479], which the Persians held. They spent the winter there and captured the city, which the Persians abandoned. After this they sailed away from the Hellespont and dispersed to their own cities [spring, 478]. [Continued in 4]

Thucydides 1.87.6-89.2

2 [106.1] When the Greeks had made an end of most of the Persians, some in the battle [of Mykale] and some as they fled, they burnt the Persians' ships and their whole fortification, after they had brought the booty out from it onto the shore and had found various chests of money. After burning the fortification and the ships, they sailed away. [106.2] When they reached Samos, the Greeks took counsel about uprooting from Ionia and about the best place to found an Ionian settlement in the Greece of which they had control, abandoning Ionia to the Persians. They thought, I should explain, that it was impossible for them to defend the Ionians and keep a constant guard over them, and they had no expectation that if they did not defend the Ionians, the Persians would leave the Ionians alone. [106.3] In addition, those in command of the Peloponnesians had it in mind to uproot from their centres of trade those Greek peoples who had collaborated with the Persians, and to give their land to the Ionians to live in. But the Athenians were not happy to see Greek rule in Ionia ended, nor to have the Peloponnesians taking decisions about people who were Athenian colonists. After a keen argument, the Peloponnesians gave way. [106.4] It was in this way that they brought the Samians, Khians, Lesbians and other islanders who had fought on the Greek side into the alliance [Hellenic League], taking pledges and oaths from them to be faithful and not to revolt. Once these oaths were secured, they sailed off to break down the bridges, for they thought that they would find the bridges still stretched in position across the Hellespont.

Herodotos 9.106

Although often passed over in accounts of the Athenian empire, this episode is in fact crucial in determining that the war against Persia goes on. By their action here the Athenians establish that they intend to continue the role of protectors of the Ionians which they had rather fitfully played in the Ionian Revolt. The emphasis here on oaths and on not revolting should be compared with the account of the origin of the Delian League given in **16**.

3   [114.1] The Greeks who set sail from Mykale towards the Hellespont first moored around Lekton, held up by contrary winds. From there they came to Abydos and found that the bridges, which they thought that they would find still stretched out, had been broken. It was those bridges that were the main cause of their coming to the Hellespont. [114.2] The Peloponnesians with Leotykhidas decided to sail away to Greece, but the Athenians and their General Xanthippos decided to stay and make an attack on the Khersonesos. So the Peloponnesians sailed away; but the Athenians crossed from Abydos to the Khersonesos and began the siege of Sestos.

                                                                          Herodotos 9.114

The Herodotean account is followed quite closely by Diodoros 11.37, which must ultimately derive from it. Comparison of **2** and **3** with **1** reveals how Thucydides cuts out Herodotos' debate and so does not indicate Spartan desire to evacuate the Ionian Greeks.

The behaviour of Themistokles and increasing tension between Sparta and Athens

4   [89.3, continuing **1**] The Athenian people, when the Persians left their territory, immediately began bringing back their wives and children and those goods that remained from the places to which they had been evacuated, and they began preparations to rebuild the city and its walls. Only short sections of the city walls were standing and most of the houses were in ruins, although the few houses in which the high-ranking Persians had made their quarters survived.

[90.1] When the Spartans perceived what was going to happen, they sent ambassadors. It was partly that they themselves would rather see neither the Athenians nor anyone else having a wall, but more that their allies were urging them, frightened of the size of the Athenian fleet, which had not previously been of the same order, and of the daring which the Athenians had shown in the Persian war. [90.2] They expressed the view that the Athenians should not build a wall, but should join them in pulling down all the walls standing outside the Peloponnese. The Spartans did not reveal to the Athenians their intentions and suspicions but said the purpose was to deprive the Persians, if they invaded again, of any secure base for operations, as Thebes had been in the recent invasion. They said that the Peloponnese provided a refuge for all, and a sufficient base for counter-attack.

[90.3] After the Spartans had said this, the Athenians immediately sent them away, replying, on Themistokles' proposal, that they would send ambassadors to the Spartans to discuss what they proposed. Themistokles told the Athenians to send him to Sparta as quickly as possible, and to choose further ambassadors in addition to himself but not to send them immediately, but to keep them back until such a time as they had raised the wall to the necessary height for fighting from. He urged all in the city to help in the fortification, sparing no private or public building that might give them any material assistance in the task, but demolishing them all. [90.4] Once he had given these instructions and suggested what he himself would do in Sparta, he left. [90.5] When he reached Sparta, Themistokles did not go straight to the authorities, but wasted time and made excuses. Whenever one of those in power asked him why he did not come before the Spartan assembly, he replied that he was waiting for his fellow ambassadors, and that they had some business which detained them but that he was expecting them to come soon and was surprised that they were not yet present.

[91.1] The Spartan magistrates were prepared to believe Themistokles because of their friendship with him, but when others kept coming and making clear allegations that a wall was being built and was reaching some height, they did not see how they could disbelieve those stories. [91.2] Becoming aware of this, Themistokles told them not to be misled by tales, but to send their own men who would be reliable and would report back faithfully when they had seen the situation. [91.3] So they sent men to investigate, and Themistokles sent secretly to the Athenians about them, urging them to detain the envoys as unobtrusively as they could, and not to let them go until he and his colleagues returned (for his fellow ambassadors, Habronikhos son of Lysikles and Aristeides son of Lysimakhos, had now arrived and reported that the wall was high enough). Themistokles was afraid that when the Spartans received an unequivocal report, they might no longer let them go. [91.4] So the Athenians detained the Spartan ambassadors, as they had been directed, and Themistokles appeared before the Spartans and told them openly that their city had already been fortified and so was capable of defending the inhabitants, and that if the Spartans or their allies wished to send to them, they should come in future on the understanding that they were dealing with men who knew quite well what was for their own and the common good. [91.5] The ambassadors explained that when they had decided that it was better to abandon the city and embark on their ships, they had made this daring decision without the Spartans, and as to the decisions that they had made jointly with the Spartans, they had shown themselves second to none in good judgement. [91.6] So now the Athenians thought it better that their city should have a wall, and considered that this was to the greater advantage both of the citizens of Athens on their own account and of the allies as a whole. [91.7] It was not possible to deliberate on a fair and equal basis at meetings to decide common policy unless there was comparable military preparedness. Either all the allies had to be without walls, or what the Athenians had done had to be considered correct. [92] When they heard this, the Spartans did not display anger openly to the Athenians. They claimed that they had sent their embassy not to prevent fortification but to advise the Athenians in their decision for the common good, and that they were particularly friendly at that time to the Athenians because of the eagerness they had displayed against the Persians. But they concealed their annoyance at the Athenians for ignoring their advice. The ambassadors of both states returned home without making any complaints.

[93.1] It was in this way that the Athenians walled their city in a short time. [93.2] It is evident even today that the building was done in haste. The foundations consist of all sorts of stones, sometimes not shaped to fit together, but laid down just as each was brought in at the time, and there are many tombstones and fragments of sculpture mixed together into the structure. For the circuit-wall of the city was extended on all sides, and it was for this reason that in their

haste they laid hands on everything indiscriminately. [93.3] Themistokles also persuaded them to complete the walls round Peiraieus - a start had been made on this task earlier, during his year of office as archon at Athens [493/2]. He realised that it was a fine place with its three natural harbours, and that if the Athenians became a naval people, that would contribute greatly to their obtaining power. [93.4] He was the first who dared to say that the Athenians should take control of the sea, and he lost no time in helping to lay the foundations of their empire. [93.5] They built the wall to the thickness which he proposed, as can still be seen today around Peiraieus: two wagons could carry stones from opposite directions. The inside was filled neither with rubble nor clay, but with large stones, cut square and fitting together, bound to one another on the outside with iron clamps and lead. About half the height he planned was completed. [93.6] He wanted to resist the enemy attacks by the size and thickness of the wall, and he considered that a guard consisting of a few of the most useless men would be sufficient, and that the others could embark on the ships. [93.7] For Themistokles devoted himself particularly to the navy because, as it seems to me, he saw that it was easier for the Persian King's force to approach by sea than by land. He thought that Peiraieus was more useful than the upper city [Athens], and he often advised the Athenians, if they were ever hard-pressed by land, to move down to Peiraieus and resist all comers in ships. This, then, is how the Athenians built their walls and set themselves up in other respects immediately the Persians had retreated.
[Continued in 7]

Thucydides 1.89.3-93.8

Themistokles' foresight

5   [41.1] At this time [477/6] Themistokles, because of his skill as a General and his shrewdness, enjoyed the approval not only of [Athenian] citizens but of all the Greeks. [41.2] Buoyed up by his repute, he went in for new enterprises that were much bigger, designed to increase the dominance of his homeland. Peiraieus at that time was not a harbour; the Athenians used what is called the Phaleron ship-yard which was very small. Themistokles conceived the plan of making Peiraieus a harbour, since with a small amount of construction it could become the finest and largest harbour in Greece. [41.3] He hoped that when this was added to Athenian facilities, it would be possible for the city to compete for leadership at sea. For at that time they had already obtained the largest number of triremes, and because of their experience of a succession of sea battles had gained a great reputation in naval contests. [41.4] In addition to this he surmised that they would get the Ionians on their side because of their kinship links, that with their help they would free the other Greeks of Asia, who would then incline their goodwill to the Athenians because of that good service, and that all the islanders, struck by the size of their naval power, would readily side with those capable of doing them the greatest good and the greatest harm. [41.5] He saw that the Spartans were well equipped in infantry forces, but not naturally well endowed for contests at sea.

Diodoros 11.41

Themistokles and the Delphic Amphiktiony

6   At the meeting of the [Delphic] Amphiktiony [in 479/8?] the Spartans proposed that those cities who had not belonged to the alliance against the Persians should

be excluded from the Amphiktiony. Themistokles was afraid that if the Spartans threw out the Thessalians and the Argives, and also the Thebans, they would completely dominate the votes and what they wanted would be done. By speaking in support of the cities Themistokles changed the minds of the members: he pointed out that only thirty-one cities had actively shared the war-effort, and that most of these were very small, and concluded that it would be a terrible thing if the rest of Greece was excluded and the meetings fell into the hands of just the two or three biggest cities. It was from this point on that Themistokles particularly clashed with the Spartans and they started trying to seduce Kimon with honours and make him a rival to Themistokles in Athenian politics.

Plutarch Themistokles 20.3-4

The Delphic Amphiktiony was the group of cities which controlled the sanctuary at Delphi and punished those who committed offences against it. The Amphiktiony kept the sanctuary at Delphi with its influential oracle from being manipulated by any single city.

The behaviour of Pausanias

7   [94.1, continuing 4] Pausanias son of Kleombrotos was sent out from Sparta [in 478] with 20 ships from the Peloponnese to be General of the Greeks. The Athenians accompanied him with 30 ships and there was a large number of allies. [94.2] They campaigned against Cyprus and subdued most of it, and later against Byzantion, which the Persians held, and besieged it during the period of Pausanias' leadership.

[95.1] Because Pausanias had already begun to behave violently, the other Greeks, and particularly the Ionians and all who had only just been liberated from the Persian king, found him burdensome. They kept going to the Athenians and asking them as their kinsmen to become their leaders, and not to leave them in the hands of Pausanias, in case he proved violent. [95.2] The Athenians listened to their proposals and put their minds to ensuring that they did not miss any opportunity to arrange matters in their own best interest. [95.3] Meanwhile the Spartans sent for Pausanias to face an inquiry in connection with what had been reported. Many accusations of misconduct had been made against him by Greeks who arrived at Sparta, and his behaviour seemed modelled on the tyrant rather than the general. [95.4] It happened that he was recalled at just the time that the allies, because of their hatred of him, went over to the Athenians, with the exception of the soldiers from the Peloponnese. [95.5] When he reached Sparta, Pausanias faced scrutiny of the offences against individuals, but he was acquitted of the most serious charges. Not the least accusation against him was that he had conspired with the Persians, and that seemed to be very clear. [95.6] The Spartans did not send Pausanias out again as commander, but sent Dorkis and some others with a small force; but the allies no longer entrusted the leadership to them. [95.7] When they realised this, they went away, and the Spartans did not send any further leaders after that, because they were afraid that any sent out might be corrupted, as they had seen happen to Pausanias, and because they wanted to be rid of the Persian wars and thought that the Athenians were quite able to exercise leadership and were currently friendly to them. [Continued in 11]

Thucydides 1.94-95

This famous final judgement is particularly puzzling given the indications already in Thucydides' account [4] of tension between Athens and Sparta.

8   [130.1] Up until this time [the exchange of letters between Xerxes and Pausanias
        at Byzantion] Pausanias had been held in high regard by the Greeks because of
        his leadership at the battle of Plataia. But from that point on he gave himself more
        and more airs and graces and was no longer able to live in the usual style but
        wore Persian dress as he went out of Byzantion, had a Persian and Egyptian body-
        guard as he marched through Thrace, had his table served in the Persian way, and
        could not conceal his intentions but showed his great ambitions for the future in
        little deeds. [130.2] He made himself difficult to approach and displayed so violent
        a temper to all alike that no one could go near him. That in particular is why the
        alliance switched to the Athenians.

                                                              Thucydides 1.130

Pausanias' behaviour, cause of or pretext for Athens taking over?

9   Aware of this [that in 480 the other Greeks would not follow their leadership]
        the Athenians did not insist but yielded, but only for as long as they particularly
        needed allies, as they showed. For when the Persians had been forced back and
        the struggle was on Persian territory, they made Pausanias' overweening
        behaviour an excuse and took the leadership away from the Spartans.

                                                              Herodotos 8.3.2

Compare **16**.

Aristeides' role

10   [23.1] When Aristeides was sent out along with Kimon as general for the war, he
        saw Pausanias and the other Spartiate [=Spartan citizen] commanders proving
        harsh and tiresome for the allies. He himself mingled with them in a kindly and
        considerate way and made sure Kimon was accommodating and even-handed to
        all the contingents. In this way he took over the leadership without the Spartans
        noticing, not by force of infantry, navy or cavalry but by kindness and diplomacy.
        [23.2] Pausanias' greed and harshness were particularly important in making the
        Athenians desirable, the Athenians being agreeable to the Greeks because
        Aristeides was fair and Kimon noble. Pausanias always met the allied comman-
        ders with a short temper and rough treatment, and he punished the troops with
        beatings and making them stand holding an iron anchor all day. [23.3] No one was
        allowed to fetch bedding or fodder or approach a spring to get water before the
        Spartans did, servants with whips driving away anyone who tried. When
        Aristeides once tried to make known the complaints on their behalf, Pausanias
        scowled, said he had no time, and did not hear him out. [23.4] As a result of this
        the various Greek naval and military commanders, and particularly the Khians,
        Samians, and Lesbians, went along to Aristeides and tried to persuade him to
        accept the leadership and to take command of the allies who had long wanted to
        be rid of the Spartiates and to transfer their allegiance to the Athenians. [23.5]
        Aristeides replied that he saw that their arguments were compelling and fair, but
        that he needed a pledge in the form of an action which, once taken, would not
        allow the troops to transfer their allegiance back again. As a result, the friends
        of Ouliades the Samian and Antagoras the Khian, who had hatched the plot at
        Byzantion, launched an attack on Pausanias' trireme when it was sailing out in
        the middle of the fleet. [23.6] When Pausanias saw this, he rose up and angrily
        threatened that in a short time he would show that they had not attacked his ship

but their own homelands. They told him to go away and think himself lucky to have had a share of their glory at Plataia; for they thought that it was because the Greeks still felt embarrassed over that that they had never exacted proper justice from him. Finally they revolted and went over to the Athenians. [23.7] It was here that Sparta's wisdom revealed itself as remarkable. For when they became conscious that their commanders were being corrupted by the amount of power they were exercising, they willingly gave up the leadership and stopped sending generals to the war; they chose to have citizens who were self-controlled and continued to behave according to traditional values rather than to rule the whole of Greece.

Plutarch *Aristeides* 23

The concluding sentence here must derive from Thucydides (**7**, 1.95.7). Plutarch's other information has traditionally been thought to derive from the fourth-century historian Theopompos of Khios, but that does not help us to decide whether its circumstantial details are a mark of fictitious anecdotes or genuine information. For the behaviour of Kimon compare **33**. For the way Khios, Samos and Lesbos are picked out here compare **2**: they were the islands which longest continued to meet their obligation to the Delian League by providing ships, rather than paying a money tribute.

The purpose of the Delian League

11 [Continued from **7**] The Athenians took over the leadership in this way, as the allies wanted because they hated Pausanias. They made an assessment of which allied cities should provide money for the war against the Persians and which were to provide ships. They did this because a pretext for the alliance was to take revenge for their losses by devastating the Persian King's territory. [Continued in **15**]

Thucydides 1.96.1

The allies were committed to continued naval warfare, and naval warfare was enormously expensive. For the obligation of allies to provide ships or money compare **13** (6.76.3), **29** (1.99.3), **26**. The term 'pretext' (*proskhema*) is important here: by using it Thucydides implies that the real purpose was different, even perhaps that the real enemy was not Persia (modern scholars have suggested Sparta or the allies themselves as alternative candidates).

An allied view

12 [Speech of Mytileneans at Olympia in 428 as they seek support for their revolt]. [10.2] 'We first became allies of the Athenians when you [the Spartans] abandoned us after the Persian War and they remained to see to the rest of the job. [10.3] We became allies, however, not in order to subjugate the Greeks to the Athenians, but to free the Greeks from the Persians'.

Thucydides 3.10.2-3

For more of this speech see **126**. For speeches in Thucydides see p. 6.

The outside observer

13 [Speech of Hermokrates to the Kamarinans, warning them against Athenian ambitions]. [76.3] 'The Ionians and other allies who were descended from Athens voluntarily accepted their leadership to punish the Persians, but the Athenians brought them all under their control, accusing some of refusing military service, others of fighting each other, and bringing some specious accusation against each. [76.4] The Athenians did not resist the Persians because they were concerned about the freedom of the Greeks, nor did the Greeks resist because they were concerned about their own freedom; the Athenians wanted the Greeks enslaved to themselves rather than to

the Persians, and the Greeks wanted a new master, who proved not less astute
but astute for ill.'

Thucydides 6.76.3-4

For more of this speech see **160**.

A fourth-century Athenian version

14 [67] If [critics] say something about our exacting tribute, we can make the following reply: we will demonstrate that our forebears acted more expediently than
the Spartans for the cities who paid tribute. First, they paid tribute not in response
to any order of ours but of their own decision when they gave us the leadership
at sea. [68] Second, they paid money not to save us but for democracy and their
own freedom, and to avoid falling into the enormous troubles they had when they
got oligarchy under dekarkhies [boards of ten, imposed by Sparta on some former
Athenian allies at the end of the Peloponnesian War] and the rule of the Spartans.
Also they paid not from what they themselves saved, but from what they had
thanks to us. [69] If they made even a summary calculation, they would properly
thank us for all that. For we took on their cities when some had been completely
uprooted by the barbarians and others had been sacked, and we brought them to
the condition where they gave only a small part of the profit that they got through
us, but their households were no less prosperous than those of the Peloponnesians
who paid no tribute.

Isokrates 12 (*Panathenaic Oration*) 67-9

The Constitution of the Delian League

15 [96.2, continued from **11**] It was at that time [spring 477] that the Athenians first established the office of *Hellenotamiai* [Treasurers of the Greeks]. These were the men
who received the tribute, as the money that was contributed was called. The first
tribute that was assessed amounted to 460 talents. Delos was their treasury and
it was at the sanctuary there that meetings were held. [97.1] They were leaders of
allies who at first were independent and took counsel in meetings open to
all...[Continued in **29**]

Thucydides 1.96.2-97.1

We hear almost nothing of League Common Meetings (see only **40**) - indeed perhaps the best evidence that
they continued to occur is that allies in revolt do not include the failure of the Athenians to hold Meetings
among their list of complaints (cf. esp. **126** (3.10.5)). The Mytileneans do there say that the Athenians began
on a footing of equality with the allies, which implies that, unlike the Second Athenian Confederacy of the
fourth century, the Delian League Meetings involved Athens and the allies all voting together, not one
chamber for allies and one for Athenians. The figure of 460T for the first tribute is a great puzzle, being a
higher figure than the Athenians were getting at the time of the first Athenian Tribute Quota Lists. Despite
the natural sense of this passage, it appears that if Thucydides' figure has any validity at all, it must include
the commuting of ship contributions to a money figure (cf. below p.92).

Oath of alliance?

16 It was Aristeides who procured the revolt of the Ionians from the Spartan alliance,
taking advantage of a moment when the Spartans had been slandered because of
Pausanias. And so it was he who assessed the first tribute payments for the cities
in the third year after the sea battle at Salamis, in the archonship of Timosthenes
[478/7], and he had the Ionians swear oaths to have the same friends and enemies,
oaths over which they sank iron bars in the sea.

[Aristotle] *Constitution of the Athenians* 23.4-5

This is part of an extremely tendentious history of the years after the Persian Wars given by the *Ath. Pol.* in chapter 23. In this account (with which **10** is to be compared) the Hellenic League against Persia is treated as simply a 'Spartan Alliance', and the Delian League presented as, from the beginning, an 'Athenian Alliance'. The bilateral alliance formula ('have same friends and enemies') used here should be compared with the formula ('be faithful and not revolt') which Herodotos says was used when these same Ionians joined the Hellenic League (**2**). It is very uncertain whether we can trust the detail over the oath and the iron bars, the point of which is that they would never float to the surface, although Plutarch (**17**) records the same story, probably from the same source.

17   Aristeides administered the oath to the Greeks, and took the oath on behalf of the Athenians, sealing the oath by throwing lumps of metal into the sea. Later, when events forced the Athenians, as it seems, to rule by force, he ordered them to divert the perjury onto him, and deal with matters to their own advantage.

Plutarch *Aristeides* 25.1

Aristeides' Assessment of Tribute
See above **15, 16**.

18   [Part of the treaty made between Athens and Sparta, and the allies on both sides, under the Peace of Nikias in 421]. 'With regard to all the cities surrendered to Athens by the Spartans, their inhabitants shall be allowed to go where they wish with all they possess; the cities are to pay the tribute as assessed by Aristeides and are to be independent. Neither the Athenians nor their allies shall begin any fighting with harm in mind, so long as the cities go on paying the tribute, now that the treaty has been agreed.'

Thucydides 5.18.5

19   [46.4] Aristeides' conduct as General was compared [to the notorious behaviour of Pausanias] among the allies, and because of the way he got on with his subordinates and his other virtues, he made them all incline, as it were with one accord, towards the Athenians. [46.5] So they no longer took any notice of leaders sent from Sparta, but as a result of their admiration for Aristeides they enthusiastically submitted to him in every matter, and so enabled him to take over the supreme command by sea without having to face any danger. [47.1] Immediately, therefore, Aristeides advised all the allies, who were holding a general meeting, to choose Delos as their common Treasury, to deposit there all the money they collected, and to impose a levy on all the cities according to their means for the war which they suspected would come from Persia. The total collected as a result was 560 talents. [47.2] Aristeides was put in charge of the tribute assessment, and he shared out the amount so precisely and fairly that all the cities were well pleased. Since he seemed to have accomplished something impossible, Aristeides got the greatest reputation for justice, and because he was so excessively just he was known as 'Aristeides the Just'.

Diodoros 11.46.4-47.2

On the amount of the original assessment see **15** and note.

20   [24.1] Even while the Spartans were leading them, the Greeks made contributions towards the war. Wanting the burden on each city to be moderate, they asked the Athenians for Aristeides' help, and instructed him to consider the land and income of each city and to fix the contributions according to the resources of each. [24.2] When he acquired such powers and Greece had, in a way, put all her affairs in his sole charge, he went out to the job poor and returned poorer, and he assessed the contributions not only justly but in a way that was kind and fitting for everyone. [24.3] As the men of old praised the age of Kronos [as the Golden Age], so the allies of the Athenians sang the praises of Aristeides' assessment as a stroke of good fortune for Greece, and particularly when not long afterwards tribute was doubled and then tripled. [24.4] To explain, Aristeides' assessment was 460 talents; Perikles added practically a third to this, for Thucydides says [111] that at the beginning of the [Peloponnesian] war 600 talents were coming in to the Athenians from their allies; [24.5] after Perikles' death, the demagogues [popular political leaders] increased it little by little until they brought the total to 1,300 talents. They did this not so much because of the length and fortunes of war, but because they enticed the people into distributions of money, payments for public shows [*theorika*], and constructing cult statues and temples.

Plutarch *Aristeides* 24.1-5

That Aristeides did indeed take into account the resources of cities, and not simply their population or total area, seems borne out by the tribute figures themselves: see below p.89 and L. Nixon and S. Price 'The size and resources of Greek Cities' in O. Murray and S. Price edd. *The Greek City from Homer to Alexander* (Oxford, 1990) 137-70. For the history of tribute amounts see below p.91-2.

On the source of this account see on **16** above. Plutarch and others collect a number of stories, all dubious, which further exploit the contrast between the amounts of money Aristeides handled and his own poverty.

Aristeides' honesty
21   Aristeides too was convicted of taking bribes, Diophantos of the deme Amphitrope prosecuting him, it being claimed that when he assessed the tribute, he took money from the Ionians. He was unable to pay the fine of 50 minas [=5000 drachmas], sailed away from Athens and died somewhere in Ionia.

Plutarch *Aristeides* 26.3

22   When Aristeides was in charge of assessing the tribute, his own property did not increase by one drachma, but when he died, the city buried him at public expense. But you [Athenians], if you needed anything, had the most money of all Greeks in your public treasury, so that you had sufficient pay for an expedition of any length you chose.

Demosthenes 23.209 *Against Aristokrates* (352/1)

Less favourable views of Aristeides' actions and pragmatism
23   Aristeides son of Lysimakhos and Pausanias son of Kleombrotos were not given the title 'Benefactor of Greece', Pausanias because of his subsequent misdemeanours, Aristeides because he assessed tribute on the Greeks who inhabited the islands. Before Aristeides the whole Greek world was free of tribute.

Pausanias 8.52.2

Pausanias' statement here ignores the money that Ionian cities within the Persian empire had paid to Persia. See below **164** and note.

24   They say that when there was discussion of a Samian proposal to bring the money from Delos to Athens contrary to the agreement, Aristeides said that this was not just but it was expedient.

Plutarch *Aristeides* 25.3

Aristeides seems to have died in the early 460s; the treasury in fact seems to have moved to Athens in 454: see below **66** and pp.36, 98.

The *Hellenotamiai*
See **15**.

25 [69] 'What is more, your *Hellenotamiai* were once falsely blamed over handling of money, as I am now, and they all, except for one, died as a result of your anger rather than your considered judgement. The truth of the matter came to light later. [70] The death penalty had been passed against the one who survived (it is said that his name was Sosias), but he had not yet been executed. When it was discovered how the money had disappeared, the man was released, although he had been handed over to the Eleven [prison authorities] by your popular decision, and the others had died although they were not guilty. [71] I think that the older men among you remember this, and the younger have heard of it, as I have.'

Antiphon 5.69-71 *On the murder of Herodes* (*c*.420)

If the story is true, this incident must have occurred in the 450s or 440s

The *Hellenotamiai* came to be a powerful symbol of the achievements of the Athenian empire, to be manipulated in fourth-century arguments over foreign policy:

26 [37] 'There was once a time, Athenians, when we had neither walls nor ships. When we acquired them, we began our run of success. If that is what you now desire, work for those things. They were the starting point from which our ancestors acquired power for the city such as no other city has ever yet obtained: they used a mixture of persuasion, concealment, bribery and force. [38] They persuaded the allies to put *Hellenotamiai* at Athens in charge of the common funds, to collect the ships together at Athens, and that Athens should provide triremes for the cities that did not have any; they concealed from the Peloponnesians that they had built walls; they used bribery so as not to pay the penalty for this; and they used force to counter the opposition. So we won our empire over the Greeks, and this success was enjoyed over a period of 85 years.'

Andokides 3.37-8 *On the Peace with Sparta* (392/1)

Andokides made this speech in an unsuccessful attempt to persuade the Athenians to accept the peace terms which he and other ambassadors had negotiated at a conference in Sparta. Those peace terms allowed Athens a navy and walls, and here Andokides tries to suggest that this can be the basis of future Athenian power. His 85 years appear to involve counting from the construction of the walls of the Peiraieus in the late 490s (see above **4**, 1.93.3).

27 Some men who want the city [Athens] to take leadership of the Greeks once more think that this would have been achieved through war rather than peace. They should first bear in mind the Persian wars: was it by force or by having done good to the Greeks that we became leaders of the fleet and held the office of *Hellenotamiai*?

Xenophon *Poroi* ('Revenues') 5.5 (*c*.355)

In this work Xenophon urges the Athenians to increase their prosperity by exploiting their resources in peace rather than by war.

Further evidence of hostility between Athens and Sparta

28 [50.1] In this year [475], the Spartans showed their resentment that they had lost command of the sea for no good reason. They were ill-disposed towards the Greeks who had revolted from them and threatened to impose an appropriate punishment upon them. [50.2] When the Gerousia [Council of Elders] met, the Spartans debated whether to go to war with the Athenians over the command by sea. [50.3] Similarly when the popular Assembly met, the younger men, and many of the others, were ambitious to get the command back, in the belief that, if they got it, they would enjoy much revenue, would make Sparta in every respect greater and more powerful, and the households of individuals would be made prosperous. [50.4] They reminded themselves of the old oracle in which the god had ordered them to beware the lame leadership, and they interpreted the oracle as having a bearing on the present situation. For they said that their rule would indeed be lame if when there were two commands [on land and at sea], they were to lose one of them.

[50.5] Practically all the citizens supported this interpretation, and when the Gerousia met to discuss these matters, no one expected that anyone would dare to give contrary advice. [50.6] But one of the members of the Gerousia, whose name was Hetoimaridas, who traced his ancestry back to Herakles, and who enjoyed favour among the citizens for his excellence, made an attempt at advising that the Athenians be allowed to keep the command. He said that Sparta should not dispute command at sea, supplied a wealth of fitting arguments to this unlikely claim, and contrary to expectation succeeded in persuading the Gerousia and the people. [50.7] In the end the Spartans judged that Hetoimaridas gave the right advice and they turned away from their intention of making war on the Athenians. [50.8] The Athenians at first expected to face a major war against the Spartans over the command at sea, and because of this built more triremes and accumulated a large amount of money. But when they learned what the Spartans had decided, they were relieved of their anxiety about war and lost no time seeing to increasing the power of their city.

Diodoros 11.50

This story is preserved only in Diodoros, and scholars are divided over whether it should be credited. If it is true, it is the only unequivocal evidence that the Spartan Gerousia deliberated over policy rather than simply being a judicial body. Even if it is true, Diodoros' date cannot necessarily be trusted.

1.2. THE GROWTH, DEVELOPMENT AND CHANGING NATURE OF THE DELIAN LEAGUE
1.2a) The first fifteen years

The original extent of the League
Certain or highly probable members:
    Khios, Lesbos, Samos, the cities of the Khalkidike (these last on the basis of **18**)
Possible members:
    the Aiolid (because party to Ionian Revolt, Hdt. 6.8), Cyprus (but Phoenician ships based there at time of Eurymedon, Plut. *Kimon* 12.5), Rhodes (Timokreon of Rhodes praises Aristeides, Plutarch *Themistokles* 21.4)
    See further **47**, **159**, p.24 and Bibliography (p.132).

Thucydides' narrative
29 [97.1, continued from **15**] The Athenians led allies who were at first independent and deliberated in meetings open to all, and increased their power greatly by war and by their handling of affairs between this [Peloponnesian] war and the Persian War. Their fighting was directed both against the Persians and against their own rebellious allies and those Peloponnesians who clashed with them from time to time. [97.2] I wrote up these events and made this excursus from my story because

this area was left untreated by all those before me who have composed accounts either about events before the Persian Wars or about the Persian Wars themselves. Hellanikos, who did touch on these events in his *Athenian History*, gave a brief treatment, inaccurate in its chronology. The narrative will also serve to explain how the Athenian empire grew up.

[98.1] First [476/5?] the Athenians under the command of Kimon son of Miltiades besieged and took Eion on the Strymon, which the Persians held, and enslaved it. [98.2] Then [475?] they enslaved the island of Skyros in the Aegean, which the Dolopes inhabited, and settled it themselves. [98.3] War arose between the Athenians and the Karystians [472?], who were not supported by the other Euboians, and in time a settlement was made by agreement. [98.4] After this [c.469-8] they made war on the Naxians, who had revolted, and besieged and subdued them. This was the first allied city deprived of its freedom contrary to Greek custom, but subsequently the same thing happened to each of the others as occasion arose. [99.1] The causes of revolts were various, but the main ones were their failure to pay tribute or to provide ships. For the Athenians were exacting and troublesome, using coercion on those unaccustomed and unwilling to bear hardship. [99.2] For various reasons they began to prove less congenial leaders than at first; they no longer campaigned from a position of equality and it was easy for them to rein in those who revolted. [99.3] The allies themselves were responsible for this situation arising, for because most of them disliked military service and absence from home, they agreed to contribute their share of the expense instead of ships. As a result the Athenian fleet grew from the money that the allies brought in, and when they revolted, the allies were unprepared and short of experience in war.

[100.1] After this [467?] the sea and land battle at the river Eurymedon in Pamphylia took place between the Athenians and their allies and the Persians. The Athenians under the command of Kimon son of Miltiades were victorious on the same day in both battles, capturing and destroying some 200 Phoenician triremes.

[100.2] Some time later [465/4] the Thasians revolted. A quarrel had arisen about the trading posts on the Thracian mainland opposite and the mine, all of which they gained profit from. The Athenians sailed against Thasos with their fleet, defeated them in a sea battle, and made a landing. [100.3] They sent 10,000 settlers, drawn from themselves and their allies, to the Strymon at about the same time in order to occupy what was then called Ennea Hodoi (Nine Ways), but is now called Amphipolis. They got control of Ennea Hodoi, which the Hedonians held, but when they advanced into inland Thrace they were all cut to pieces at Hedonian Drabeskos by the Thracians, who treated the founding of Ennea Hodoi as a hostile act.

[101.1] The Thasians, defeated in battle and under siege, appealed to the Spartans and asked them to aid them by invading Attica. [101.2] Unknown to the Athenians, the Spartans promised to do so, and would have done so, but were prevented by the earthquake which had taken place, during which the helots and the *perioikoi* [free inhabitants of the towns of Lakonia who were not Spartan citizens] from Thouria and Aithaia revolted and occupied Ithome. [Continued in **39**]

Thucydides 1.97.1-101.2

The number of settlers sent by the Athenians to Ennea Hodoi is extremely large.

Thucydides' last comment here raises a nice question about his sources. When and in what circumstances did the Athenians discover about the Spartan promise? Thucydides evidently believed in the promise, but it will have served the purpose of many in Athens who wanted war with Sparta to have invented such a promise.

Athenian hyperactivity

30   CHORUS. In those days, wasn't I great when I didn't fear anything, and wiped out the opposition sailing here and there in those triremes? We weren't going to hang about then for fine speeches with fancy phrases, nor was it quibbling with someone that we put our minds to, but who was the best rower. We captured loads of cities from the Persians and we were the ones that made them pay Athens the tribute these youngsters are stealing.

Aristophanes *Wasps* (422)1091-1101

Doriskos: a Persian stronghold

31   [106.2] All [the Persian governors] from Thrace and the Hellespont, except for the one at Doriskos, were expelled by the Greeks sometime after this [Xerxes'] expedition. But the Greeks were unable to expel the governor of Doriskos, although many attempted it. As a result the reigning King in Persia always sends him gifts. [107.1] Of the governors expelled by the Greeks, the only one whom King Xerxes regarded as a man of any worth was Boges, the governor of Eion. He never stopped praising him and gave special honour among the Persians to his surviving sons because Boges showed himself deserving of great praise. When the Athenians under Kimon son of Miltiades were besieging him, he had the opportunity to leave the town under a truce and return to Asia, but he refused, not wanting the King to think that he preserved his life through cowardice, and endured to the very end. [107.2] When no more food was left within the walls, he kindled a great pyre and slaughtered his children, his wife and his concubines and then threw them onto the pyre. After this he scattered all the gold and silver from the city into the river Strymon from the city wall. This done, he threw himself onto the pyre. For this reason he is deservedly praised by the Persians even to this day.

Herodotos 7.106.2-107.2

Kimon's activities in the north Aegean and Karia

32   [60.1] In this year [470] the Athenians chose Kimon son of Miltiades as General, gave him a sizeable force, and sent him out to the coast of Asia to help the allied cities and liberate those still under the control of Persian garrisons. [60.2] Kimon took over the fleet at Byzantion, and sailed to the city called Eion, which he took from Persian control. He besieged Skyros, which Pelasgians and Dolopes inhabited, set up an Athenian as founder, and divided up the land between settlers (*kleroukhoi*). [60.3] After this he set his mind to embarking on greater ventures, sailed to Peiraieus, added more triremes to his fleet and prepared other considerable gear, and then set sail with 200 triremes. When he had sent for ships from the Ionians and others, he reached a grand total of 300 ships. [60.4] So he sailed with his whole fleet to Karia, persuaded the coastal cities founded from Greece to revolt from the Persians, and attacked and besieged cities that used both languages and had Persians garrisons. When he had brought over the cities of Karia, he also persuaded the cities of Lykia, and took them over in the same way.

Diodoros 11.60.1-4

Part of 60.4 occurs almost verbatim in a papyrus fragment of the fourth-century historian Ephoros, who was much used by Diodoros. Diodoros' narrative is derived from Ephoros, but that does not mean that we can trust his chronology, and he almost certainly compresses into one year here events that took place over several years.

Athens' changing relations with allies

33   [11.1] The allies continued paying tribute but failed to provide men and ships according to their assessment, and were already refusing to go on campaign and did not man ships or send men, on the grounds that there was no need for warfare and that they wanted to live quietly and farm, since the barbarians had been removed and were not causing trouble. The other Athenian Generals applied compulsion to make them do this, put those who failed on trial and by their punishments made Athenian rule grievous and hard to bear. [11.2] But when Kimon was General he went in the opposite direction, and did not apply force to any Greek; he accepted money from those who were not willing to campaign, and empty ships, and he let them be enticed by leisure and spend their time on their own affairs, turning themselves from warriors into money-makers and farmers not fit for war through luxury and folly. He put many Athenians on the ships in turn and made them labour on the campaigns, and in a short time used the money and pay from the allies to make the Athenians masters of those who paid. [11.3] As a result of their own shyness of warfare, the allies became accustomed to fearing and flattering the men who were maintained and trained, and were always sailing and handling arms; they failed to realise that they were turning themselves into subjects and slaves.

   [12.1] No one did more to humble the Great King and abase his pride than Kimon. He did not let him go when he departed from Greece, but following hard on the Persians' heels and not letting them pause for breath, as it were, he ravaged and destroyed some of their territories and made others revolt and come over to the Greeks, so that he completely cleared Asia of Persian arms from Ionia to Pamphylia. [12.2] When he learned that the King's generals were lying in wait in Pamphylia with a large army and many ships, he set out from Knidos and the Triopion peninsula with 300 ships, with the intention of inducing such fear as to make the sea this side of the Khelidonian islands an area they would not sail into or trespass upon. These ships had been made by Themistokles to be very swift and manoeuvrable, and on that occasion Kimon made them broader, and gave them a gangway on the decks so that they would carry large numbers of hoplites and so be more effective at fighting the enemy. [12.3] He sailed to the city of Phaselis, whose inhabitants were Greek, but they did not receive the fleet or wish to revolt from the King, and so he began to ravage their territory and attack their walls. [12.4] The Khians, who were part of his fleet, and had long enjoyed friendly relations with Phaselis, induced Kimon to be more gentle and shot pamphlets attached to arrows over the walls with messages for the people of Phaselis. In the end this brought reconciliation on condition that Phaselis pay ten talents, join the League, and take part in the campaign against Persia.

Plutarch *Kimon* 11-12.4

A Thraco-Persian alliance

34   Some of the Persians were unwilling to leave the Khersonesos and even summoned the Thracians from the north, since they thought that Kimon, who had sailed out from Athens with very few ships, was not worth bothering much about.

He attacked them with four ships and captured thirteen of theirs. He drove the Persians out, got control over the Thracians and claimed the whole Khersonesos for Athens.

Plutarch *Kimon* 14.1

Themistokles as Persian governor

35   There is a monument to Themistokles in the agora of the Asiatic Magnesia [on the Maiander], where he was governor. The Persian King gave him Magnesia, which brought in 50 talents a year, for bread, Lampsakos for wine (it seems to have been the biggest producer of wine at that time) and Myous for fish.

Thucydides 1.138.5

36   Most authorities say that the King gave Themistokles three cities for his bread, his wine and his fish: Magnesia, Lampsakos and Myous. But Neanthes of Kyzikos and Phanias add two others: Perkote and Palaiskepsis for his bedding and his clothing.

Plutarch *Themistokles* 29.11

Coins issued in Magnesia confirm that Themistokles lived there, and there was a festival to Themistokles at Lampsakos in the Hellenistic period; there is no good reason to doubt Thucydides' testimony. Whether the testimony of the Hellenistic historians Neanthes and Phanias is equally trustworthy is more doubtful. From the point of view of the history of the Delian League the crucial question is whether the Persian King being in a position to 'give' cities to Themistokles means that those cities were outside the League at the time. Lampsakos, Myous, Perkote and Palaiskepsis appear to have been paying tribute by 451, but if some cities paid to Persia and the Delian League at the same time (see **164** and note), they may have already been within the League when given to Themistokles.

Khios, Lesbos and Samos acquire special status

37   [24.1] Aristeides ... advised the Athenians to assert their leadership of the Greeks... [24.2] Persuaded of this, the Athenians took over imperial rule and treated the allies in a more tyrannical way, except for the Khians, Lesbians, and Samians. They used them as guards of the empire and allowed them to keep their own constitutions and continue to rule over what they then ruled over.

[Aristotle] *Constitution of the Athenians* 24.1-2

For Khios, Lesbos and Samos singled out in the traditions about the early Delian League see **2** and **10** above. There is no evidence that Athens in fact applied different rules to Khios, Lesbos and Samos from those that she applied to other allies. For the changing nature of Athenian rule see **29** and **33**.

Athens and a Persian rebel.

38   The story goes that a Persian called Rhoisakes, in revolt from the King, came to Athens with a large sum of money. Troubled by threats of prosecution, he took refuge with Kimon and put two bowls down in Kimon's front court, one full of silver coins and one of gold. Kimon saw this, smiled and asked the man whether he wanted to hire Kimon or have him as a friend. When he said he wanted him as a friend, Kimon said, "Go away then, and take this with you. I will have the use of it when I need, once I am your friend."

Plutarch *Kimon* 10.9

1.2b) War at home and abroad: from 465 to 450
Thucydides' narrative.

39 [101.2, continuing 29] Unknown to the Athenians, the Spartans promised to invade Attica, and would have done so, but were prevented by the earthquake which had taken place, during which the helots and the *perioikoi* from Thouria and Aithaia revolted and occupied Ithome. Most of the helots were descendants of the Messenians of old who had then been enslaved, and as a result they were all called Messenians. [101.3] So there was war between the Spartans and the men at Ithome, and in the third year of being besieged [463] the Thasians came to an agreement with the Athenians, demolished their wall, handed over their ships, were assessed as to the amount of money they had to pay both immediately and for the future, and lost the mainland and the mine.

[102.1] The Spartans, as their war against those at Ithome grew longer, summoned [462?] various allies, including the Athenians, who came in a considerable force under the command of Kimon. [102.2] They particularly summoned the Athenians because of their perceived capacity for siege warfare and the Spartans' own weakness at this, revealed by the long-continued siege; otherwise they would have taken the place by storm. [102.3] It was from this campaign first that an open quarrel broke out between the Spartans and the Athenians. For when the place was not taken by force, the Spartans grew frightened at the bold and revolutionary character of the Athenians and also because they thought of them as alien in race. They feared that if they stayed, they would be persuaded by those on Ithome to instigate something revolutionary, and so they sent them, alone of the allies, away, although without making clear what their suspicions were but simply saying that they did not need them any longer. [102.4] The Athenians realised that they were not being sent away for any creditable reason, but because some suspicion had arisen. They took this badly, thinking they should not be treated like this by the Spartans, and as soon as they returned home put an end to the alliance which they had made with them against the Persians, and to spite the Spartans made an alliance with the Argives, who were the Spartans' enemies, and both Athens and Argos made identical alliances with the Thessalians, confirmed by the same oaths.

[103.1] In the tenth year [often amended to 'fourth', 'fifth' or 'sixth'] those at Ithome, unable to resist any longer, made an agreement with the Spartans to leave the Peloponnese under truce and never more set foot in it, and if anyone was caught doing so he was to be the slave of the man who caught him. [103.2] The Spartans had previously received an oracle from Delphi instructing them to release the suppliant of Zeus of Ithome. [103.3] So they departed [456?] with their wives and children, and the Athenians, because of their hostility to the Spartans, received them and settled them at Naupaktos which they had captured from the Ozolian Lokrians who had recently occupied it. [103.4] The Megarians also revolted from the Spartans [461/0] and went over to an alliance with the Athenians, prompted by the fact that the Corinthians were winning a war over border territory. The Athenians came to hold Megara and Pegai, and built and garrisoned the Megarian long walls which run from the city to Nisaia. This was the original and main cause of the intense hatred between the Corinthians and the Athenians.

[104.1] Inaros, son of Psammetikhos king of the Libyans bordering on Egypt, started out from Mareia, the city just south of Pharos, and led the revolt of most of Egypt from King Artaxerxes. Having made himself ruler, he called in the Athenians. [104.2] The Athenians were at that time campaigning against Cyprus with two hundred ships of their own and of their allies, and leaving Cyprus they sailed from the sea into the Nile, got control of the river and of two-thirds of Memphis, and made war on the other part, which is called White Fort, which was occupied by Persians and Medes who had taken refuge there and Egyptians who had not joined the revolt.

[105.1] A battle occurred [459 or 458] between an Athenian fleet which had landed at Halieis and the Corinthians and Epidaurians, and the Corinthians won. Later the Athenians fought a sea battle at Kekryphaleia against a Peloponnesian fleet, and the Athenians won. [105.2] After this war broke out between the Athenians and the Aiginetans, and a great sea battle took place at Aigina between the Athenians and Aiginetans, with the allies of each taking part, and the Athenians, under the command of Leokrates son of Stroibos, won, captured 70 ships, landed, and laid siege to Aigina. [105.3] Then the Peloponnesians, wanting to aid the Aiginetans, sent three hundred mercenary hoplites who had been in the service of the Corinthians and Epidaurians across to Aigina; the Corinthians with their allies occupied the heights of Geraneia and descended to the Megarid, taking the view that the Athenians would not be able to help the Megarians when they had a large army on Aigina and in Egypt, and that if they did help Megara, they would have to withdraw from Aigina. [105.4] But the Athenians did not disturb the force besieging Aigina; instead the oldest and the youngest of those remaining in the city went to Megara under the command of Myronides. [105.5] A battle against the Corinthians took place that was finely balanced, and the two sides parted, each thinking that they had held their own in the action. [105.6] When the Corinthians withdrew, the Athenians, who had indeed had the better of it, set up a trophy. The Corinthians, taunted by the older men in the city, made preparations and then, twelve days later, went and tried themselves to set up a trophy as victors. The Athenians marched out from Megara, cut down those trying to erect the trophy, and were victorious in battle with the rest. [106.1] Defeated, the Corinthians withdrew, and under pressure no small part of their force lost their way and fell into a private estate surrounded with a deep ditch and with no way out. [106.2] When the Athenians realised this they hemmed them in at the front with their hoplites, encircled them with light troops, and stoned all who had entered. Great suffering was here inflicted on the Corinthians. But the bulk of their army returned home.

[107.1] At around this time [c.458] the Athenians also began to build the Long Walls down to the sea at Peiraieus and at Phaleron. [107.2] The Phokians launched an expedition against the people of Doris, who are the mother people of the Spartans, attacking Boion, Kytinion and Erineon and capturing one of those small towns. The Spartans sent a force of 1,500 of their own men and 10,000 allies under Nikomedes son of Kleombrotos (acting for the king, Pleistoanax son of Pausanias, who was under age) to help the people of Doris. They forced the Phokians to come to terms and to hand back the town, and then retreated again. [107.3] If they wished to go by sea and cross the Gulf of Krisa, the Athenians had sailed round with their fleet and were intending to block their way. But it did not appear to them safe to march through Geraneia when the Athenians held Megara and Pegai, for the pass through Geraneia was difficult and always guarded by the Athenians, and at that moment they could see that the Athenians were intending to block this route too. [107.4] They decided to wait in Boiotia and there consider how they could cross to the Peloponnese with least risk. What is more, certain Athenians were secretly making overtures to them, in the hope that they would put an end to democracy and the building of the Long Walls. [107.5] The Athenians marched out against them in full force, with a thousand Argives and contingents from the other allies to give a total force of 14,000. [107.6] The Athenians took the field against the Spartans because they realised that they were at a loss as to how to cross and because they suspected an attempt to overthrow democracy. Some Thessalian cavalry also assisted the Athenians in accordance with the alliance, but in the battle they deserted to the Spartans. [108.1] Battle took place at Tanagra in Boiotia, and the Spartans and their allies were victorious, heavy casualties being incurred on both sides. [108.2] The Spartans headed for the Megarid, cut down trees, and returned home again through Geraneia and the Isthmus. Sixty-two days after the battle, the Athenians marched out under Myronides [108.3] and in a battle at Oinophyta defeated the Boiotians, became masters of Boiotia and Phokis, demolished the fortifications of Tanagra, took the hundred richest men of the Opuntian Lokrians hostage, and finished building their Long Walls. [108.4] Subsequently [c.457] the Aiginetans came to terms with the Athenians, demolished their fortifications, handed over their fleet, and were assessed for tribute for the future. [108.5] The Athenians under the command of Tolmides son of Tolmaios sailed around the Peloponnese [456/5], burnt the Spartan shipyard, captured the Corinthian city of Khalkis [in Aitolia], landed at Sikyon and defeated the Sikyonians in battle.

[109.1] The Athenians and their allies were still in Egypt, and they experienced the many different forms and fortunes of war. [109.2] Initially the Athenians gained control of Egypt, and the Persian King sent a Persian, Megabazos, to Sparta with money to persuade the Peloponnesians to invade Attica and so have the Athenians withdraw from Egypt. [109.3] When this plan got nowhere and the money was spent in vain, Megabazos returned to Asia with the rest of the money and the King sent the Persian Megabyzos son of Zopyros to Egypt with a large army. [109.4] He marched in over land, defeated the Egyptians and their allies in battle, drove the Greeks out of Memphis, and finally confined them to the island of Prosopitis where he besieged them for 18 months, until he had diverted the water elsewhere, dried up the channel, put the ships on dry land and made most of the island part of the mainland; then he crossed to the island on foot and captured it. [110.1] So it was that after six years of war Greek fortunes and forces were destroyed. Of the many men involved a few were saved by marching through Libya to Cyrene, but the greatest part of the force perished. [110.2] Egypt again came under the Persian King, except for Amyrtaios, the king in the marshes; because of the size of the marshes and because the marsh people are the most warlike of Egyptians, they could not capture this man. [110.3] Inaros, the king of the Libyans, who precipitated the whole Egyptian affair, was betrayed, captured and crucified. [110.4] Fifty triremes from Athens and the rest of the alliance which were sailing to Egypt as a relief force put in at the Mendesian mouth of the Nile, unaware of what had happened. An army fell upon them from the land and a Phoenician fleet from the sea, destroying many ships, the smaller part fleeing back home. Thus ended the great Egyptian expedition of the Athenians and their allies.

[111.1] Orestes son of Ekhekratidas, king of Thessaly, was exiled from Thessaly and persuaded the Athenians to restore him. The Athenians took Boiotians and Phokians, who were their allies, and campaigned against Pharsalos in Thessaly [454/3?]. They got control of the countryside in as far as it fell directly under their armed presence (the Thessalian cavalry kept them confined), but they did not capture the town or succeed in any of the other objects of their expedition, but retreated again with Orestes without having achieved anything. [111.2] A little later [454/3?] one thousand Athenians embarked on their ships at Pegai, which was then in Athenian control, and sailed across to Sikyon under the command of Perikles son of Xanthippos. They landed, clashed with the Sikyonians in battle, and were victorious. [111.3] Straightaway they added Akhaians to their force, sailed to the opposite coast, attacked Oiniadai in Akarnania and besieged it. But they returned home without capturing it.

[112.1] Three years later [451] there was a truce between the Peloponnesians and the Athenians for five years. [112.2] The Athenians stopped fighting in Greece, but made an expedition [451] against Cyprus with two hundred ships manned by themselves and their allies under the command of Kimon. [112.3] Sixty of these ships sailed to Egypt, sent for by Amyrtaios, the king in the marshes; the rest laid siege to Kition. [112.4] After the death of Kimon and a famine, they retreated from Kition, sailed beyond Cypriot Salamis and fought simultaneous sea and land battles against the Phoenicians, Cypriots and Cilicians, in both of which they were victorious. They then sailed home and the sixty ships from Egypt came back with them. [Continued in **64**]

Thucydides 1.101.2-112.4

This narrative may seem artlessly straightforward, but is in fact extremely artful. The interweaving of events in Greece and in Egypt in these chapters of Thucydides vividly conveys the way in which the Athenians sustained war on many fronts (compare **42**). Thucydides' decision to dwell on the minor incident of the slaughter of Corinthian troops ('Great suffering was here inflicted' 1.106.2), even though on his own account 'the bulk of their army returned home', raises the emotional tension and suggests an unaccustomed bloodiness in this warfare between Greeks. The vague phrases in 1.110 about the defeat in Egypt, (especially 'Of the many men involved a few were saved...'), and the finality of the conclusion of that chapter ('Thus ended the great expedition...') heighten the drama of that episode.

Athens, Aigina and allied reactions

40   [70.1] In this year [465/4] the Thasians revolted from the Athenians following a dispute about mines. They were besieged and forced to capitulate by the Athenians and compelled to become subject to them again. [70.2] Similarly the Athenians tried to besiege Aigina to bring the Aiginetans, who had revolted, under control. For this city, because it had often enjoyed success in naval engagements, was full of pride and well provided with money and triremes, and was generally at odds with the Athenians. [70.3] So the Athenians campaigned against it, ravaged its territory, besieged it and hurried to take it by storm. For generally the Athenians' power was much increased and they did not use the allies fairly, as they had previously, but ruled them in a violent and overweening manner. [70.4] Many of the allies were unable to put up with this harshness, and they talked to each other about revolt, and some gave up attending the Common Meetings and made their own private dispositions.

Diodoros 11.70.1-4

This passage of Diodoros gives a fuller version of Athenian actions with regard to Aigina than is given by Thucydides, and it adds a rare mention of the Common Meetings (compare **15**).

Allies die in Athenian wars

The following items excerpted from surviving Athenian lists of war dead indicate both the range of places in which Athenians were active and the contribution which their allies, both from the League and from outside the League, made towards their hyperactivity. As **44** shows, valuable historical information can be gleaned from the names to be found in these lists.

41 The list of 'Athenian' war dead from, probably, 464, which seems to have had a separate stone slab ('stele') for each tribe, includes:

one man from Madytos who died at Kardia (ll.34-6)

men from Byzantion who died at Sigeion (ll.118-27 or 29)

another casualty at Sigeion (ll.32-3)

casualties at Eion (ll.37-8, 141-4)

casualties at Thasos (ll.43-53, 130-4)

Inscriptiones Graecae i³ no.1144

We know about fighting for Thasos from the literary accounts, but this inscription shows not just that Athenians were also engaged at nearby Eion but also that Athenian allies were fighting in quite different theatres of war, at Sigeion in the Troad and at Kardia in the Thracian Khersonesos (compare **34** above).

42

Of the tribe Erekhtheis.

These died in the war: on Cyprus, in Egypt,
in Phoenicia, at Halieis, on Aigina, at Megara,
in the same year

ML 33.1-4

The names of some 188 members of a single Athenian tribe, including two Generals, perhaps successive. Except for one case where it is recorded that they died in Egypt, the list is not divided to indicate where each died. The Athenian army was tribally organised, individual tribal units might be detached for particular tasks, and when a battle line was drawn up, different tribal contingents would stand at different parts of the line. Unless we are to contemplate more than 1,500 Athenians dying in this one year, we must suppose that this tribe met particularly heavy losses either in an engagement unique to it, or because of its position in one particular battle. The second alternative is perhaps the more plausible, for part of another very similar tribal list (perhaps of the tribe Aegeis) with 49 names survives, which seems likely to belong to this same year (*SEG* 34.45).

43 Concerning this action many [bear witness, when] furious Ares set up a sea battle between Greeks and Persians around lovely Memphis, and the Samians captured fifteen Phoenician ships. Hegesagoras son of Zoïlotes and...

ML 34

This appears to refer to the sea battle mentioned in **39**, Thuc. 1.104.2.

44 Delodotos, Kean

Inscriptiones Graecae i³ 1150 line 13

This monument, made up of a number of separate stelai, seems to date from *c*.460-455. It must originally have recorded well over 100 names, but among almost 100 surviving names only this man from Keos is not an Athenian.

The name Delodotos is only ever attested for this man. Keans seem to have been unusually fond of names connected with Delos: the name Delikos is attested only on Keos and Delos, the name Delothemis only at Keos and Samos. Delodotos' name ('Delos' gift') has a form familiar from such names as 'Theodotos'

('God's gift) or 'Herodotos' (Hero's gift) and may imply that either this man or an ancestor had been born after supplications at the sanctuary of Delos for a child. This name is therefore good evidence for the central importance of the Delian sanctuary for the inhabitants of the Cyclades (compare below pp.65, 100).

45   The following Argives died at Tanagra at the hands of the Spartans; they endured grief fighting for land.

ML 35.1-2

The Argives who fought and died at Tanagra (Thuc. 1.107.5, **39**) were buried in the Kerameikos cemetery at Athens, and this monument, which was inscribed by an Argive stone-cutter and seems originally to have listed around 400 Argive names, was erected on their grave. The scale of Argive losses here puts the losses of the Delian League allies into perspective.

46   [The temple] holds [a gold bowl], which [the Spartans] and their alliance dedicated after [Tanagra], [a gift from the Argives], Athenians [and Ionians, and a tithe because of the victory] in the war.

ML 36.1-4

This marble stele found at Olympia can be restored on the basis of the text which Pausanias (5.10.4) quotes, although he says it was 'on the shield', rather than on a stele. 'Bowl' in the first line is a poetic expression for the shield.

47   It was in this year [455/4] that the Athenians ruled the greatest number of cities, and gained a great reputation for courage and good generalship.

Diodoros 11.85.2

This statement comes after Diodoros has just mentioned Perikles' campaign in Akarnania (cf. **39**, Thuc. 1.111.3). For the size of the League/Empire see p.95. The fullest literary description of the extent of the Empire is **159**.

League Treasury moved to Athens
For the transfer of the League Treasury to Athens in 454/3 see pp.3, 36, 98 and **24, 66** and **113**.

Athens changes its rules on citizenship
48   In the archonship of Antidotos [451/0] the population had increased to such an extent that it was resolved on the motion of Perikles to exclude from civic rights all who were not born of two citizen parents.

[Aristotle] *Constitution of the Athenians* 26.4

49   When Perikles was at the height of his power ... he proposed a law that only those who could claim Athenian parentage on both sides should be counted as Athenian citizens.

Plutarch *Perikles* 37.3

This law has often been thought to be aimed at least partly at the Athenian upper class, who were inclined to marry into the nobility of other Greek cities, but whatever the arguments used to persuade the Athenian assembly, there is no doubt that the effect was to exclude any possibility of men from allied cities gaining access to the privileges that went with Athenian citizenship (owning land in Attica, grants of land in settlements abroad, meat from sacrifices at festivals, cf. **222-3, 234-43**). If an Athenian serving abroad formed an attachment to a local woman, he could marry her only if he was prepared that any sons of his would not become citizens. See further p.37.

Peace with Persia?
Embassy of Kallias
50   Kallias son of Hipponikos and those who went to Persia with him as ambassadors from Athens happened to be at Sousa, the city of Memnon, on some other busi-

ness when the Argives sent ambassadors to Sousa at the same time to ask Xerxes' son Artaxerxes if the friendship which they had formed with Xerxes still abided or whether they were considered by him to be enemies. King Artaxerxes replied that the friendship certainly abided, and that no city was more friendly to him than Argos.

Herodotos 7.151

Any date down to the death of Artaxerxes in 424 would be possible for this embassy, and historians debate whether the middle 460s, before Argos allied with the anti-Persian Athenians, or *c*.450, provides a more plausible occasion.

Conditions imposed on Persians by Kallias

51   [13.4] This deed [Kimon's victory at Eurymedon] so humbled the King's pride that he made that famous peace, in which he promised that he would always keep a horse's journey from the Greek Sea and not sail inside [west of] the Kyanean and Khelidonian islands with a long and bronze-beaked ship [i.e. a warship]. Yet Kallisthenes [late fourth-century historian] denies that the Persians made a treaty on these conditions, but says that because of the fear inspired by that defeat they acted as if such a peace was in force and kept so far away from Greece that Perikles with fifty ships and Ephialtes with just thirty could sail beyond the Khelidonians without any barbarian fleet meeting them. [13.5] But Krateros in his collection of decrees [made in the early third century] includes a copy of the treaty as one that was made. And they say that the Athenians put up an altar of peace because of this treaty, and gave special honour to the ambassador Kallias.

Plutarch Kimon 13.4-5

This extract shows Plutarch at his best, carefully recording variant traditions and the reasons given by various authors for their actions. Whether Athens had made a Peace with Persia in the fifth century on advantageous terms became a big political issue in the fourth century, first because Sparta brought about a rather degrading Persian-guaranteed peace treaty in 386 which compared unfavourably with Athenian exclusion of Persians not just from mainland Greece but also from the Ionian seaboard, and then because Alexander and the Macedonians liked to think that they were taking revenge for the Persian Wars and did not like to think that their achievements had been anticipated (compare **54**). Kallisthenes was the official historian of Alexander until he showed too little respect for the extraordinary nature of Alexander's achievements and died in suspicious circumstances.

52   [2.1] The Athenians were renowned throughout practically the whole inhabited world as remarkable for bravery and glory. For they had increased their hegemony to such an extent that on their own, without the Spartans and the Peloponnesians, they had defeated the great Persian forces in contests both by land and by sea, and they so humbled the famous Persian hegemony as to compel them to make an agreement to free all the cities of Asia. [2.2] But of these things we have given a quite precise and detailed account in two books, this and the preceding...

Diodoros 12.2.1-2

This is from the preface to the twelfth book of Diodoros, which begins with the year 450.

53   [4.4] When Artaxerxes the Persian King learnt about the defeats around Cyprus, he took counsel with his friends about the war, and decided that it was in his interests to make peace with the Greeks. In consequence, he wrote to the generals in Cyprus and to the satraps [provincial governors] laying down the conditions on which they could end the quarrel with the Greeks. [4.5] So those with Artabazos and Megabyzos sent ambassadors to Athens to discuss a settlement. The Athenians heard what they proposed favourably and sent ambassadors with full powers under Kallias son of Hipponikos. An agreement was made between the Athenians and their allies and the Persians about peace, whose central clauses were: that all the Greek cities in Asia be autonomous; that the Persian satraps should not come closer than three days' journey to the coast and no long ship sail inside [west of] Phaselis and the Kyanean Rocks; that if the King and his generals observed these terms, the Athenians should not invade the land that the King ruled. [4.6] Once the treaty had been concluded, the Athenians withdrew their forces from Cyprus after having achieved a brilliant victory and a most famous peace. It happened that Kimon died from illness while on Cyprus.

Diodoros 12.4.4-6

The dating of Kimon's expedition and death is difficult. Diodoros spreads it over two archon-years, 450/49 and 449/8 which may be right, with Kimon's death perhaps in 450 (see *CAH* v² 501-2 against *AE* 124-6).

Doubts about the authenticity of the 'Peace of Kallias'

54   Theopompos [a fourth-century historian] in book 25 of his *History of Philip* says [*FGH* 115 F154] that the treaty with the Persians is a fake, being written up not in the Attic but in the Ionic alphabet.

Harpokration s.v. *Attikois grammasin*

The point of this claim is that Athens officially changed from using the Attic alphabet (which lacked e.g. omega and eta) to the Ionic alphabet for public inscriptions only in 403/2, so that any stele inscribed in the middle of the fifth century should have been written in the Attic alphabet. Theopompos seems to have made a great attack on the Athenian presentation of their success against Persia in book 25 of his *History of Philip* (see also *FGH* 115 F153).

55   Someone would get an idea of the extent of the change if he compared the treaty which we imposed and the one now agreed: it will be apparent that then we imposed boundaries on the King's realm, assessed some cities in it for tribute, and prevented him using the sea; now...

Isokrates 4 (*Panegyrikos*) 20

This is one of a number of fourth-century speeches which made more or less explicit reference to the Athenians imposing peace terms on the Persians in the fifth century. Compare the claims made in Plato's spoof Funeral Oration, *Menexenos*, 241e-242a or Demosthenes 19 (*False Embassy*) 273.

Kallias' fellow ambassador?

56   No one in the whole continent of Asia is said to appear to be a more beautiful or greater man than your [i.e. Kharmides'] uncle Pyrilampes, on all the occasions when he goes as ambassador to the Great King or to someone else on the continent.

Plato *Kharmides* 158a

Pyrilampes became famed as a bird-fancier, and particularly for the peacocks which he perhaps acquired in Persia (see **58**). Said to have acquired his aviary at a date probably to be put in the 440s, he may have been a fellow ambassador with Kallias.

The route of the embassy of Diotimos

57   Eratosthenes [the Hellenistic geographer] identifies one of the nonsenses of Damastes [of Sigeion, a fifth-century writer], when Damastes suggests that the Arabian Gulf is a lake, but repeats that Diotimos son of Strombikhides, leading an Athenian embassy, sailed up the Kydnos from Cilicia to the river Khoaspes, which flows along by Sousa, and arrived in Sousa in 40 days, and that Diotimos himself told him [Damastes] this. He should have wondered whether it was possible for the Kydnos to cut through the Euphrates and Tigris to flow into the Khoaspes!

Strabo 1.3.1

Diotimos was an Athenian general in 433, although his embassy could have taken place substantially before or after that.

The long absence of Athenian ambassadors to Persia ridiculed

58 HERALD. The Ambassadors from the King!

DIKAIOPOLIS. What sort of a king? I'm fed up with ambassadors and peacocks and flattery.

HERALD. Silence.

DIKAIOPOLIS. Bless me! The shape of Ekbatana!

AMBASSADOR. You sent us to the Great King, paid at 2 drachmas a day, in the archonship of Euthymenes (437/6).

DIKAIOPOLIS. Aaaagh! the cost!

AMBASSADOR. We were worn out with wandering through the plain of the Kayster, lying on soft cushions in our carriages, done for.

Aristophanes *Akharnians* (425) 61-71

59 DIKAIOPOLIS. What then, Drakyllos or Euphorides or Prinides, have any of you seen Ekbatana or Chaonia? No? But your son of Koisyra and Lamakhos...

Aristophanes *Akharnians* 612-614

Lamakhos is the name of a famous Athenian general, and Koisyra is an aristocratic name: Dikaiopolis is implying that no 'ordinary' Athenians got to go on exotic embassies. The Athenians preferred to send wealthy men to the wealthy rulers of other countries or cities, no doubt because such men were more aware of the behaviour that would be expected of them.

Abortive embassy of 425/4

60 [50.1] During the following winter [425/4] Aristeides son of Arkhippos, one of the commanders of the Athenian money-collecting ships which were sent out to the allies [see below **117, 118**], captured Artaphernes, a Persian on his way from the King to Sparta, at Eion on the Strymon. [50.2] When he was brought to them, the Athenians had his despatches translated and read. They were written in the Assyrian script. There was much else in them, but the chief thing was addressed to the Spartans and said: that the Persian King could not understand what they wanted; that many ambassadors had come and that no two had said the same thing; and that if they wanted to say something he could understand, they should send men along with Artaphernes. [50.3] Later the Athenians sent Artaphernes off on a trireme to Ephesos, and ambassadors with him. But when the ambassadors heard that Artaxerxes son of Xerxes had recently died (he died at about this time), they came back home.

Thucydides 4.50

Peace of Epilykos

61 We are the people who first made a treaty with the Great King - I must remind you of past events in order to give you the best advice - and agreed to friendship for all time, a treaty which Epilykos son of Tisander, my mother's brother, was responsible for as ambassador, and then, persuaded by the King's banished subject Amorges, we cast off the King's power, as if it was worth nothing, and took up the friendship of Amorges, considering him to be stronger.

Andokides 3.29

Epilykos' embassy must precede his death in Sicily, presumably during the expedition of 415-413. The favoured date is 424/3, a year in which he served on the Council at Athens and in which both Neokleides and Thoukydides, whose names occur in **62**, are known to have been active. 424/3 makes good sense as the year in which an embassy should be sent to Persia, since that is the year in which Artaxerxes died and Dareios II (Dareios the Bastard) succeeded to the throne. But making a treaty with the new King makes best sense if there had been an existing treaty with the old King, and hence this 'Peace of Epilykos' is itself strong testimony in favour of an earlier 'Peace of Kallias' agreed during the long reign of Artaxerxes.

Herakleides honoured for assisting Athenian ambassadors to Persia

62   The [Secretary of the Council] should write up [this decree and the earlier decree passed for Herakleides] and place the stele on the Akropolis.

The Council [and People decided], in the prytany of [—], when S[— was Secretary] and Neokleides was President, on the proposal of [—], that the Secretary [of the Council should write up] Herakleides [of Klazomenai as *proxenos*] and benefactor, [as the People have decided], and place [the stele on the Akropolis, since he did good] to the Athenian [embassy and is] a man good [to the Athenian people in all things]. Thoukydides [said: in other respects I agree with the proposal] of the Council, but since [the ambassadors who have come] from the King [report that Herak]leides helped [them eagerly both] to secure the peace treaty [with the King and on] other matters that they report, [Herakleides should be given] the right to own land and [a house] at Athens and be exempt from [the metic] tax [on resident aliens] just like other *proxenoi*. And if he [is killed] by violence, [punishment in his case should be just as if an] Athenian were killed, [and the same to apply to the descendants] of Herakleides.

Herakleides son of G[—], of [Klazo]menai, *proxenos* and benefactor.

ML70, with Addenda (*SEG* 39.9)

This stone was inscribed in the early fourth century, probably on the occasion when Herakleides was given citizenship for further services subsequently rendered (that being the decree referred to in the first line). The most appropriate peace treaty with the King with which Herakleides could have assisted would be that referred to in Andokides. For the term *proxenos* see Glossary; for other examples of this honour bestowed see **235-238**.

Extent of Athenian power

63   It was only the coast itself that the Athenians controlled for 70 years, and not all of that, but the section between the Black Sea and the sea of Pamphylia, when they were at the height of their sea power.

Dionysios of Halikarnassos *Roman Antiquities* 1.3.2

The interest of this extract lies in the suggestion that there was an alternative tradition in antiquity, poorly represented in surviving sources, which cut the Athenian empire down to size.

Note E   The Character of the Athenian Empire: the importance and use of inscriptions as evidence.

The character of the empire in literary sources

a) Thucydides   Thucydides in the Pentekontaetia presents the Athenians as increasingly harsh to their allies, converting an association of free allies—what has become known as the Delian League—to an empire. He does this by such features as noting, of Athenian treatment of Naxos, that 'this was the first allied city deprived of its freedom' (**29** (1.98.4)), so that we anticipate worse to come, as well as by explicit statements that the Athenians 'began to prove less congenial leaders' (**29** (1.99.2)).

Speakers in Thucydides reinforce this view. The Mytileneans justify their revolt by claiming that what the Athenians do now is not what they originally did (**12, 126**); Hermokrates warns Kamarina that the Athenians have changed their tune towards old allies and so cannot be trusted with new allies (**13, 160**). Thucydides presents Athenians as themselves brutally realistic about possessing the empire for their own benefit and being hated by at least their upper-class subjects (**106, 114, 129, 132, 157**).

b) Other Literary sources   There are indeed frightening things in some other literary sources, perhaps most of all in Aristophanes' *Birds*, but elsewhere texts present a milder picture. [Xenophon] *Constitution of the Athenians* is notable here. This rather naïve political analysis is written from the viewpoint of an Athenian who dislikes democracy, explaining to a Greek from another city how it is that democracy flourishes in Athens and those with reservations about it fail to overthrow it. [Xenophon] draws attention throughout the pamphlet to the way in which the Athenians arrange everything in their own interest, but his picture is a very genial one, in which the behaviour of Athenian democrats is clever, almost admirably so, rather than ruthless.

Thucydides, and even Aristophanes, are much more perceptive than [Xenophon], but should we believe their picture? Crucial in our decision about this will be the way we read inscriptions.

The inscribed evidence
The pros and cons of inscriptions: a) Inscriptions have the great merit of being direct products of political actions, recorded at the time and in the way that those responsible for them wanted. In a world where almost all literary texts are produced by rich men with reservations about democracy, Athenian decrees are texts produced by men at the heart of democratic government. b) But inscriptions have the great demerit of not carrying their context with them. Records of decisions tell us nothing about any debate that preceded their passage unless that debate produced an amendment (Athenian procedure was to pass the substantive motion and then adjust it, rather than amend before passing), and proposals defeated in the Assembly simply do not make it onto stone. Even when an Athenian decree is passed in response to particular events, we are left to deduce those events from the response; there is no preamble describing the background. Only in the case of the bestowing of honours is there any significant exception to this, and even then it is rare to be told much more than that a man has been 'good to the Athenian People'. The Athenians seem to have taken the view that the less that is said, the less difference of opinion there can be over whether it should be said, and the sensitivity of both cities and individuals over wording suggests they were wise to take that view (see **179**.58-9 and **238**).

Competing ways of interpreting the inscriptions
a) What then are we to make of the inscriptional evidence? One view takes decrees to be official documents whose terms were carefully weighed. Changes in wording, on this view, signify general changes in attitude. Thus it is a significant moment when the Athenians first refer to 'the cities whom the Athenians rule' rather than 'their allies' (see note on **235**), and it is a significant matter that Athenian interference in government at Erythrai in the 450s (**216**) seems a matter of setting up institutions in a posi-

tive way, whereas the extraordinary tribute re-assessment of 425 (**138**) is a jumble of peremptory orders.

b) A contrasting view takes Athenian decision-making to be a far more random matter. Although epigraphists refer to a 'chancellery' style of Athenian letter-cutting, the professionalism that this suggests did not extend to formulating the decrees themselves; Athens did not have a body of civil servants busy drafting documents. Even if what was proposed to the Assembly emerged after a lengthy discussion in the Council, the Assembly was essentially presented with the more or less well organised thoughts of a Council member. Few decrees of any length are at all well planned; rather they tend to dart about from one matter to another with little logic to the order in which matters are considered (**138** is a good example of this). That one speaker one day referred to 'the Athenian allies' and another the next day referred to 'the cities whom the Athenians rule' can, on this view, bear no sinister interpretation. And indeed formulae do not change in any simple way over time: nothing is said of Athens' allies to Kolophon in ?447 (**219**) or Khalkis in 445 (**78**), but they are back for Samos in similar circumstances in 439 (**91** cf. Erythrai in ?453 **216**). Some Athenians dressed up what they said in one way, some in another, and it may be that more came to speak harshly later than earlier, but we have insufficient data to draw statistically valid conclusions; in particular we have almost no inscriptional evidence before the late 450s: we do not know what language the Athenians used in addressing Naxos in the 470s or Thasos in the 460s, and we cannot assume it to have been mild.

The evidence for changes in Athenian demands
a) Tribute

There is, of course, no doubt that things did change over time, but it is easier to document when new demands first appear in our evidence than to be sure when those demands were first made, and it is more problematic still to use the evidence for those demands to argue for a change of attitude. One area of changing demands in which changes can often be dated with some confidence is payment of tribute (see further Note **F**). From 454 onwards the Athenians listed 1/60th of the tribute as dedicated to Athena, and despite **24** it is likely that it was in 454/3 that the League treasury was moved from Delos to Athens. We do not know how much tribute payments had gone up, or down, before that, but from then on we can trace changes, and although there are many minor variations it is clear that substantial alterations in demands came only during the Arkhidamian War (although not only with the 425 re-assessment, and perhaps not particularly then; see note to **138** and also **185**).

b) Gratuitous demands

Another change concerned what may be called 'gratuitous demands', demands made of the allies from which there was scant profit for the Athenians. One example is the demand that allies bring a cow and a panoply to the Great Panathenaia (perhaps a demand made on all in the early 440s (if that is where **190** belongs), but foreshadowed by a similar demand made on Erythrai in 453 (**216** and compare **232**)). Another example is perhaps the Megarian exclusion order (**97-9**): allies are expected to police this order although Megarians offered no threat to them and the offence was against Athenian territory alone. The imposition of Athenian coins, weights and measures falls into the same category (**198**). Although the Megarian exclusion order was presumably not permanent, gratuitous obligations were in general cumulative.

The stelai themselves represent a demand made on the allies which, if not exactly gratuitous, will certainly have constituted an unwelcome burden. Although Athenian behaviour in this as in other respects was not entirely consistent (see **182, 183**) Athens seems to have been in the habit of asking those it honoured to pay for the inscription if they wanted the honour recorded on stone (so **179, 237**). It extended this practice to demanding that allies pay for copies of Athenian decisions about them to be displayed in their own cities and/or at Athens (**234**), a practice unlikely to have been welcome when, as often, those decisions were disadvantageous to members of the allied city. The Athenians themselves often determine where the ally is to place the inscription (**78.60ff.**, **198, 220**), an indication of the importance that they attached to their decisions being visible. The Coinage, Weights and Measures decree (**198**) declares that the purpose of its being set up at Athens is 'for anyone who wants to see (*skopein*)'. These Athenian inscriptions with their regularly spaced letters, no word breaks, and somewhat breathless style can never have been easy to read; that they can be seen is what matters: they are visible symbols of Athenian power and control. The stelai came to represent the 'letter of the law' that the Athenians might insist upon (**199**.1051), and which might come to be the object of physical abuse by those subjected to them (**199**.1055).

c) Exclusions: i) Formal

As the Athenians increased the demands upon the allies, so also, formally or informally, they increasingly excluded them from opportunities. For a formal exclusion we can point to Perikles' citizenship law (**48-9**): until 451/0 a member of an allied city could hope to acquire Athenian in-laws by marrying a son to an Athenian girl, or better still, perhaps, acquire Athenian grandchildren by marrying a daughter to an Athenian man. Among the rich, in particular, such marriages across political boundaries had been common in the archaic period. Once Perikles' law was in force no new kinship links between Athenians and allies could be formed; the allies, who were increasingly being asked to act like Athenian citizens in bringing offerings to Athenian festivals, were excluded from any route to Athenian citizenship itself. We do hear from Lysias (34.3) that the Athenians made, at a date unknown, an arrangement (*epigamia*) legitimising marriages with Euboians, and may suspect that to be connected with Athenians being settled there in the 440s; it is unlikely that it was an arrangement made in the allied interest.

Exclusions: ii) Informal

Informal exclusion may have been no less oppressive. The empire undoubtedly brought enormous prosperity to Athens, and individual Athenians, most of all no doubt those already rich, became quite colossally rich. Rich Athenians, largely relieved by tribute of the burden of funding their own navy and only occasionally subject to a capital levy (*eisphora*, see **135**), were in a position to dominate the market in money-lending and acquire revenue-bearing assets whatever the capital cost. That they did so is suggested by a variety of evidence, all of it epigraphic: at the time that the Second Athenian Confederacy was formed the Athenians made promises *not* to acquire property among their new allies (see **246**), and the records of the sale of the property of those Athenians found guilty of impiety in 415 reveal a number of them to have had property holdings abroad (**239-43**) (and note also the vexatious Athenian prosecutor in *Birds* (1459-60) gobbling up confiscated property). All the property abroad revealed by these sales is within the Empire, and the scale of some of these properties is enormous: Oionias' 81-talent property on Euboia is by far the most valuable land-holding known to us and should have yielded him an <u>income</u> of more than 6 talents a year. We do not know at what date these private land-holdings among the allies were formed by rich men, nor how individuals got round the legal restriction of land-owning in a city to its own citizens, which seems to have been general.

Poor Athenians unable to use financial power to acquire assets among the allies benefited from the military power of Athens. Poor Athenians were among those given land that the Athenians confiscated from their allies after revolts. In this case it is clear, from literary as well as epigraphic evidence, that the practice of confiscating land to give to settlers sent out from Athens certainly dates back to the 440s (**64** (1.114.3), **68-70, 72-5, 77, 229-31** cf.**232**) and was continued during the Peloponnesian War (**119** (3.34.4), **133-4, 159** (7.57.2), **245**.107). A significant number of Athenians were still resident in these settlements abroad at the end of the Peloponnesian War when Lysander sent them back to Athens in order to increase pressure on food there (Xen. *Hell.* 2.2.2, *Mem.* 2.8.1). A dozen years later Andokides notes continuing Athenian desire for overseas property and the recovery of (foreign) debts (3.15 and compare 36).

Allied reactions to Athens

Just as different Athenians expressed themselves in different ways when they talked of Athens' allies, so not all Athens' subjects will have thought of themselves, or of the Athenians, in the same way. Thucydides has Diodotos claim that the common people favour the Athenians (**132** cf.**211**), and for all that this suits Diodotos' argument, there may be some truth in that view (just how we should interpret the actions of the people on Mytilene (**128** (iii.27)) is a matter for debate). Fourth-century retrospectives on empire (**244, 245**) stress that Athens kept her allies free of civil strife, and she did so largely by favouring democracies (**212-216**), democracies that most often would not have come into existence at all without Athens' assistance. Democracy brought political power to men who would otherwise have been dominated by their rich neighbours, and unlike those neighbours they will have been little hit by losing opportunities they never had for marriage to Athenians and the like. No doubt some came, wrongly, to take democratic government for granted and hope to have it and freedom from Athens too (cf. **175-6**), but others who remained loyal to the end arguably did so for their own advantage (**183**), just as some who revolted did so for immediate material gain rather than long-standing political hostility (cf.**145**).

Just as both rich and poor Athenians had an interest in maintaining empire, so we should not take it that it was only ever poor allies who looked favourably on Athens. The individuals whom the Athenians honour as *proxenoi* (**235-38**) are unlikely to have been in general poor men. They were men who saw more profit for themselves in collaboration than in resistance, and who were prepared to risk local hostility (see Thuc. 3.70; and compare Tod 142 from the fourth century) for the advantages of acquiring Athenian friends. Some got more material advantages than just friendship: Herakleides of Klazomenai (**62**) is the first non-Athenian we know of to have been given the right to own land at Athens (*gês enktêsis*). Rich Athenians likewise will have championed allied interests (as Antiphon did in taking on the case of Samothracian tribute (**186-9**)) at least in part to foster friendships with wealthy men among the allies - one might compare the historian Thucydides with his friends in Thrace (4.105.1).

The balance sheet?

The Athenian Empire was not without its costs - power corrupted even Perikles, if Douris's story about his behaviour on Samos is true (**89**). But whether we enter a positive or a negative figure at the end of the balance sheet will depend upon the importance we attach to peace and to democratic government, and on what sort of freedom we regard as most valuable, and for whom.

1.3 THE ATHENIAN EMPIRE FROM C.450 TO THE OUTBREAK OF THE PELOPONNESIAN WAR

Thucydides' narrative.

64 [112.5 continuing 39] After this [449] the Spartans fought the so-called Sacred War, got control of the sanctuary at Delphi and restored it to the Delphians. Then later, when the Spartans had retreated, the Athenians marched out, got control and handed it over to the Phokians. [113.1] Some time after this [447], the Athenians went on campaign with 1,000 of their own hoplites and contingents from each of the allies under the command of Tolmides son of Tolmaios against Orkhomenos, Khaironeia and certain places in Boiotia which Boiotian exiles were holding. They captured and enslaved Khaironeia, established a garrison there and withdrew. [113.2] As they were on the march, the Boiotian exiles from Orkhomenos, together with Lokrians and Euboian exiles and others who were of the same mind, attacked them at Koroneia, got the upper hand in the battle, killed some of the Athenians and took others alive. [113.3] The Athenians then evacuated the whole of Boiotia after having made a treaty under which they recovered the men. [113.4] The Boiotian exiles returned and all the Boiotians regained their independence.

[114.1] Not much later [446] Euboia revolted from the Athenians, and when Perikles crossed there with an Athenian army, reports came in of the revolt of Megara, of the Peloponnesians being about to invade Attica, and of the Athenians' garrison troops, except for those who had managed to escape to Nisaia, having been destroyed by the Megarians. The Megarians revolted once they had brought in Corinthians, Epidaurians and Sikyonians. Perikles quickly brought the army back from Euboia. [114.2] After this the Peloponnesians, under the command of Pleistoanax son of Pausanias, the Spartan King, invaded Attica as far as Eleusis and Thria and ravaged, but they advanced no further and withdrew back home. [114.3] The Athenians, under the command of Perikles, crossed back to Euboia, subdued the whole island, settled most of it by agreement, but ejected the Hestiaians from their homes and appropriated their territory. [115.1] The Athenians withdrew from Euboia and a little later made a treaty with the Spartans and their allies for thirty years, giving up Nisaia and Pegai and Troizen and Akhaia, places in the Peloponnese that the Athenians held.

[115.2] Six years later [441/0] the Samians and Milesians came to war over Priene, and the defeated Milesians went to the Athenians and denounced the Samians. Some individuals from Samos itself who wanted to change the constitution there joined in the attack. [115.3] The Athenians sailed to Samos in forty ships, established a democracy, took fifty boys and an equal number of men as hostages, whom they set down on Lemnos, and withdrew leaving a garrison behind. [115.4] Some Samians did not stay, but fled to the mainland after making an alliance with the most powerful men in the city and with Pissouthnes son of Hystaspes, who at that time was in charge at Sardis. They collected 700 mercenaries, crossed by night to Samos, [115.5] first raised a revolt against the people and got power over the majority of them, and then stole their own hostages away from Lemnos, revolted, handed over to Pissouthnes the Athenian garrison troops and magistrates who were on Samos, and prepared an immediate campaign against Miletos. The people of Byzantion joined them in revolting.

[116.1] When the Athenians heard they sailed to Samos with 60 ships. They did not employ 16 of the ships, for some went off to the Karian area to ward off the Phoenician fleet, and others to Khios and Lesbos to tell them to come and help. With 44 ships, under the command of Perikles and the nine other Generals, they fought a sea battle by the island of Tragia against 70 Samian ships, of which 20 were troop-carriers and all had sailed from Miletos, and the Athenians were victorious. [116.2] Later 40 ships came from Athens to help them, and 25 from Khios and Lesbos, and they landed, got the upper hand on land, and besieged the city simultaneously with three walls and from the sea. [116.3] Perikles took 60 of the ships lying offshore and made a rapid expedition towards Kaunos and Karia, following a report that Phoenician ships were sailing against them. For Stesagoras and others had gone from Samos with 5 ships to fetch the Phoenician fleet. [117.1] Meanwhile the Samians suddenly sailed out and attacked the unfortified Athenian camp, destroyed the ships which were an advance guard, and were victorious in a sea battle against the ships that put to sea. They were in control of the sea around Samos for about two weeks and imported and exported what they wanted. [117.2] When Perikles came back, they were blockaded again. Later 40 ships with Thoukydides, Hagnon, and Phormio came from Athens to give additional aid, along with 20 with Tlepolemos and Antikles and 30 from Khios and Lesbos. [117.3] The Samians fought a short battle at sea but were unable to resist and in the ninth month the city was taken by siege [439], and they reached an agreement that they would pull down their walls, give hostages, hand over their fleet, and pay a full indemnity by regular instalments. The people of Byzantion also agreed to be subjects as before.

[118.1] The events narrated earlier concerning Corcyra and Poteidaia and the various other causes of this war happened not many years after this. [118.2] All these events involving Greek relations with each other and with the Persians occurred in the period of about fifty years between Xerxes' retreat and the beginning of this war. During this time the Athenians made their rule stronger and themselves became very powerful, but the Spartans, although they perceived this, did little to prevent it; they kept quiet most of the time, being people who even earlier had not been quick to go to war, unless compelled, and who were in some difficulties through wars near home, until Athenian power was manifestly growing and the Athenians were laying hands on their allies. At that point they no longer held back but decided to attack with all energy and to clear away Athenian power, if they could, by setting out on this war.

Thucydides 1.112.5-118.2

Thucydides devotes much more space here to the revolt of Samos than to the crisis caused by the defeat at Koroneia and the simultaneous revolt of Euboia and Megara. He passes over what Athens agreed to give up (some of which he had never noted that Athens had gained - e.g. Troizen and Akhaia) on the mainland to emphasise the way Athens strengthened her hand against her major Ionian allies. In this way he preserves the emphasis on Athenian power growing, although in terms of amount of territory under her control Athens' power was actually shrinking in these years.

The 'Congress Decree'

65   [17.1] When the Spartans began to be annoyed at increasing Athenian power, Perikles increasingly urged the Athenians to think big and consider themselves capable of great achievements. He moved a decree to summon all Greeks living in any part of Europe or Asia, small cities and great, to send representatives to a meeting in Athens to discuss the Greek temples, which the Persians had burnt down, and the sacrifices, which they owed to the gods because they had vowed them at the time of the battles against the Persians, and the sea, that all might sail about with impunity and keep the peace [of Kallias?]. [17.2] 20 men aged over fifty were sent about these matters, 5 to summon the Ionians and Dorians in Asia and the islands as far as Lesbos and Rhodes, 5 went to the places in the Hellespont and Thrace as far as Byzantion, 5 to those in Boiotia, Phokis and the Peloponnese and from there via the Lokrians to the next part of the mainland as far as Akarnania and Ambrakia. [17.3] The rest went via Euboia to Oita, the gulf of Malia, the Akhaians of Phthia, and Thessaly, trying to persuade them to come and share in counsels on peace and united Greek endeavours. [17.4] Nothing was accomplished. The project was first mooted in the Peloponnese and because of Spartan opposition, so it is said, the Greeks did not come together. I put this incident in, however, to show Perikles' proud and ambitious designs.

Plutarch *Perikles* 17

This is the only evidence for this initiative, which has become known as the 'Congress Decree'. If historical, this decree must belong after the removal of the Treasury from Delos to Athens (454) and before the building of the Parthenon, begun in 447. But there has been much modern doubt whether the story can be trusted. The language Plutarch employs to describe the aims is not the language of the fifth century, but this may simply be his own summary of his unknown source.

The 'Periklean' Building Programme

66 [12.1] What brought most pleasure and adornment to Athens, most startled other men, and is the only evidence that claims about Athens' power and ancient prosperity are not lies, was the erection of sacred buildings. But it was this, of all Perikles' policies, that his enemies begrudged and slandered at meetings of the Assembly. They said that the people would lose its good reputation and be criticised if it brought the money that belonged to all Greeks alike from Delos to itself, and that Perikles had removed the most presentable response to critics, that they had taken the common treasury from Delos and were guarding it securely for fear of the Persians. [12.2] They seemed to be displaying dreadful insolence towards Greece and to be openly acting as tyrants if those who were forced by Athens to contribute to the war saw them gilding and decking out the city like a loose woman, applying expensive stones and statues of gods and temples costing a thousand talents.

[12.3] In response, Perikles explained to the people that they did not owe their allies an account of the moneys, since they fought on their behalf and kept the Persians at bay while the allies provided no cavalry, ships, or infantry, but money alone; money which belonged not to those who gave it but to those who took it, provided they supplied the services for which the money was given. [12.4] Since the city was sufficiently provided with what was needed for warfare, it was right that it should turn its prosperity towards those things from which, when complete, it would gain eternal fame and, while they were being completed, ready prosperity. Since all kinds of workmanship would be displayed and demands of all sorts created which would excite every skill and involve every craft, it would provide employment for practically the whole city as well as adorning and nourishing it. [12.5] Military expeditions provided prosperity at the expense of the community for the young and strong, but Perikles wanted the unorganised working people to have a share in resources without being idle and unemployed.

He proposed to the people great projects for buildings and intricate work plans
which kept them occupied, and in that way those who stayed at home had no less
reason than those who rowed in ships or were part of garrisons or took part in
campaigns for sharing in and benefiting from public funds.

Plutarch *Perikles* 12.1-5

This passage, again without substantiation from other sources, raises similar problems to the last: are the
florid language, the inaccuracies (some allies were still contributing ships), and the probable anachronisms
(the Periklean building programme as a means of ensuring full employment) at the core of the passage, or
simply later accretions around a historical account? Even the extent of Perikles' responsibility for the building programme is uncertain.

Fighting in the north Aegean and Hellespont

67   Athenian casualty list of ?447 B.C., recording casualties from all ten tribes in three theatres of war:
one general (Epiteles) and 27 others 'in the Khersonese', 12 'at Byzantion', and 17 plus one man from
Eleutherai 'in the other wars'. The list concludes:

These lost their glorious youth fighting by the Hellespont. Like enemies, the
harvest they brought to their famous homeland was the grief of war, but they set
up for themselves an immortal memorial of their valour.

ML 48

The date of this list is uncertain: it can only be dated by the mention of fighting in the Khersonesos and at
Byzantion. The decision to place this passage and the next in 447 is based on an interpretation of the evidence
of the tribute lists (see pp.96-7). Although the number of casualties in each of the three sections of the list
is similar, the pattern of distribution across the tribes differs. In the Khersonesos all but five of the 27 deaths
come from five tribes; in the 'other wars' all but four deaths come from 4 tribes; but at Byzantion there are
casualties from every tribe with two each from two tribes. This would suggest that the nature of the fighting was rather different at Byzantion from that elsewhere.

Establishment of settlements abroad

68   After this [Periklean activity at Sikyon and in Akarnania, 454/3 or 453/2 as
Diodoros has it] Perikles went to the Khersonesos and established a settlement
(*kleroukhia*) on the territory with 1,000 citizens. At the same time that this was
done, Tolmides, the other General, went to Euboia with another 1,000 settlers
and distributed that territory, along with the land of the Naxians, to them.

Diodoros 11.88.3

This seems to be one of those Diodoran passages in which events of a number of different years have been
incorporated together. For settlers on Euboia see below **73-7**.

69   The feat of Perikles as General that was most admired was his campaign around
the Khersonesos, which saved the Greeks who lived there. He not only strengthened the cities in manpower by bringing 1,000 Athenian settlers, but girdled the
neck of the Khersonesos from sea to sea with fortifications and towers, providing a defensive wall against the incursions of Thracians who were scattered
around the Khersonesos and ending a war that had been long and hard.

Plutarch *Perikles* 19

Crisis in central Greece and Euboia

70   Later [following his campaigns around the Peloponnese, Tolmides], after returning to Athens, led Athenian settlers (*kleroukhoi*) to Euboia and Naxos. He also
invaded Boiotia with an army, ravaged the greater part of the territory and laid
siege to Khaironeia, advanced against Haliartos and died fighting in a battle [at
Koroneia] in which the whole army was defeated.

Pausanias 1.27.5

71   [23.1] When Perikles included an entry of 10 talents 'as was needed' in his account of expenditures from his generalship [in 446/5] [23.2] the people did not quibble with this or look further into the secret. But some, including the philosopher Theophrastos, have stated that Perikles had ten talents sent <u>annually</u> to Sparta, and that by looking after the authorities in Sparta in this way he deferred the war, not purchasing peace but time during which he could make preparations quietly and ensure that the Athenians fought better.

Plutarch *Perikles* 23.1-2

72   Of the Lemnians from Myrina. Of the tribe Erekhtheis: Solon, Euteles, Peisippos; of the tribe Aigeis: Arkhias, Kallisthenes, Neaios, Paionios, Philoxenos, Drakalion, Aristoteles [——] Of the tribe Hippothontis: Phaeinos, Andriskos, Olympikhos; of the tribe Aiantis: Phollos, Dexiphilos, Art..e-, Thotim-, Ame-, A-

Inscriptiones Graecae i^3 1164

Athenians seem to have been settled on Lemnos around 500, and a settlement may have been sent there in the early 440s. The precise date of this inscription is uncertain but letter forms suggest a date in the 440s or 430s, and casualties at Koroneia have been suggested. That 19 casualties are recorded from just four tribes may imply that the total number of Lemnian casualties in this year was between 40 and 50.

73   In Greece [in 445/4] the Athenians regained control of Euboia, expelled the people of Hestiaia from their city, and sent out a colony there under the command of Perikles. They sent out 1,000 settlers (*kleroukhoi*) and divided the city and its territory into lots for them.

Diodoros 12.22.2

74   Theopompos says that when Perikles subdued Euboia, he sent the Hestiaians off under the settlement terms to Macedonia. 2,000 Athenians came and settled Oreos, a town which had formerly belonged to the Hestiaians.

Theopompos *FGH* 115.F387 quoted by Strabo 10.1.3

75   He expelled the so-called 'Hippobotai' at Khalkis, who were particularly rich and famous, and uprooted all the Hestiaians from their land and settled it with Athenians. He reserved ruthlessness for the Hestiaians, because they had captured an Athenian ship and killed the men on board.

Plutarch *Perikles* 23.4

Arrangements for Hestiaia

76   Let the magistrates in charge of court cases to do with shipping [introduce the case] in the same month [—— and] ensure a fully manned court, [or else each be fined 1,000 drachmas] at their scrutiny. Let actions to recover money be [in Hestiaia for an individual from Hestiaia, just as] in Athens those from the dikasts [—— Concerning] violence and offences the [cases shall be heard by the Thesmothetai for anyone whose] appointed time has not yet run out. If anyone [is condemned for these and punishment is decided,] let the condemned man of Hestiaia [be put in chains] until [he pays. Let the archon choose seven] men from those who live at Hestiaia [—— and these] undergo scrutiny in Hestiaia, [giving an account of what has been done in the Council] at Hestiaia [each year. These seven are] publicly, three times a year, in Hestiaia [to judge any court actions that anyone wants to bring]. The same are also [to judge] actions in Dion [and before the people of Dion resident in Athens]. Another judge is [to be appointed] in Ellopia, [and he is to judge whatever cases the] Ellopians living in Ellopia [want.] The archon in Athens [is to take responsibility for appointing] judges [now, but for the future] let those in Hestiaia hold an annual election by lot [for the seven men to judge cases in] Hestiaia as the [people of those living in Hestiaia decides each year] from those living [in Hestiaia —] these [are to judge all the cases arising from agreements with other cities up to a value of 10 drachmas,] those over ten drachmas...

Inscriptiones Graecae i³ 41.90-109

This is the most substantial section, lines 90-109, that can be restored of an inscription on both sides of a stele making arrangements for Hestiaia. Much of what survives evidently concerns judicial arrangements, but there is also an intriguing mention of 'horse, donkey or sheep' in line 60, and stipulation of fares for ferry crossings, including ?3 obols for Oropos to Hestiaia, at lines 67-75.

Ellopia and Dion are places near Hestiaia. Although the restorations are likely to be wrong in detail, they give an impression of the sorts of stipulation made by the Athenians for this settlement.

Arrangements for Khalkis

77   When the Athenians had subdued the Khalkidians, they turned their territory, which is called the Horse-rearing (*Hippobotos*) land, into an Athenian settlement, providing 2,000 lots of land. They set aside sacred land for Athena in the place called Lelanton, and they rented out the rest according to the inscribed stelai on display in the Royal Stoa [on the west side of the Athenian Agora] which had a record of the leases. They kept the prisoners in chains, but even this did not extinguish the anger felt against the Khalkidians.

Aelian *Varia Historia* 6.1

78   The Council and People decided. The tribe Antiokhis were prytaneis, Drakontides was President, Diognetos made the proposal: The Athenian Council and dikasts are to swear an oath on the following terms: [4] 'I will not expel Khalkidians from Khalkis, nor will I uproot their city; I will deprive no individual of civic rights nor punish any with exile nor take any prisoner, nor execute any, nor confiscate the money of anyone not condemned in court unless that is the decision of the Athenian people; [10] whenever I am a prytanis, I will not put anything prejudicial to the interests of an individual or the community to the vote without due notice, and any embassy that is sent I will bring before the Council and People within ten days, as far as I can; [14] I will maintain this while the Khalkidians obey the Athenian people.' An embassy is to come from Khalkis with the commissioners for oaths and administer the oath to the Athenians and list the names of those who have sworn; the Generals having responsibility to see that all take the oath.

[21] The Khalkidians are to swear an oath on the following terms: 'I will not revolt from the people of Athens by any means or device whatsoever, neither in word nor in deed, nor will I obey anyone who does revolt, and if anyone revolts I will denounce him to the Athenians, and [26] I will pay to the Athenians whatever tribute I persuade them to agree, and I will be the best and fairest ally I am able to be and will help and defend the Athenian people, in the event of anyone wronging the Athenian people, and I will obey the Athenian people'. [32] All the Khalkidians of military age and above are to swear. If anyone does not swear, he

is to be deprived of his civic rights and his property is to be confiscated [35] and a tithe of it dedicated to Olympian Zeus. An embassy is to go from Athens to Khalkis with the commissioners for oaths and administer the oath in Khalkis and list those of the Khalkidians who have sworn.

[40] Antikles made a proposal. In the name of good fortune for the Athenians: the Athenians and Khalkidians should make the oath just as the Athenian People voted for the people of Eretria, and the Generals should have responsibility to see that that happens as quickly as possible. [45] The People as soon as possible should choose 5 men to go to Khalkis to exact the oaths. And on the matter of hostages, they should reply to the Khalkidians that for the moment the Athenians have decided to leave matters as decreed. [50] But whenever they decide, they will deliberate and draw up an agreement [or 'exchange'] on conditions which seem suitable for the Athenians and the Khalkidians. The foreigners who live in Khalkis and [54] do not pay taxes to Athens, even if they have been given tax exemption by the Athenian people, should pay taxes in Khalkis along with the rest, just like the other Khalkidians.

[57] The Secretary of the Council is to write up this decree and oath at Athens on a stone stele and set it up on the Akropolis at the expense of the Khalkidians, and let the Council of the Khalkidians write it up and deposit it in the sanctuary of Zeus Olympios at Khalkis. This is the decree about the Khalkidians.

[64] Three men, chosen by the Council from their own number, should go with Hierokles as quickly as possible to make the holy sacrifices demanded by the oracle about Euboia. So that this happens as quickly as possible, the Generals should take responsibility and provide the money for it.

[70] Arkhestratos made a proposal. In other respects I agree with Antikles, but the Khalkidians should themselves subject their officials to scrutiny on Khalkis, just as the Athenians at Athens, except in cases involving exile, execution, or loss of civic rights. [74] On these matters there should be reference to Athens to the court of the Thesmothetai in accordance with the People's decree. As to guarding Euboia, the Generals are to take responsibility for doing that as best they can in the best interests of the Athenians.

[80] Oath.

ML 52 (*SEG* 42.10)

There is no firm date provided by evidence internal to the decree, although Drakontides is quite likely to be the man known to be active in the 430s as an opponent of Perikles and General on the second Athenian expedition to Corcyra. The content of the decree presupposes a major disturbance in relations between Athens and Khalkis and Eretria and this can only be that of 446-5.

Two features of the decree deserve especial comment: that the oaths involve only the Athenian People, and not the allies (contrast the settlement with Samos **91**); and that (compulsory?) reference to Athens is required in the case of judicial action involving ex-magistrates. This provision was designed to prevent Athenian supporters being arraigned by enemies at home on trumped-up charges and then excluded from politics by the severity of the penalty imposed. The phrase used in line 76 'in accordance with the People's decree' may imply that this rule was being enforced on all allies (see bibliog. p.134). See also **205** and note.

Part of the Athenian decree setting out the oath to be sworn at Eretria survives, and the surviving clauses are exactly parallel to those of the Khalkidian oath.

79 Eretrian Register: In the Archonship of Diphilos [442/1] a decree was passed to list the sons of the richest men from Eretria as hostages. This decree has the title 'Eretrian Register'.

Hesykhios *Lexicon* s.v. Eretrian Register

80   [After Perikles' and Ephialtes' Areopagite reforms] the people, under the influence of their greater freedom, like an unmanageable stallion, are described by
the comic poets as "no longer willing to obey authority, but biting at Euboia and
mounting upon the islands".

Plutarch *Perikles* 7.8

Although connected by Plutarch with the results of the Ephialtic reforms of 462/1, the quotation from a
comic poet seems most likely to relate to the 440s.

81   PUPIL. And here, as you see, is Euboia. It is stretched out very long indeed.
STREPSIADES. Yes, I know. It was stretched on the rack by us and by Perikles.

Aristophanes (423) *Clouds* 211-13

Foundation of Thourioi

82   [10.3] [Under 446/5] The Sybarites, expelled from their homeland a second time,
sent ambassadors to Greece to the Spartans and Athenians, asking them to help
return them home and share in making a settlement. [10.4] The Spartans paid them
no attention, but the Athenians replied that they would help, filled 10 ships, and
sailed back with the Sybarites, under the command of Lampon and Xenokritos.
They sent a message to the cities in the Peloponnese inviting volunteers to take
part in the settlement. A large number took up the invitation...

[Disputes follow in which most of the original Sybarites are killed.] [11.2] Because
the land was large and of good quality, they sent [in 444/3] for large numbers of
additional settlers from Greece, divided up the city and distributed the territory on
a basis of equality. [11.3] Those who stayed quickly gained great wealth, made a
friendly agreement with the people of Kroton and ruled themselves well. They established a democratic constitution and divided the city into ten tribes which they named
according to the ethnic origin of their members: there were three tribes of those who
had come from Peloponnese, named Arkadian, Akhaian, and Eleian; an equal
number from related peoples from outside the Peloponnese, named Boiotian,
Amphiktionid, and Dorian; and the remaining four from the other peoples of Greece,
named Ionian, Athenian, Euboian, and Nesiotic [from the Aegean islands].

Diodoros 12.10.3-4; 11.2-3

83   When Athens sent the settlement to Sybaris which later changed its name to
Thourioi, Lysias went with Polemarkhos, the oldest of his brothers (he had two
other brothers, Euthydemos and Brakhyllos), his father being dead, to share in
the allotment of land. This was the archonship of Praxiteles [444/3], and he was
15 at the time.

[Plutarch] *Lives of the Ten Orators* 835d

The accounts of the Eleusinian commissioners for 408/7 record timbers from Thourioi (*IG* I³ 387.101): see
R. Meiggs *Trees and Timber in the Ancient Mediterranean World* (Oxford, 1982) 354; the Athenians may
have been aware in the 440s of Thourioi's importance as a point from which access could be had to such
resources. See also **231**.

The revolt of Samos

84   Those in positions of power do the same [i.e. weaken their rivals] with regard to
cities and nations, as for example the Athenians with regard to Samos, Khios and
Lesbos: for as soon as they had a firm hold over their empire, they humbled these
islands contrary to the agreements.

Aristotle *Politics* 1284a38

85 The Samian affair happened nineteen years before the *Wasps* [422], in the archonship of Timokles [441/0]. The Milesians and Samians were at war, and the
Athenians, summoned to alliance by the Milesians, campaigned against the
Samians, under the leadership of Perikles son of Xanthippos. The Samians, in a
bad way, tried to approach the Persian King. When the Athenians learnt this, they
got special war triremes ready against them, at the suggestion of Perikles. When
the Samians discovered this, they built a device against them, which the
Athenians learnt about from one Karystion and guarded themselves against. They
made conditions bad for the Samians, but they highly honoured Karystion with
his family, and thought him worthy of Athenian citizenship... The Athenians ...
put in a garrison to Samos and established a democracy through the action of
Perikles.

Scholiast on Aristophanes *Wasps* 283

86 'On the occasion that the Samians revolted, we did not vote against you, when
the rest of the Peloponnesians voted separately [from the Spartans] as to whether
to go to the defence of Samos, but we spoke openly against helping, on the
grounds that anyone should be able to punish their own allies.'

Thucydides 1.40.5

This is a passage from the speech of the Corinthians at Athens in 435 when they try to dissuade Athens from
agreeing to a request for alliance from Corcyra, a colony of Corinth.

87 Samos was no weak city, but had indeed come extremely close to depriving the
Athenians of control over the sea when it fought its war against them.

Thucydides 8.76.4

88 [Under 441/0] [28.3] Perikles was the first man to have siege engines, both the so-
called 'rams' and 'tortoises', built by the engineer Artemon of Klazomenai. He
besieged the city actively and got control of Samos by throwing down the walls.
He punished those responsible and exacted from the Samians the expenses of the
siege, which he set at [one thousand] two hundred talents. [28.4] He took away
their ships, demolished their walls, and set up democracy, before returning home.

Diodoros 12.28.3-4

This is part of an account of the war with Samos which in other respects adds nothing to Thucydides.

89 [28.1] In the ninth month the Samians surrendered and Perikles pulled down the
walls, took away the ships and inflicted a large fine, part of which the Samians
paid immediately, part they were assessed to pay at a stated time, giving hostages
as security. [28.2] Douris of Samos writes about this in tragic terms, accusing the
Athenians and Perikles of much cruelty not recorded by Thucydides, Ephoros,
or Aristotle. But it seems unlikely to be true that Perikles brought the Samian
trierarchs (i.e. trireme captains) and marines to the marketplace in Miletos, tied
them to boards for ten days and when they were already in a bad way ordered the
Milesians to execute them by bludgeoning their heads and then to throw out the
bodies without burial. [28.3] Even when he has no personal links, Douris does not
usually control his narrative by reference to truth, and he is very likely here to
magnify the misfortunes of his own homeland to slander the Athenians.

Plutarch *Perikles* 28.1-3

Douris wrote in the early third century when he was himself tyrant of Samos. Although he may have had
access to some good local information, other ancient sources too suggest that he was given to sensationalism.

90   Only the left hand edge and one other small fragment of the stele recording expenditure from the
Treasury of Athena in 440-39 survives, but this is enough to give three figures: more than 128 and
less than 130 talents; more than 368 and less than 370 talents; and more than 908 and less than 910
talents. The fourth figure follows a heading 'Total' and must be more than 1,400 and less than 1500
talents. The words 'against the Samians' occur between the first and the second figures, and it
has been suggested that the first figure is the expense of the Byzantion campaign, the second and
third, totalling more than 1276 and less than 1280 talents the expense of the Samian campaign.

ML55

If the figures are correctly interpreted here, they raise the question of why the total expenses of these two
campaigns were borne from the Treasury of Athena, rather than paid by the *Hellenotamiai*; this seems to be
the earliest instance of secular use of sacred money. See further on **196**.

91   [15] [I will do, say and advise the Athenian people as] best [I can; I will not revolt
from the people of] Athens in word [or deed, nor from the] Athenian allies. [20]
[I will be faithful to] the people of Athens. [The Athenians swear:] I will do, say
and [advise the people of] Samos [as best I can, and I will look after the
[Samians...

ML56.15-23 (*SEG* 39.3)

Fragments of the first 14 lines contain the words 'Lemnos' and 'Peloponnes[ians]. The oaths preserved here
should be compared with those sworn at Khalkis (**78**). Lines 27-32 contain a fragmentary list of the Athenian
Generals who swore the oath.

The foundation of Amphipolis

92   29 years after [the disaster at Drabeskos (1.100.3 **29**)], the Athenians came, with
Hagnon son of Nikias sent out as founder, drove out the Hedonians and founded
a settlement at this same spot, which was formerly called Nine Ways. Their base
of operations was Eion, a coastal trading post which they possessed. It was at the
mouth of the river, 25 stades [c.3 miles] distant from the present city. Hagnon
called the new foundation 'Amphipolis' because the Strymon flowed around it
on both sides: because he planned to enclose it, he cut it off by a long wall from
river to river, and made it a conspicuous landmark by sea and land.

Thucydides 4.102.3

A scholiast on Aiskhines 2.31 gives the archon date for the foundation of Amphipolis as 437/6

93   The Athenians [in 437/6] founded Amphipolis and enrolled in it some of their
own citizens and some from garrisons in the neighbourhood.

Diodoros 12.32.3

The composition of the citizen body of Amphipolis was to prove crucial during the Peloponnesian War: see
below **147-8**.

Perikles' expedition to the Black Sea

94   [20.1] Perikles sailed into the Black Sea with a large fleet, brilliantly equipped.
He did all that the Greek cities asked him to and dealt with them in a kindly way,
but he showed the extent of his power, his ability to do what he would with
impunity and his boldness to the foreign peoples living in the area and their kings
and rulers. The Athenians sailed where they wanted, subjected the whole sea to
themselves and left 13 ships for the people of Sinope along with Lamakhos and
soldiers against the tyrant Timesileos. [20.2] When Timesileos and his compan-

ions were expelled, Perikles had a decree passed that 600 Athenian volunteers should sail to Sinope and help the people of Sinope make a new foundation, distributing among themselves the houses and land which the tyrants had previously possessed.

Plutarch *Perikles* 20.1-2

This expedition is dated to the early 430s because of the casualties at Sinope recorded in the following inscription.

95   A monument to the war dead includes:

[3-8] at [Sin]ope: Dorotheos; foreigners: Deinias, Noemon, Syrot-

Two more locations seem to have been indicated at lines 17 and 20, with two deaths recorded at one and one death at the other.

[25-9] [against] Thracians: barbarian archers: Nomenios, Kallistratos

Inscriptiones Graecae i³ 1180

This list seems best to fit a time when the Athenians were still engaged around Amphipolis but also in the Black Sea.

Akarnania allies with Athens

96   [68.6] So after a while the Ambrakiots expelled the [Amphilokhian] Argives and themselves occupied their city. [68.7] When this happened, the Amphilokhians placed themselves under the protection of the Akarnanians, and both additionally called in the Athenians, who sent them Phormio as a General and 30 ships. When Phormio arrived, they took Argos by force and enslaved the Ambrakiots, and the Amphilokhians and Akarnanians together settled the city. [68.8] After this the alliance between the Akarnanians and the Athenians was first made.

Thucydides 2.68.6-8

This action by Phormio and alliance can only be dated by plausible context, and increasing Athenian interest in areas of Corinthian influence in the 430s would seem to provide the most likely background. See Hornblower *Greek World* 88-9.

The Poteidaian and Megarian affairs

97   [67.1] [During the siege of Poteidaia [432, **101-02**] the Corinthians] invited the [Peloponnesian League] allies to Sparta and denounced the Athenians for breaking the Peace [of 446/5] and wronging the Peloponnese. [67.2] The Aiginetans did not send an embassy openly, for fear of the Athenians, but secretly were major supporters of the Corinthian pressure for war, saying that they were not allowed to be independent as the Peace had stipulated. [67.3] The Spartans proceeded to invite in addition any of their own allies, and anyone else, who had other charges to bring against the Athenians, and asked them to address a meeting of the Spartan assembly. [67.4] Various others came forward and made complaints, and the Megarians laid out various serious grievances, and particularly that they were being excluded from the harbours within the Athenian empire and from the Athenian Agora contrary to the Peace.

Thucydides 1.67.1-4

Although first mentioned by Thucydides in his relation of events of 432, the passing of the Megarian decree may well belong earlier in the 430s.

98   [139.1] Later [in 432] the Spartans sent another embassy to Athens ordering the
Athenians to leave Poteidaia, and restore independence to Aigina. They particularly emphasised that the Athenians would not face war if they repealed the decree
about the Megarians in which the Megarians were banned from using the
harbours within the Athenian empire and the Athenian Agora. [139.2] The
Athenians were not prepared to give in on the other matters and did not repeal
the decree, citing the working of the sacred land and the undefined land by the
Megarians and their harbouring of runaway slaves.

Thucydides 1.139.1-2

99   DIKAIOPOLIS. Some drunken young men from a party went off to Megara and
kidnapped a prostitute named Simaitha. Then the Megarians, their anger fuelled
with garlic, came and kidnapped two prostitutes belonging to Aspasia in return.
It was as a result of that that war broke out for the whole of Greece - over three
prostitutes. It was that that caused angry Olympian Perikles to thunder and lighten
and stir Greece up: he made laws that were written like drinking songs and said
that the Megarians should be banned from earth, from the Agora, from the sea
and from heaven. It was this that made the Megarians, who were dying by inches,
ask the Spartans to get the decree repealed - the decree over the prostitutes. But
we were not willing, even when they often begged us. And it was that that brought
about this din of shields.

Aristophanes *Akharnians* 524-39

Perikles' responsibility for the Megarian decree, and thus for the war, is mentioned again by Aristophanes
at *Peace* 606-610, where he is said to have moved it to distract Athenian attention and so avoid prosecution.
Plutarch *Perikles* 30 has details, supported also by other ancient writers, of further Athenian action following the death in Megara of the herald Anthemokritos, but the date of that incident is quite unclear, and while
it may be relevant to the Peloponnesian War, it has little relevance for Athens' empire.

100   [56.1] Immediately after this [the battle of Sybota in 433] the following dispute
leading to war also occurred between the Athenians and the Peloponnesians. [56.2]
For as the Corinthians were casting about for how to revenge themselves on them,
and the Athenians had a shrewd idea of their hostility, the Athenians ordered the
Poteidaians, who live on the isthmus of Pallene and are Corinthian settlers, but
Athenian tribute-paying allies, to pull down their fortifications on the Pallene
[south] side, give hostages, and send away the magistrates they annually received
from Corinth and not receive them in the future. The Athenians were afraid that
the Poteidaians would be persuaded to revolt by Perdikkas [King of Macedon
*c.*452-413] and the Corinthians and would induce the other Thraceward allies to
revolt also. [57.1] The Athenians made these advanced preparations about
Poteidaia immediately after the sea battle at Corcyra [Sybota]. [57.2] The
Corinthians were openly at variance with them already, and Perdikkas son of
Alexander, King of the Macedonians, who hitherto had been the friend and ally
of Athens, had been made an enemy [57.3] because the Athenians had made an
alliance with his brother Philip and Derdas, who were jointly opposed to him.
[57.4] Frightened, he entered negotiations with Sparta, sending ambassadors to
try to secure war between Athens and the Peloponnesians, and he was trying to
win over the Corinthians to get Poteidaia to revolt. [57.5] He also negotiated with
the Khalkidians in Thrace and the Bottiaians to get them to revolt too, thinking
that it would be easier to make war with the Athenians if he had these places,

which were on his borders, as allies. [57.6] The Athenians, aware of this, wanted to anticipate the cities' revolts. They had just [early summer 432] sent thirty triremes and 1,000 hoplites to Perdikkas' territory under the command of Arkhestratos son of Lykomedes and two others, and they now ordered the commanders of these ships to take Poteidaian hostages and demolish their wall, and to keep an eye on the neighbouring cities so that they did not revolt. [58.1] The Poteidaians sent ambassadors to Athens to see if they could persuade them that they were not instituting anything revolutionary. These ambassadors also went to Sparta with the Corinthians to ask them to get ready to punish Athens if necessary. In long dealings with Athens they received no gesture of friendship; the Athenian fleet was sailing both against Macedon and equally against themselves. The Spartan authorities promised them that if the Athenians attacked Poteidaia they would invade Attica. Then, choosing that opportunity, the Poteidaians made a common revolt with the Khalkidians and Bottiaians.

Thucydides 1.56-58.1

101 [60.1] Meanwhile the Corinthians, now that Poteidaia had revolted and the thirty Athenian ships were in the Macedonian area, were concerned for the place and thought that the danger touched them themselves, and they sent in all 1,600 hoplites and 400 light-armed troops, volunteers serving for pay from their own city and from the rest of the Peloponnese. [60.2] Their commander was Aristeus son of Adeimantos, and it was because they were friendly with him that most of the Corinthian soldiers volunteered - he was someone who was always friendly with the people of Poteidaia. [60.3] These troops arrived in Thrace on the 40th day after Poteidaia revolted.

[61.1] The Athenians got immediate news that the cities had revolted, and when they heard also about the troops on their way with Aristeus, they sent 2,000 hoplite troops of their own and 40 ships against the places that had revolted, with Kallias son of Kalliades and four other Generals. [61.2] When they reached Macedonia, they first joined the earlier 1,000 troops who had just captured Therme and were besieging Pydna. [61.3] They first joined in the siege of Pydna, but then made an agreement and an alliance with Perdikkas on the best terms they could get, since Poteidaia and Aristeus' arrival made haste essential, left Macedonia and came to Beroia and from there to Strepsa and after they had made an unsuccessful attack on that place marched by land to Poteidaia. They had 3,000 hoplites of their own, besides a large force of allies and 600 Macedonian cavalry under Philip and Pausanias [Macedonian princes].

Thucydides 1.60-61.4

102 [Athenian arrival at Poteidaia results in a battle in which the Athenians achieve a rapid victory] [63.3] After the battle the Athenians set up a trophy and gave back the bodies of the dead to the Poteidaians under truce. Just under 300 of the Poteidaians and their allies died, along with 150 Athenians including the General Kallias. [64.1] The Athenians immediately built and garrisoned a wall. But they left the side towards Pallene unfortified. They did not think that they were sufficiently numerous both to garrison the isthmus side and to cross to Pallene and build a fortification there, and they were afraid that the Poteidaians and their allies would attack them if they divided their forces. [64.2] When the Athenians at home learned that there was no wall on Pallene, they sent a little later 1,600 troops with Phormio son of Asopios as General. When he arrived at Pallene, Phormio made Aphytis his base and brought his army to Poteidaia, advancing slowly and ravaging the territory. But when no one came out to meet him in battle, he built a wall cutting them off from Pallene [64.3] so that Poteidaia was besieged by force from both sides and from the sea by the ships blockading them.

Thucydides 1.63.3-64.3

1.4   THE STATE OF THE EMPIRE AT THE OUTBREAK OF THE PELOPONNESIAN WAR

Thucydides' view

103   The Spartans did not take tribute from the [Peloponnesian League] allies who acknowledged their leadership, but took care that they should be governed by oligarchies in the exclusive interest of Sparta. The Athenians took away the ships of the cities after a time and assessed them all for tribute in money, except for Khios and Lesbos. The individual force available to each side for this war was greater than [their combined force] when they were at the height of their intact alliance [against Persia].

Thucydides 1.19

104   [9.4] The Athenian allies were: Khios, Lesbos, Plataia, the Messenians at Naupaktos, most of the Akarnanians, Corcyra, Zakynthos, and other tributary cities among many other peoples, coastal Karia, the Dorian neighbours of the Karians, Ionia, the Hellespont, the Thraceward region, islands between the Peloponnese and east to Crete, all the Cyclades except Melos and Thera. [9.5] Of these Khios, Lesbos and the Corcyreans provided ships; the others provided land forces and money.

Thucydides 2.9.4-5

The views of Thucydides' Corinthian and Athenian speakers

105   'If it was not manifest that the Athenians were wronging Greece, some instruction of those who did not know would be necessary; but as it is, what need is there of long speeches when you can see that they have enslaved some, are plotting against others - not least our allies - and have been making advanced preparations for the event of war?'

Thucydides 1.68.3

The Corinthians are here addressing the Spartan Assembly in 432.

106   [75.1] 'Do we deserve, Spartans, to be subject, in return for our keen action [in the Persian Wars] and our intelligent planning, to such excessive criticism from the Greeks of our current empire? [75.2] It was not, after all, by force that we took that empire; it was because you were not willing to stay in for the rest of the action against the Persians, and because the allies came to us and themselves begged us to stand in as leaders. [75.3] We were compelled by the situation itself, primarily, to develop the empire to its current state; fear was our first motive, afterwards honour, and finally advantage. [75.4] It still did not seem safe to risk relaxing our grip, when we had incurred the hatred of most of our allies, when some had

revolted and been subdued, and when you were not as friendly to us as you had been, but were suspicious and hostile. Had we done so there would have been revolts over to your side. [75.5] No one is to be reproached for putting their own interests first in circumstances of the greatest danger.

[76.1] You, Spartans, have set yourselves up as leaders of the cities in the Peloponnese to suit your own interests. And if you at that time had endured everything and your leadership was hated, as we are hated, we know well that you would have been equally hard on your allies and would have been compelled either to use force or to put yourselves at risk. [76.2] There is nothing remarkable, then, or out of the usual way of mankind, in what we have done. There were three most powerful forces that made us accept the empire we were offered and not give it up: honour, fear and advantage. We are setting no precedent in this; it has always been the rule that the weaker is held down by the stronger. We think that we deserve our power, and there was a time when you thought so too, but now you calculate what is in your interests and then use the language of justice, which no one yet brought forward to prevent him improving his position when he had the opportunity to gain something by force. [76.3] Those deserve praise who, ruling others in accordance with human nature, act more fairly than the power available to them requires. [76.4] It is our opinion that if others were to take over our position they would show that we display moderation. Yet, quite unreasonably, our reasonable behaviour has given us a bad reputation rather than praise.

[77.1] Because, finding ourselves at a disadvantage in law-suits against our allies in cases controlled by inter-state agreements, we transferred such cases to Athens where the laws are the same for all, we are supposed to be too fond of dragging people into court. [77.2] No one asks why this reproach is not made against those who exercise imperial power elsewhere and show less moderation to their subjects than we do. After all, those who can use force do not have to take things through the courts. [77.3] We accustom our allies to dealing with us on equal terms, and if they experience some minor set-back that they do not think they should have suffered, over some decision or exercise of imperial power, they do not feel gratitude that they have not been deprived of more, but get more annoyed by their loss than if we had set aside law from the beginning and openly taken advantage of them. If we had done that they would not have kept saying that it was not right that the weaker be controlled by the stronger. [77.4] It seems that men get more angry at being wronged than being forced, I suppose because in the former case they seem to be taken advantage of by an equal, in the latter to be compelled by a stronger party. [77.5] They endured suffering much more terrible things at the hands of the Persians, but find our imperial rule harsh. Fair enough, present conditions are always burdensome for subjects. [77.6] You, if you defeated us and took over our empire, would quickly lose the goodwill which you have received because people fear us, particularly if you showed that you still think now as you did when you briefly took the lead against the Persians. Your ways are simply incompatible with others', and when any of you goes abroad he acts neither according to those home conventions nor according to the conventions which the rest of Greece observes.'

Thucydides 1.75-7

This is part of the Athenian speech to the Spartan Assembly on the same occasion.

107 'Those of us who have past experience of exchange of goods with the Athenians do not need to be instructed to be on our guard against them. But those who live in more inland parts and not by the sea need to know that if they do not defend those on the coast they will find it increasingly difficult to import and export seasonal produce that needs to cross the sea. They should not make hasty judgements about what is being said now, on the grounds that it does not affect them, only to discover later that, if cities on the coast are abandoned and the trouble approaches them, it is for themselves just as much that they now take counsel.'

Thucydides 1.120.2

This is part of the Corinthian speech at the meeting of the Peloponnesian League in 432 which decides in favour of war with Athens. For the suggestion here that the Athenians controlled imports and exports by other Greek cities, compare the following passage and **121-2** (with note to **121**) as well, perhaps, as the Megarian Decree (**97-9**).

The view of a contemporary Athenian

108 [2.2] Those who are subject to a land power can get the forces of small cities together and fight in a body; but those who are subject to a sea power, if they are islanders, cannot unite their cities; for the sea lies in between and those who rule them have control of the sea. Even if it were possible for the islanders to get together into one island without being noticed, they would be starved out. [2.3] As to the cities on land ruled by the Athenians, the big cities are ruled by fear, and the small by necessity: there is no city which does not need to import and export, and no city can do that unless it obeys those who rule the sea. [2.4] Those who are sea powers can also do what land powers can do only sometimes: ravage the land of stronger powers. They can sail to a place where the enemy are not present or are few in number, and if the enemy attack, they can re-embark and sail away. Acting like this they get into difficulties less than those who go to help on foot. [2.5] Those who rule by sea can sail as far away from their own land as they want, but those who rule by land cannot go many days' journey from their land: progress is slow and it is impossible for an army going by land to take much food. A land army has either to go through friendly territory or fight its way and win; the sea power can land wherever it is stronger and not land when it is weaker but sail on until it reaches friendly territory or people weaker than it. [2.6] Also blight on crops that comes from Zeus is more difficult for land powers, easier for sea powers; for the whole land does not suffer blight at the same time and those who rule the sea can get provisions from where the land is healthy.

[2.7] To consider less important matters, it is by ruling the sea that the Athenians discovered various cuisines, mixing with different people in different places. Because they rule the sea, they have gathered into one place whatever is sweet in Sicily and Italy and Cyprus and Egypt and Lydia and the Black Sea and the Peloponnese and everywhere else. [2.8] Also they hear every dialect and can select one feature from one and another feature from another. The Greeks all have individual dialects and lifestyles and clothing; but the Athenians mix up what they get from all Greeks and foreigners.

[Xenophon] *Constitution of the Athenians* [*c*.424?] 2.2-8

The general Greek view?

109 [8.4] Feeling in Greece was strongly on the side of the Spartans, for they professed to be the liberators of Greece. Every individual and every city was eager to assist them in any way they could, in word or deed, and everyone thought that there was an obstacle to progress if they were not themselves present. [8.5] Most were angry with the Athenians, some wanting to be rid of their imperial control, and others fearing that they would fall victims to it.

Thucydides 2.8.4-5

An Aristophanic view

110 HERMES. Then, when the cities that you ruled realised that you [the people of Athens] were at each other's throats and showing your teeth as you grinned, they plotted against you in every way that they could because of their fear of the tribute, and they used bribes to persuade the most powerful men in Sparta.

Aristophanes *Peace* (421) 619-22

Views ascribed to leading men in Athens and Sparta

111 [13.2] Perikles repeated his previous advice to make preparations for the war, to bring things in from the fields, not to go out to battle but to come into the city and guard it, to equip the navy, which was their strength, and to keep the allies in hand [i.e. prevent/suppress revolts]. He said that their power stemmed from the money which they received from the allies and that most successes in war came from good decisions and abundance of money. [13.3] He told the Athenians to be confident since they generally had 600 talents of tribute coming in to the city annually from the allies, not counting other income, that they had at that time 6,000 talents of coined silver on the Akropolis (at its greatest this reserve had amounted to 9,700 talents, but they had spent on the Propylaia, other buildings, and the Poteidaia campaign out of that), [13.4] without counting the gold and silver contained in private and public dedications and all the sacred equipment used for processions and contests, and the Persian War spoils, and such like, amounting to at least 5,000 talents. [13.5] He added in the considerable resources from the other temples, which he said that they could use, even if they were deprived of all else, and the gold which made up the statue of Athena. (He demonstrated that the statue had 40 talents weight of refined gold, all of which was removable, and if they used this to save the city, they would have to replace it all again).

Thucydides 2.13.2-5

Thucydides has Perikles make this speech immediately before the invasion of Attica by Peloponnesian forces in 431. Diodoros, in an account of the origins of the war which he takes from Ephoros, transfers these statements about resources to Perikles' speech in response to the Spartan ultimatum (i.e. the speech which Thucydides gives at 1.140-144). Mention of the resources of sanctuaries other than those on the Akropolis links in with the first Kallias decree, for which a date of 434 or 431 seems probable; that decree orders that the treasures of outlying sanctuaries be brought to the Akropolis for safe-keeping (ML 58/Fornara 119 A 18-27).

112 [80.3] 'When dealing with Peloponnesians and neighbours, our strength is comparable, and we can quickly attack wherever we wish; but when dealing with men whose land is far off, and, what is more, who are extremely experienced at sea and are the best equipped in all other ways - in both private and state wealth, in ships, in cavalry, in arms, in having a population unequalled by any other Greek state, and what is more in having many tribute-paying allies - how could we lightly make war on them?

[83.2] The Athenians have as many allies as we have and they pay tribute. War is not a matter of arms, for the most part, but of money. It is money that makes arms useful, particularly when a land power is fighting a sea power. [83.3] So first let us acquire money, and not become excited by our allies before we do...'

Thucydides 1.80.3, 83.2-3

King Arkhidamos' speaks to the Spartan Assembly in 431, trying to dissuade it from voting for war.

113 The Athenians, keeping tight hold on their naval hegemony, transferred to Athens the moneys collected on Delos for common use, some 8,000 talents, and handed it over to Perikles to look after. Perikles was outstanding among the citizens for nobility, reputation, and skill in speaking. But after a time he had privately spent no small part of these moneys, and when asked to render an account he fell ill, unable to give an account of the money entrusted to him.

Diodoros 12.38.2

This is one of several passages (see also 12.40.1, 12.54.3; cf. 13.21.3) in his narrative of the beginning of the war in which Diodoros refers to the transfer of the Treasury from Delos to Athens, an event most probably to be dated to 454/3 (**24, 66** and see p.36). It is not clear that the figures given here or elsewhere in Diodoros have any authority. Stories of Periklean peculation are found also in Plutarch (*Perikles* 32.3-6) and implicitly rejected by Perikles at Thucydides 2.60.5 and by Thucydides at 2.65.8.

114 '[63.1] You must defend the prestige which derives from the empire - an empire in which you all take pride - and not run away from the labour it involves, or else not run after the rewards. Do not think that the contest is just about slavery or freedom, it is about loss of empire and about the danger to which the hatred felt for your imperial rule has brought you. [63.2] Nor can you resign your power, if someone, frightened by the present crisis, wants to play at being noble by adopting a life of inactivity. The empire you have now is like a tyranny: in the opinion of mankind it may seem to have been acquired unjustly, but it cannot be safely surrendered.'

Thucydides 2.63.1-2

So Perikles, defending his policies to the Athenians in 430. For the sentiment in 63.1 compare Perikles at 2.41.3 and 2.64.3; for that in 63.2 compare Kleon at 3.37.2.

1.5   ATHENS AND HER EMPIRE DURING THE ARKHIDAMIAN WAR

Problems at Kaunos in Karia, and in Lykia

115 The Megabyzos who fought in Egypt against the Athenians and their allies was the son of this Zopyros, and his son Zopyros deserted from the Persians to Athens.

Herodotos 3.160.2

For Megabyzos see **39** Thuc. 1.109.3

116 When his father and mother died, Zopyros, the son of Megabyzos and Amytis, revolted from the King and went to Athens because his mother had been a benefactor of the Athenians. He sailed to Kaunos, and the Athenians followed at the same time. When Zopyros ordered them to hand over the city, they asserted that they were willing to hand the city over to him, but not yet to the Athenians who followed with him. As Zopyros entered the city wall a Kaunian by the name of Alkides threw a stone onto his head, and so Zopyros died. His grandmother, Amestris, had the Kaunian crucified.

Ktesias *Persika* (*FGH* 688. F14.45)

Kaunos seems to have revolted from Athens in the early 420s, suggesting that Zopyros' stay in Athens probably began sometime in the 430s.

117 [69.1] During the following winter [430/29] the Athenians sent ... six ships to the regions of Karia and Lykia under Melesander as General in order to collect money and prevent piratical activity by the Peloponnesians moored there from harming merchant ships sailing from Phaselis and Phoenicia and that part of the world. [69.2] Melesander marched up into Lykia with a force from the ships and from the allies, and was defeated in battle and killed, losing part of the army.

Thucydides 2.69

118 [19.1] The Athenians still needed money for the siege [of Mytilene]..., and sent out 12 ships [428/7] to collect money from the allies under Lysikles and four other Generals. He collected money in other places, sailed around, and made an expedition from Myous in Karia through the plain of the Maiander to the hill of Sandios. [19.2] There he was attacked by the Karians and the Anaians [= Samians from Anaia], and he and much of the rest of his force were killed.

Thucydides 3.19.1-2

The record of this part of the empire for paying tribute was not good: see S. Hornblower *Mausolus* 27ff. For other mentions of money-collecting missions see **60**, **144**. For the passage omitted, see below **135**.

Trouble at Kolophon

119 [34.1] As he was sailing along the coast [427], Pakhes put in at Notion, the port of Kolophon. The Kolophonians were living at Notion following the capture of the upper city by Itamenes and the Persians who had been brought in during political conflict. This capture had taken place at the time of the second Peloponnesian invasion of Attica [430]. [34.2] The refugees at Notion fell into political conflict again after they had settled there. Some of them had introduced Arkadian and foreign mercenaries hired from Pissouthnes and quartered them behind a crosswall, and the pro-Persian faction of Kolophonians from the upper city joined them in a single political community, while those who had run away to escape them and were in exile called in Pakhes. [34.3] Pakhes summoned Hippias, the commander of the Arkadians in the fortified part of the town, to negotiate, undertaking that if no progress was made in the negotiations, he would restore him to the fortification again safe and well. Hippias came out to Pakhes, and Pakhes then kept him under guard, without putting him in chains, while he launched a surprise attack on the fortification and, because no attack was expected, took it. He had the Arkadians and foreigners who were there killed and later took Hippias back there, as he had undertaken, and when he was inside arrested him and had him shot. [34.4] Pakhes handed Notion over to those Kolophonians who did not belong to the pro-Persian faction. Later the Athenians colonised the place under new founders whom they sent out from Athens and gave it laws like their own, bringing in all the Kolophonians they could find anywhere.

Thucydides 3.34

120 Antikl[es (?) said: in other] respects I agree with the proposal of the Council, [but add of Apollophanes] of Kolophon ['since] he is [a man] good to the people [of Athens] and the soldiers'. He is to look after the security of the sacred [land] of Zeus, to ensure that it is safe for the Athenians; the Generals in office at any time are to help him look after its needs along with the Council that is in office and the prytaneis. He is to have access to the prytaneis and the Council and the People first after sacred matters whenever he needs something. He is not to be punished [in any way unless] the Athenian people so decides. [The same rights are to be permitted also] to the descendants [of Apollophanes], and if anyone breaks these rules...

Inscriptiones Graecae i³ 65.7-24 (*SEG* 38.4)

These honours for Apollophanes seem to belong to the period just after the recapture of Notion.

Athens, Methone and Macedon

121   The people of Methone from Pieria. Phainippos son of Phrynikhos was Secretary [424/3].

(1) The Council and People decided, in the prytany of the tribe Erekhtheis, when Skopas was Secretary [430/29?] and Timonides President, on the proposal of [Diopei]thes [5] that the People should vote at once about the people of Methone, whether they should assess tribute at once or whether it was sufficient for them to pay the share for Athena which they had been assessed to pay at the last Panathenaia, and should be free from tax as to the rest.

[10] As to the debts which the people of Methone are recorded as owing to the [Athenian] treasury, if they are as friendly to the Athenians as they are now, and even more so, the Athenians [allow a special] assessment concerning their payment, and if a [general] decree is passed about the debts recorded on the [boards], [15] the people of Methone need pay nothing [unless] a separate decree is passed about the people of Methone.

Three [ambassadors] aged over 50 are to be sent to Perdikkas and say to Perdikkas that [fairness] dictates that the people of Methone be allowed to use the sea and [20] their movement not be limited, and allow them to import goods to the land [just as] before, and neither doing [nor suffering injury], and that he should not [lead] an army through the territory of Methone without permission from Methone. If [both sides] agree, the ambassadors are to broker a treaty; if not, [25] each side is to send an [embassy] to the Athenian Council and [People] at the Dionysia, with power to decide disputed matters. And to say to Perdikkas that if the soldiers at Poteidaia praise him, the Athenians [will be] well-intentioned towards him.

The People voted that Methone [30] should pay the goddess's share of the tribute which they had been assessed to pay at the last Panathenaia, and for the rest be free of taxes.

(2) The Council and People decided, in the prytany of the tribe Hippothontis, when Megakleides was Secretary [426] and Niko[.....] was President, on the proposal of Kleonymos that the [people of Methone] [35] be allowed to import from Byzantion up to [....] thousand medimnoi of corn each year, and that the Athenian officials at the Hellespont (*Hellespontophylakes*) should neither themselves prevent this import nor allow any other to prevent it, on pain of a fine of 10,000 drachmas each at their scrutiny. After the *Hellespontophylakes* have been informed in writing, [40] they may import the stated amount. The ships that carry the imported grain shall not be liable to any penalty.

Any general decree that the Athenians pass concerning aid or any other demand made of the cities either about themselves or about the cities, any that they pass mentioning by name the [45] [city] of Methone, this shall apply to them, but the others not; they should guard their own land and so do what they have been assessed to do.

As to the offences which they say Perdikkas has committed against them, the Athenians shall take counsel as to what it is right to do when [50] the ambassadors returning from Perdikkas, those who went with Pleistias and those with Leogoras, report to the People. The People shall hold an Assembly at the beginning of the second prytany immediately after the [Assembly] in the dockyard to consider the other cities, and continue [55] [sitting] until these affairs are sorted out, giving nothing else priority in the discussion unless the Generals make some request.

(3) The Council and People [decided], in the prytany of the tribe Kekropis, when [-]es was Secretary and Hierokleides was President [?426] on the proposal of...[text breaks off]

ML 65 (SEG 40.7)

This stone originally included no fewer than four decrees. The heading gives the magistrates at the date of the most recent decree, when the decision to inscribe was taken, but the decrees are then given in the order in which they were passed, the first probably in 430/29, the second and perhaps the third in 426 and the last (which does not survive at all on the stone) in 424/3.

Methone seems to have been brought into the Athenian Empire only in the late 430s, when the Athenians were becoming more active in the Thraceward area (see p.94). This seems to have annoyed Perdikkas, King of Macedon, and Methone here uses her important strategic position and the difficulties which this brought her, both to bargain for exceptional treatment and to secure Athenian diplomatic intervention with Perdikkas.

The cross-reference to Methone in **122** may suggest that this set an important precedent. The Corinthian complaint before the war (**107**), however, along with the Megarian decree (**97-9**) and the general reflections of [Xenophon] (**108**, 2.3) make it not unlikely that the *Hellespontophylakes* may have been set up before the war. Just how far the Athenians did operate a 'closed sea' policy, even during the war, is unclear: note that Mytilene <u>is</u> able to import grain from the Black Sea in 427 (**124**, Thuc. 3.2.2).

The care which the Athenians take here over Methone suggests that they were extremely sensitive about their relations with the Greek cities of this area in the wake of the siege of Poteidaia.

122 ...eight hundred medimnoi [—-] war, the total. Concerning [—-] the Aphytaians up to 10,000 medimnoi. They are to pay the same [price] as [5] the people of Methone. Let the Thrambaians supply corn from their own resources to the magistrates in Aphytis, in proportion to the number. Let the [other cities contribute taxes] just as for the people of Methone according to the decree. The Secretary [of the Council] is to write up the oath which the Aphytaians swore to the additional settlers at Poteidaia and to the Athenians along with this decree [10] on a stone stele and set it up on the Akropolis at [their] expense. If anyone, a *Hellenotamias* or any other official, fails to obey any of these decisions voted by the People [concerning Aphytis, let him be liable to the penalty stipulated] in the decree. And praise the Aphytaians because they are men good to the Athenians both now and in former times, [and [15] to declare] to the people that they will get what they ask for [from the Athenians]. The People decided that the Aphytaians should contribute 500 drachmas for the goddess.

This is the oath that the Aphytaians [swore to those in Poteidaia: If any] enemy [attacks the city] of the Athenians [or the Athenian settlers] [20] at Poteidaia, [I will help the Athenians to the best of my ability in word] and deed...

Inscriptiones Graecae i³ 62

For Aphytis see **102**. This and the following decree must both date to the first half of the 420s, perhaps to 428/7 and to 426. See also note on **121**.

123 [If any] official [or private individual proposes or puts to the vote, contrary to] this [decree, that] these [should be taken away from the Aphytaians], let him owe [10,000 drachmas, sacred to] [5] Athena. The Secretary of the Council [is to write up this] decree [on a stone stele and] place it on the Akropolis at [their] expense.

[And summon] the Aphytaian embassy [to hospitality in the] Prytaneion tomorrow. S[kopas said: otherwise as] [10] Patrokleides proposed, but no [Athenian or]
Athenian ally [is to prevent the Aphytaians from bringing money] from any place
they wish. [It is to be allowed for] any [Aphytaian] who wishes to sail to Athens
[and bring] money [for the Athenians] without risk of being attacked and without
[need to make a truce. Those who wish may] [15] also bring corn [according to
the decrees] voted by the People [and engage in trade] paying whatever taxes the
[Athenian People] decrees. And if anyone prevents the Aphytaians [from sailing
to Athens, let him owe] 10,000 [drachmas] —-

Inscriptiones Graecae i³ 63

The revolt of Mytilene

124 [2.1] Straight after the invasion [of Attica] by the Peloponnesians [in 428] the
whole of Lesbos except Methymna revolted from the Athenians. They had
wanted to revolt even before the war, but the Spartans had given them no support.
But now they were forced to make their revolt before they intended to. [2.2] They
were waiting to finish blocking up their harbours, building their walls and
constructing ships, and for the arrival of the archers and grain that they had sent
for from the Black Sea. [2.3] But the people of Tenedos were at odds with them,
as were the people of Methymna and some individual Mytileneans who were of
the opposite political faction and were Athenian *proxenoi*, and they told the
Athenians that Mytilene was forcing the cities of Lesbos into political union and
was hurrying on all the preparations for revolt in collaboration with the Spartans
and with their Boiotian kinsmen. They said that unless the Athenians anticipated
these preparations they would lose Lesbos.

Thucydides 3.2

125 In the case of Mytilene too, a conflict arising from an inheritance dispute was the
cause of a great deal of trouble, including the war against the Athenians in which
Pakhes captured the city. To explain: a rich man named Timophanes died leaving
two daughters, and when Dexandros, the Athenian *proxenos*, failed to secure
them for his sons and was rejected, he stirred up political conflict and urged the
Athenians to intervene.

Aristotle *Politics* 1304a4-10

As with the Megarian decree (**97-9**), so here another source supplies personal reasons not even hinted at by
Thucydides for major political events. For Pakhes at Mytilene see **128**.

126 [10.4] 'While the Athenians led from a position of equality we followed them enthusiastically. But when we saw that they were relaxing their efforts against the
Persians and increasingly enslaving the allies, we began to be afraid. [10.5] Since
the allies had a large number of individual votes, they could not unite to defend
themselves, and they were all enslaved except for us and the Khians; we took part
in campaigns as parties nominally independent and free. [10.6] Given the past prece-
dents we could no longer trust the Athenians as leaders. It was hardly likely that
when they had made some of those who were fellow members with us subjects,
they would refrain from doing the same to the rest if they ever had the power.

[11.1] 'If we were all still independent, we could have been more confident that
they would not alter the status quo in our regard. But since they had most of the

allies under their thumb, our continuing equality was something they reasonably would find increasingly difficult to put up with. They would contrast us who alone remained their equals with the majority who had submitted to them, particularly since they were becoming increasingly more powerful than us and we increasingly isolated. [11.2] The only safe guarantee in an alliance is an equal balance of fear; that way the party wanting to break faith is deterred by lack of sure advantage. [11.3] The only reason why we were left independent was that their policy as regards their empire was to seize control by specious arguments and aggressive plans rather than by force. [11.4] On the other hand, our position demonstrated that those who had equal votes did not take part in campaigns against their will, and that those whom they attacked must have done something wrong. In the same way, they led the strongest against the resourceless first, thinking that if they left the powerful till last they were bound to find them weaker when the rest had been dealt with. [11.5] If they had begun with us when all the other states were strong and had a place to take a stand, they would not have subjugated them so easily. [11.6] They were not without fear that our navy might join you or some other power and so put them in danger. [11.7] But we survived by being nice to the people of Athens and whoever was influential with it. [11.8] But it does not seem that we would have maintained our position long, given the example of how they have treated others, had this war not broken out.'

Thucydides 3.10.4-11.8

Part of the speech of the Mytileneans at Olympia in 428 seeking Spartan support for revolt from Athens. For the immediately preceding section of the speech see **12** above.

127 [5.1] When the Mytilenean ambassadors returned from Athens without having accomplished anything, the Mytileneans declared war along with the rest of Lesbos except Methymna. The people of Methymna gave assistance to the Athenians, together with the Imbrians, Lemnians and some few other allies...

[6.1] The Athenians were much encouraged by the inaction of the Mytileneans, and summoned the allies, who quickly joined them, since they observed that the Lesbians were not doing anything forceful. They stationed the fleet south of the city and fortified two camps, one on each side of the city, and blockaded both the harbours. [6.2] They prevented the Mytileneans from using the sea, but the Mytileneans and other Lesbians who had now come to help them had control of the land. The Athenians only had the small area of land around the camps and Malea which served them as a place to moor ships and a market place. This was the situation in the war around Mytilene.

Thucydides 3.5.1, 6.1-2

128 [27.1] Meanwhile [summer 427] the people of Mytilene, when the fleet from the Peloponnese had not reached them but was taking a long time, and their corn had run out, were compelled to make an agreement with the Athenians because of the following events. [27.2] Salaithos [a Spartan general on loan to Mytilene], who had himself ceased to expect the ships, gave arms to the people, who had previously only had light arms, in order to attack the Athenians. [27.3] But when the people gained possession of the arms, they no longer obeyed the commanders but organised meetings and demanded that those who could do so should bring the corn into the open and distribute it to everyone, threatening that if they did not, they would make an agreement with the Athenians and hand over the city to them. [28.1] Those at the centre of the affair knew that they were helpless and risked being left out of the agreement, and so they joined in making an agreement with Pakhes [the Athenian general] and the camp. The agreement was that the Athenians could take any decision they wanted about the people of Mytilene and that they accepted the army into their city; and that the Mytileneans would send an embassy to Athens about themselves. Pakhes was not to imprison, enslave or execute anyone until the embassy came back.

Thucydides 3.27-28.1

How should we interpret the action of the people of Mytilene here? Thucydides has Diodotos suggest (below **132**) that the people of Mytilene handed over the city to the Athenians when they got arms in their hands because they were friendly to Athens. But Thucydides' own account allows us to put emphasis rather on the fact that they wanted food.

Debate at Athens over the punishment of the Mytileneans

129 [39.2] 'I myself am prepared to forgive those who revolt because they are unable to bear our imperial power or are compelled by our enemies. But the people who have revolted in this case are people who live on an island, with their own fortifications, have to fear our enemies only by sea, are equipped with triremes to face those enemies, are independent and are especially honoured by us. How can one describe what they have done other than as a plot and an uprising rather than a revolt - revolt is what people do in response to the application of force? They have tried to join with our bitterest enemies to destroy us. This is much worse than getting a force of their own and fighting against us.'

Thucydides 3.39.2

Part of Kleon's speech in the debate at Athens in summer 427 over what punishment was appropriate after the Mytilenean revolt had been crushed.

130 [39.8] '[If you are lenient with Mytilene, other cities will decide that revolt is a good idea]. We shall have risked money and lives over each of these cities, and if we take the city once it has been destroyed, we shall not after that have the income from it on which our strength depends, while if we fail, we shall add yet another enemy to our present enemies, and the time we should be spending fighting the enemies we have now we shall spend fighting our own allies.'

Thucydides 3.39.8

A further section of the same speech.

131 [46.1] 'You must not make unwise decisions because of misplaced trust in the effectiveness of the death penalty, and you must not deprive those who have revolted of the hope that they can change their minds and make up for their mistake in a very short time. [46.2] You should reflect that, as it is, if a city that has revolted decides that it is not going to succeed, it can come to terms while it is still able to pay the expenses [incurred by Athens] and pay tribute in the future.'

Thucydides 3.46.1-2

An extract from Diodotos' speech opposing Kleon's views.

132 [47.2] 'At the moment in all the cities the people are your friends; either they do not join the few in revolting, or, if they are forced to revolt, they become at once the enemy of those who have revolted, and when you go to war with the hostile city, you have the people, who are the majority, on your side. [47.3] But if you put the people of Mytilene to death, when they had no part in the revolt and, when they got arms in their hands, willingly handed the city over to you, you will in the first place be doing wrong in killing people who did you good, and in the second place you will be doing exactly what the oligarchs want: when they get cities to revolt in future, they will have the people as their ally from the beginning if you have indicated that the same punishment falls on those who offended and those who did not.'

Thucydides 3.47.2-3

A further extract from Diodotos' speech. On Diodotos' interpretation of the people's action see on **128** and p.38.

133 [50.1] [Diodotos' view having prevailed, the citizens of Mytilene were not executed.] But the Athenians, acting on a proposal moved by Kleon, executed the other men, whom Pakhes had sent away on the grounds that they were those most responsible for the revolt; they numbered just over a thousand. The Athenians also demolished the walls of Mytilene and took away its fleet. [50.2] Later they did not assess Lesbos for tribute, but divided the land, except for the land of Methymna, into three thousand plots. They dedicated three hundred plots as sacred to the gods, and settled Athenians chosen by lot (*kleroukhoi*) on the other plots. The Lesbians agreed to pay to these settlers 200 drachmas a year for each plot and went on farming the land. [50.3] The Athenians also took away the towns which Mytilene controlled on the mainland opposite, which from then on were subject to Athens.

Thucydides 3.50

The 200 drachmas which the Athenians receive approximates to cost of paying a hoplite for a year, and thus the settlement here may be thought of as a way of maintaining a large garrison at no expense to Athens. But it is odd to choose garrison troops by lot, and no garrison appears in any subsequent passage of Thucydides (not, for example, at 4.52 when there is further trouble in the region). See also p.91.

Subsequent Athenian regulation of land plots on Lesbos (*c.*426)

134 [Only a small proportion of the letters in the first 10 lines of the inscription can be read, and although plausible restorations have been suggested, I here give a text only from 10 onwards]

The Athenian People also [grants them the land] and resolves that they be independent [inhabiting what is] their [own, except for handing over the land on the mainland which] the Athenians command them [to hand over], and deciding with Athenians [according to agreements and [15] having cases decided by] the former agreements. [They are to calculate the value of] anything that was sold to the settlers from the plots of land] before they were handed over to them, [having inquired] after whichever Athenian General or soldier [or other Athenian] [20] now has it. The Secretary of the Council is to write all this up on a stone stele and [set it up] on the Akropolis at [Mytilenean] expense. Write these things up and [summon the] Mytilenean [embassy] to hospitality [at the Prytaneion] [25] tomorrow. And [grant] to the settlers the right to sell back the land...

Inscriptiones Graecae i[3] 66.10-27 (*SEG* 36.9)

Although all restorations here are highly speculative this inscription would seem to be evidence for on-going negotiation about land and property between the Athenians and the Mytileneans after the initial settlement. The Athenians seem to treat the Mytilenean embassy to all the usual hospitality.

Athens raises a capital tax

135 Needing money for the siege [of Mytilene, 428], the Athenians then for the first time themselves contributed an *eisphora* of 200 talents...

Thucydides 3.19.1

For an explanation of the *eisphora* system, see Glossary. Thucydides' 'for the first time' should refer to the amount raised, not to the fact of an *eisphora*, if the second Kallias decree, which refers to the *eisphora* (ML

58B 17, 19 (both restored)), dates to before 428. (But for a 418 date see L. Kallet-Marx, *CQ* 39 (1989) 94–113).

For the continuation of this passage see **118**.

Tribute collection procedures revised, 426: the Kleonymos Decree

136 [First line of heading fragmentary] Of tribute. The Council and People decided, in the prytany of the tribe Kekropis, Polemarkhos was Secretary, Onasos was [5] President, on the proposal of Kleonymos: All the cities that pay tribute to the Athenians [are to choose] in each city [Collectors of tribute, in order that the whole tribute may be collected] from each city [for the Athenians] or else [the Collectors are to be] liable [to scrutiny].

[Lacuna]

[... after the] Dionysia; and read [out in the Assembly the cities] which pay [the tribute and the cities which] do not [15] pay and which [pay in part].

And send [five men] to the cities that owe money to exact the tribute from them. Let the *Hellenotamiai* write up on a board the [cities which have not paid enough] tribute and [the names] of those who bring it, and place the boards [20] on each occasion in front of [—].

In the case of Samos and Thera [—] the moneys which [—] of the selection of the men, and any other city that is assessed to pay money to Athens.

[25] The prytany of the tribe Kekropis is to place this decree on a stone stele on the Akropolis.

P...kritos said: In other respects I agree with the proposal of Kleonymos, but in order that the Athenians may bear the war most easily and effectively, this is to be brought before the People, and the Assembly [is to be convened] at dawn tomorrow. The [30] [Council and the People] decided, in the prytany of Kekropis, when Po[lemarkhos was Secretary] and Hygiainon was President, [on the proposal of ...: in other respects] as in the former decree...

[Lacuna]

Surviving fragments of the upper part of the stele recording the Kleonymos decree (**136**), showing the decree relief with its representation of bags of tribute. The stele is 59 cm. wide and the standard letter height is 9 mm.

... to choose men to look after [the other court cases that concern] Athenian money, [according to ....'s] decree, [40] and [to order one] of the Generals to be present whenever [a case is heard] about any of the [cities].

If anyone tries to [invalidate] the decree about the tribute by unfair means or [to prevent] the tribute being [taken away] to Athens, [45] anyone from that city may indict him [for treachery] before the Commissioners.

[The Commissioners are to bring] the case [to court] within a month, [once] the summoners have come. [Let the summoners be two in number], or whoever [wants to] may indict them. [If] the court [50] condemns [him], it is to assess the penalty [that he should] suffer or pay.

All the heralds that the prytaneis [with the Council choose], are to be sent to the cities in the prytany [of the tribe Kekropis] in order that [the men] [55] to collect the tribute may be chosen and [recorded] in the Council Chamber.

Let the Sellers (*Poletai*) put the stele out to contract.

Of the collection of tribute from the cities.

ML68

The main decree here is moved by the same Kleonymos who moved the Methone decree (121), perhaps a month earlier, and an Athenian decree found on Delos dating to the same year (see *Zeitschrift für Papyrologie und Epigraphik* 60 (1985) 108). He was almost certainly a member of the Council for 426/5. He was prominent enough to be attacked in every extant Aristophanic comedy from *Akharnians* (425) to *Birds* (414). In 415 he proposed a reward of 1,000 drachmas for information about the mutilation of the Herms.

The most important innovation in this decree seems to be the establishment of Collectors (*eklogeis*) of tribute in every city. The word 'Collector' is restored in line 7 but required by line 55. Compare also **187**.

Mention of Thera together with Samos in lines 20-21 suggests that it may have been forcibly brought into the empire between 431 (see **104**) and 426, even though Thucydides makes no mention of this.

The Athenians intervene on Delos

137A [104.1] During the same winter [426/5], the Athenians also purified Delos in accordance with some oracle. Peisistratos the tyrant had previously purified it, but not all of it, only the part that could be seen from the sanctuary. On this occasion the whole island was purified... [Thucydides goes on to discuss the evidence which the Homeric *Hymn to Apollo* gives for a Delian festival attended by Ionians and Aegean islanders.] [104.6] That is what Homer's evidence for a great meeting and festival at Delos in days of old amounts to. Later the islanders and the Athenians sent choral groups and animals for sacrifice. But most of the competitions came to an end because of the misfortunes of Ionia, as one would expect, before the Athenians recreated the competitive festival and added a horse race which had not previously been part of the festival.

Thucydides 3.104.1 and 6

137B [58.6] Because the plague was so severe, the Athenians ascribed the cause of their misfortune to the deity. Therefore, acting on the command of some oracle, they purified the island of Delos which was sacred to Apollo and seemed to have been polluted by the burial on it of the dead. [58.7] They excavated all the burials on Delos and transferred them to the island called Rheneia, which is next to Delos. They made a law that no birth or burial should occur on Delos. They also celebrated the Delian festival which had been held in the past but not for a long time.

Diodoros 12.58.6-7

137C Athens [set up] this altar of Apollo Paion and Athena [—] Let everyone [who has come from] another land or is a Delian look at it, the work of Kleoteles.

Inscriptiones Graecae i³1468bis

137C owes its place here to the presence of Apollo Paion, Apollo in his guise as Healer. This dedication, if it is right to date it to around 426, would suggest that Diodoros might be right to connect the purification of Delos with the plague at Athens.

For subsequent action with regard to the Delians see **154-5**.

Tribute reassessment, 425/4

138 Gods. Assessment of Tribute.

The [Council and People] decided, in the prytany [of the tribe —, when -] was Secretary [and -] President, [on the proposal] of Thoudippos:

[to send heralds whom the Council elects by show of hands] from the - [to the] [5] cities: 2 [to Ionia and Karia], 2 [to Thrace, 2] to the Islands, [and 2 to the Hellesp]ont. These [are to announce] in the assembly [of each city that ambassadors should come to Athens during] Maimakterion [November/December].

Magistrates in charge of introducing cases to court [are to be chosen, and these are to choose a Secretary and an Undersecretary.] The [Council —– choose ten men]. They [are to record the cities within five days] from the day when [—– or else each be fined 1,000 drachmas] [10] for each day. The magistrates in charge of oaths [are to take oaths from the Assessors on the same day when]ever [they are elected, or each will be liable to] the same fine.

[The magistrates in charge of introducing cases are to look after the court cases arising over the tribute, once the People] have voted. [Let whichever magistrate in charge of introducing cases is selected by lot] and the Polemarch hold the preliminary hearing of charges in] the Heliaia [as with other cases brought before] the members of the Heliaia. But if [the Assessors (?) fail to deal with] [15] the cities in accordance with the judgement of the court, let them be fined [10,000 drachmas each] at their scrutiny.

The [Thesmo]thetai are to set up a new [court of 1,000 dikasts].

[As to the tribute, since] it has become less, let [this court], together with the Council, hold an assessment during the month of Poseideion (January/February), [just as in the last] term of office, of [all the assessments] proportionately. They shall deal with the matter every day from the beginning of the month [to ensure that] the tribute [is assessed] in Poseideion. [The full Council] [20] is also to deal with the matter [continuously, to ensure that] the assessment happens, provided [that there is no contrary decree of the People. They must not [assess less] tribute for any [city] than the tribute that city [has brought in before now], unless there [seems to be such shortage of resources that] that territory cannot [bring in more]. The Secretary [of the Council is to] write up this decision and this [decree and this] tribute that is assessed [for each city on two] stelai and [place one in the] Council Chamber [25] and one [on the Akropolis]. The Sellers (*Poletai*) [are to put this out to contract] and the *Kolakretai* [are to provide the money].

[For the future, notice] about the tribute [is to be given to the] cities [before the] Great [Panathenaia. Whichever prytany] is in office is to introduce [the assessments at the] Panathenaia. [If the prytaneis do not introduce matters] about the [tribute then] to the People [and the Council and the court, or do not deal with it immediately] in their own term of office, [each of the prytaneis is to be fined 100 drachmas sacred to] [30] Athena [and 100 drachmas] to the public treasury, and [each of the prytaneis is to face a fine of 1,000 drachmas at their scrutiny]. And if anyone else [proposes a vote on the proposal that the cities not] be assessed at the first prytany [at the Great Panathenaia], let him lose his civic rights and the property [be confiscated and a tenth of it] given to the goddess.

These matters are to be brought to the People in the prytany of [the tribe —] compulsorily on the second day after the expedition [returns, [35] immediately] after the [religious business]. If the Assembly does not manage to deal with this on this day, they [shall take it] first on the next day and continue without a break [until] the business is dealt with in the prytany of [the tribe —]. If they do not bring it to [the People] or do not [transact the business] during their office, [each] of the [prytaneis] is to be fined 10,000 drachmas at their scrutiny [on the grounds that] they have prevented tribute being supplied to the armies.

Those who are summoned to court are to be brought by the public summoners [in order that] the Council [may judge immediately] [40] whether or not they [execute their duties correctly].

The Assessors are [to write down] the routes for the heralds [who go], according to the oath, prescribing how far they are to journey in order that they may not [—] the assessment to the cities [-] wherever it seems [—]

[—] what it is right should be said [to the cities] about the assessments and [the decree, about this the People] shall decree, along with [anything else that the prytaneis introduce as needing decision].

[45] [The Generals are to see to] the cities bringing in [their tribute as soon as the Council draws up the tribute] assessment, in order [that the People have sufficient money for the] war. [The Generals] must consider [about the] tribute [every year, reckoning what is needed for campaigns, both by land] and sea, [and any other expenditure.]

[At the] first [sitting] of the Council [let them always introduce cases about] this, [without the Heliaia or] the other courts, unless [50] the People] vote that they be introduced after the courts have] first [made a judgement.]

[The *Kolakretai* are to pay] the heralds who go.

[—] said: in other respects let it be as the Council proposed, but [—] let the prytany that [is in office] and the Secretary [of the Council bring] the [assessments by city] to the court whenever it is assessments that are at issue in order that [the dikasts may agree them].

The Council and People decided, [55] in the prytany of Aigeis, when [Phil]ip[pos] was Secretary and [-]oros President, on the proposal of Thoudippos: All the cities assessed for tribute under the [Council to which Pleisti]as was first Secretary in the archonship of Stratokles [425/4] [are to bring] a cow [and a full set of armour] to the Great Panathenaia; they are to take part in the procession [in the same way as Athenian settlers abroad].

The Council to which Pleistias was the first Secretary assessed the tribute for the cities [in the following way] in the archonship of Stratokles, when the [60] magistrates in charge of introducing cases had as secretary Ka[........].

[Lists of cities and their assessments followed in 4 columns: see Table on p.93. The total given was almost certainly between 1460 and 1500 talents]

ML 69 (*SEG* 42.14)

Although so much of the above depends upon restorations, the main elements of the decree are not in doubt. This re-assessment is particularly notable a) because it was done in a year when re-assessment was not due; b) because of the strength of the language involved; c) because of the inclusion, at the end of the list, of states that had never previously paid to Athens or which had long ceased paying. Whether the re-assessment also massively increased the tribute demanded from the allies is less clear because little is preserved from the lists from earlier in the war. See further p.92.

The way in which the war is cited as creating a need for extra income (compare **136**) links this tribute increase with those in Athens who favoured active campaigning against Sparta rather than sitting it out, but a more particular link with Kleon cannot be established as, although Thoudippos is a rare name, it is not certain whether or not the Thoudippos who proposed the decree is the same Thoudippos who married Kleon's daughter (for the case for scepticism, see F. Bourriot in *Historia* 31 (1982) 404-35).

139 After Perikles' death the demagogues increased the tribute little by little until they brought the total to 1,300 talents. They did this not so much because of the length and fortunes of war, but because they enticed the people into distributions of money, payments for public shows, and constructing cult statues and temples.

Plutarch *Aristeides* 24.5[=20]

Athenian negotiations with Persia
For the negotiations in 425/4 and subsequently see **60-62**.

Trouble in Ionia, 425/4
a) Khios

140 During the same winter (425/4) the Khians demolished their new wall on Athenian orders because the Athenians suspected that some rebellion was afoot, after they had extracted from the Athenians the most reliable pledges and assurances that they could get that they would not make any new policy about them.

Thucydides 4.51

For the immediately preceding passage of Thucydides see **60**.

141 PRIEST. To give health and salvation to the citizens of Cloudcuckooland themselves and to the Khians.

PEISETAIROS. I like adding the Khians everywhere.

Aristophanes *Birds* 878-80

142 This he took from history, for the Athenians offered prayers for themselves and the Khians together at sacrifices, since the Khians sent allies to Athens when the needs of war demanded it. Just as Theopompos says in Book 12 of his *Philippika* (trg. 104) as follows: 'Most avoided doing such things. As a consequence they made common prayers for themselves and for them, and when they poured libations at public sacrifices they made prayers to the gods to give the Khians and themselves good things in exactly the same way.' Eupolis says this about Khios in his *Cities* (frg. 246).

This is Khios, a fine city
for it sends us warships, and men should we need them
and in other respects too obeys us well, like an unspurred horse.

In his *Great Manual* Thrasymakhos says the same as Theopompos. Hypereides in his *Delian Speech* says that the Khians offered prayers for the Athenians.

Scholiast on Aristophanes *Birds* 880

This passage reminds us of how much information about allies' relations with Athens we have lost: historians such as Theopompos ranged much more widely than Thucydides in their discussions of Athens and her empire.

b) Lesbos

143 [52.1] During the following summer there was a partial eclipse of the sun [March 21, 424] and during the same month an earthquake. [52.2] The exiles from Mytilene and elsewhere on Lesbos set out from the mainland, hired mercenaries from the Peloponnese and collected others locally, captured Rhoiteion, made off with 2,000 Phokaian staters [=8 talents], and then gave the place back unharmed. [52.3] After this they made an expedition against Antandros and captured it through treachery. They intended to free the other Aktaian cities, which had once belonged to Mytilene but which the Athenians now held, and particularly Antandros, and once they got control of it to use it as a base to raid Lesbos, which was not far off, and get control of the other Aiolian towns on the mainland. Antandros had the material for building ships, since there was wood on it and Ida was close by, and also other material.

Thucydides 4.52

144 [75.1] During the same summer [424] the Lesbian exiles were about to strengthen Antandros, as they had planned, but Demodokos and Aristeides, two Athenian Generals in charge of money-collecting ships, who were in the Hellespont area because a third General, Lamakhos, had sailed to the Black Sea with 10 ships, perceived that the place was being prepared and thought that it would prove a nuisance just as Anaia was to Samos. Samian exiles had established themselves on Anaia, gave help to the Peloponnesians by sending steersmen for their fleet, caused trouble to the Samians in the city, and received exiles. So the Athenian Generals raised an army from the allies, sailed against Antandros, defeated those who came out from Antandros against them in a battle, and recovered the place.

Thucydides 4.75.1

Brasidas' campaigns in the Thraceward region
a) Akanthos
145 [84.1] In the same summer [424], a little before the grape harvest, Brasidas, along with the Khalkidians, campaigned against Akanthos, a colony of Andros. [84.2] The Akanthians were divided about whether to take him in: those who had joined the Khalkidians in inviting Brasidas on the one hand and the people on the other. But because of their fear about the crops not yet being gathered in, the people were persuaded by Brasidas to let him enter the city alone and to make up their minds when they had heard him speak, and so they let him in. He stood up before the people and made the following speech — he was not a bad speaker, for a Spartan.

[88.1] Brasidas made that speech. After much had first been said on both sides, the Akanthians took a secret vote, and both because what Brasidas had said was attractive and because of their fear about the crops, the majority decided to revolt from the Athenians. They made him pledge to keep the oaths which the Spartan authorities had sworn when they sent him out, that the allies he brought over would be independent, and then they took in his army. [88.2] Not much later Stagiros, an Andrian colony, also revolted.

Thucydides 4.84, 88

146 '[If I attack you] I will not consider myself to be doing wrong. I think that I have two good and compelling arguments: as regards the Spartans, I must not let them be harmed by your being merely sympathetic without joining them, and they will be harmed by the money you pay to the Athenians; and as regards the Greeks, they must not be prevented by you from getting free of slavery.'

Thucydides 4.87.3

This extract from Brasidas' speech to the Akanthians, shows the other side of the Athenian insistence on the need for tribute for their war effort in **138**.

b) Amphipolis

147 The people of Argilos were near neighbours of Amphipolis, had always been
suspected by the Athenians and indeed were always plotting against Amphipolis.
When Brasidas came and gave them the opportunity, they increased their pressure
on the other Argilans inside Amphipolis to get that city to give in, and then took
him into their own city and revolted from the Athenians on that night and before
dawn had the army on the bridge over the river.

Thucydides 4.103.4

On Argilos and Athenian activity in its neighbourhood see on **232-3**.

148 [105.2] [Brasidas] made a proclamation, offering moderate terms: any Amphi-
politan or Athenian inside the city who so wished could stay, keeping his property on an equal and similar basis, and anyone who did not wish to stay could
leave, taking his property, within five days. [106.1] Many who heard the proclamation had diverse reactions, particularly since only a small part of the citizen
body was of Athenian origin and the larger part was of mixed origin, and those
who had been captured outside were related to many who were within the city.
They took the proclamation to be fair, compared to what they feared: among the
Athenians there was pleasure at a chance to escape, since they thought that they
were particularly at risk and had no expectation of speedy help; among the rest
of the population there was surprise at the prospect of escaping danger without
also losing the city. [106.2] The manifest justice of what Brasidas had already done
and the fact that the majority had been swayed and were no longer listening to
the Athenian General who was present, led to an agreement being made and
Brasidas being admitted on the conditions he had proclaimed.

Thucydides 4.105.2-106.2

c) Brasidas meets some resistance

149 [109.5] Most of the towns [on the Akte peninsula] went over to Brasidas, but Sane
and Dion resisted and he spent time in their territory, ravaging it with his army.
[110.1] But when they did not take any notice, he went straight off campaigning
against Torone in the Khalkidike, which the Athenians held. A few men there
urged him to come and were ready to hand the city over to him.

Thucydides 4.109.5-110.1

d) Skione

150 [120.1] About the same time [in summer 423] when the delegates [who arranged
the truce recorded in the previous chapter] were going to and fro, Skione, a town
of Pallene, revolted from the Athenians and joined Brasidas...

[121.1] The people of Skione were encouraged by Brasidas' words and all alike
enthusiastic, even those who had not previously been pleased by what was being
done. They were minded to carry on the war vigorously and gave Brasidas a warm
reception, publicly crowning him with a gold crown as one who brought freedom
to Greece, and individually putting ribbons on him and greeting him as if he were
an athlete.

[122.6] The truth about the revolt was that the Athenians were right: Skione had
revolted two days after the truce was signed. The Athenians immediately passed
a decree, persuaded by Kleon's view, to destroy Skione and put its citizens to
death. They kept the peace in other respects but made preparations for a campaign

against Skione. [123.1] Meanwhile Mende revolted from the Athenians. It was a town of Pallene and settled by the Eretrians. Brasidas received them, not considering that he was doing anything wrong in letting them come over to him at a time clearly within the truce.

Thucydides 4.120.1, 121.1, 122.6-123.1

151 [2.2] Kleon sailed first to Skione, which was still being besieged, took some hoplites from the garrison there and sailed to the Still Harbour of Torone, which was not far from the town...

[3.4] Kleon and the Athenians set up two trophies, one by the harbour and one at the fortifications. They enslaved the women and children of Torone and sent the citizens of Torone, the Peloponnesians, and any other men from the Khalkidike, totalling 700, away to Athens.

Thucydides 5.2.2, 3.4

152 About the same time during this summer [421] the Athenians forced the people of Skione to capitulate. They killed the men of military age and enslaved the children and women; the land they gave to the Plataians to cultivate. They restored the Delians to Delos, mindful of their fortunes in battles and of the oracle of the god at Delphi.

Thucydides 5.32.1

For the lasting memories of the actions recorded in **151** and **152** see **204** and **245**. For the expulsion of the Delians see below **154**.

Persian subordinates in action

153 Pissouthnes revolted and Tissaphernes, Spithradates and Parmises were sent against him. Pissouthnes made a counter-attack with Lykon the Athenian and the Greeks whom he commanded. The King's generals bribed Lykon and the Greeks to desert Pissouthnes, then they exchanged pledges with him and took him to the King. The King removed Pissouthnes from office and gave his satrapy to Tissaphernes. But Lykon got cities and lands for his treachery.

Ktesias *Persika FGH* 688 F15.53

This episode cannot be precisely dated from its context in Ktesias, but Pissouthnes' revolt may be connected with the following episode recorded by Thucydides partly in its chronological place and partly in a ten-year flash-back.

154A At the beginning of summer [422] the year's truce expired, [but another was made, lasting] until the Pythian Games. During the truce the Athenians uprooted the Delians from Delos. They had decided that because of some ancient offence the Delians were not pure when they were consecrated... The Delians settled at Atramyttion in Asia which Pharnakes gave to them, and whoever wanted to settled there.

Thucydides 5.1

154B It was at this time [422] that the Athenians accused the Delians of secretly making an alliance with the Spartans, and they expelled them from the island and themselves occupied their town. Pharniakes [*sic*] the satrap gave the Delians who had been expelled Adramyttion as a town to live in.

Diodoros 12.73.1

155 Arsakes the Persian, Tissaphernes' subordinate, was the man who, when the
Delians, uprooted by the Athenians for them to purify Delos, settled at
Atramyttion, claimed that he had a secret enmity to settle, called up the best of
them to join his army, led them out as if friends and allies, and then, waiting his
moment, rounded on them while they were eating and had them shot down with
javelins.

Thucydides 8.108.4

This episode must have occurred between 422 and 421 when the Delians were restored to Delos (**152**).

1.6 FROM THE PEACE OF NIKIAS TO THE END OF THE EMPIRE

The Melian affair.

156 [84.1] [In summer 416] the Athenians made an expedition against Melos with 30
of their own ships, 6 Khian ships and 2 from Lesbos. They had 1,200 of their
own hoplites, 300 archers and 20 mounted archers, plus 1,500 allied hoplites.
[84.2] The Melians were settlers originally from Sparta and were unwilling to be
subject to the Athenians as the other islanders were. To start with, they kept
the peace and sided with neither party, but then, when the Athenians tried to
force them into the empire by ravaging their land, they became openly hostile
to Athens. [84.3] The Generals Kleomedes son of Lykomedes and Teisias son
of Teisimakhos took up position in their territory with this army, but before
doing any damage to the land they first sent ambassadors to enter discussions.
The Melians did not bring them before the people as a whole, but told them to
make whatever points they had come to make before the magistrates and the few.

Thucydides 5.84

Nikias had led an unsuccessful expedition against Melos already in 426 (Thuc. 3.91.1-3).

157 'We, at least, are not going to make an unconvincingly long speech with lots of
fine words about how we deserve to rule since we defeated the Persians or about
how we now attack because we have been wronged. Nor do we reckon that you
should expect to persuade us by saying that although you were settled from
Sparta, you have not campaigned against us or that you have done us no wrong.
We should both be aware of the other party's true position and try to get what is
possible, each party knowing full well that just settlements are reached in discussions between men only when each side is equally under compulsion, and that
those who have power do what that power enables them to do, and the weaker
party agrees.'

Thucydides 5.89

One of the points made by the Athenians in the so-called Melian Dialogue between the Athenian ambassadors and those in authority on Melos. In view of the dialogue form and the very abstract nature of the arguments used on both sides, it seems very unlikely that Thucydides' text is at all closely related to the words
actually spoken; Thucydides' editorial interventions have obscured the nature of the original exchange.

158 [114.1] The Athenian ambassadors went back to the army, and because the Melians
made no concessions, their Generals immediately turned to war and dividing the
work among the cities built a fortification wall around the Melians...
[116.2] About the same time [winter 416/5] the Melians captured part of the
Athenian encircling fortification, since not many troops were guarding that part.
[116.3] Because this had occurred, another army came out from Athens later under
the command of Philokrates son of Demeas and the siege was now strengthened.

An act of treachery occurred and the Melians agreed to let the Athenians decide on their fate. [116.4] The Athenians killed all the Melian men of military age that they captured and enslaved the women and children. They themselves settled the place, later sending 500 settlers.

Thucydides 5.114.1, 116.2-4

A tradition of dubious reliability (Ps.-Andokides 4.22, Plutarch *Alkibiades* 16.5-6) holds that the decision to execute the Melians was proposed or at least supported by Alkibiades.

The extent of the Athenian empire in 415

159 [57.1] The following fought on the two sides against and about Sicily, either coming to help conquer the land or to help save it, in the war against Syracuse. They did not come to support one side or the other because of the pull of justice or kinship, but by chance, because of what they judged to be their interests, or because they were forced. [57.2] The Athenians, themselves Ionians, came willingly against Dorian Syracuse and along with them campaigned the Lemnians, Imbrians and Aiginetans (that is, those who then inhabited Aigina) who still speak the Attic dialect and follow Athenian customs, and also the Hestiaians on Euboia, the settlers who were living in Hestiaia. [57.3] Of the rest who joined the expedition, some were subjects, others independent on the basis of an alliance, and others again were paid. [57.4] Of those who were subject and paid tribute, there were those from Eretria, Khalkis, Styra and Karystos on Euboia, from Keos, Andros, Tenos of the islands, and from Miletos, Samos and Khios in Ionia. Of these the Khians did not pay tribute but provided ships and were independent followers. For the most part all of these were Ionians and descended from the Athenians, except for the Karystians (who were Dryopes), but even though they were subjects and under compulsion nevertheless as Ionians they took part against a Dorian city. [57.5] In addition to these the Aiolians: Methymna, subject to provision of ships not tribute, Tenedos and Ainos, tribute-payers. These Aiolians fought against the Aiolian Boiotians, who founded their cities and were helping Syracuse, because they had to. But, as one would expect, the Plataians, who were themselves Boiotian, fought the Boiotians because they hated them. [57.6] Rhodes and Kythera were both Dorian, Kythera a Spartan colony bearing arms with the Athenians against the Spartans with Gylippos, and the Rhodians, an Argive race, compelled to fight against the Dorian Syracusans and the people of Gela, settlers they themselves had sent, who were campaigning with the Syracusans. [57.7] Of the islands round the Peloponnese, Kephallenia and Zakynthos were independent, but because islands were under pressure from the Athenians who ruled the sea, they followed Athens. Corcyreans were not only Dorian but Corinthians who openly fought the Corinthians and Syracusans, although settlers sent by the one and kin to the other; they stressed necessity as the respectable reason, but in fact their hatred of the Corinthians was equally important. [57.8] Those now called Messenians, from Naupaktos and from Pylos, which was then in Athenian hands, were brought over for the war. Also a few Megarian exiles ended up reckoning it in their best interests to fight the people of Selinous, who were Megarians. [57.9] The others had voluntarily joined the campaign. The Argives did so not so much because of their alliance as because they hated the Spartans and saw immediate private gain in fighting Dorian against Dorian with the Ionian Athenians. The Mantineans and other Arkadian mercenaries were used to fighting against whoever was pointed out to be their enemy and on that occasion regarded the Arkadians who had come with the Corinthians as no less their enemies, because they were paid to do so. The Cretans and the Aitolians also had been paid to take part. The Cretans, who had founded Gela with the Rhodians, ended up voluntarily fighting for pay against, rather than with, their settlers. [57.10] Some of the Akarnanians came to help, partly for gain but mostly out of friendship with Demosthenes and goodwill towards the Athenians with whom they were allied. [57.11] These next came from beyond the Ionian gulf: of the Italians Thourioi and Metapontion joined the campaign similarly compelled by the political conflicts they were themselves experiencing at that time. Of the Sicilians, those who joined the Athenians were Naxos and Katana, and among the non-Greeks Segesta, which had called the Athenians in, and most of the Sikels, and of those outside Sicily some of the Etruscans, because of a quarrel with Syracuse, and Iapygian mercenaries. Those were all the national contingents who campaigned with the Athenians.

Thucydides 7.57

The debate over Athenian imperial intentions in Sicily

160 [76.2] 'I don't think that [the Athenians] want to re-establish Leontinoi, but rather uproot us. It is hardly plausible that they should uproot cities back there but re-establish cities here, or look after the people of Leontinoi, who are from Khalkis, on the grounds that they are kin, but keep in slavery the Khalkidians in Euboia, from which these came as settlers. [76.3] The same thinking lies behind those events in Greece and what they are trying here. The Ionians and other allies who were descended from Athens voluntarily accepted their leadership to punish the Persians, but the Athenians brought them all under their control, accusing some of refusing military service, others of fighting each other, and bringing some specious accusation against each. [76.4] The Athenians did not resist the Persians because they were concerned about the freedom of the Greeks, nor did the Greeks resist because they were concerned about their own freedom; the Athenians wanted the Greeks enslaved to themselves rather than to the Persians, and the Greeks wanted a new master, who proved not less astute but astute for ill.'

Thucydides 6.76.2-4

An extract from the speech of Hermokrates to the people of Kamarina in 415, encouraging them to join the Syracusans in resisting the Athenian expedition against Sicily. For this and other views about the purpose of the Delian League see **11-14**.

161 [82.3] 'After the Persian Wars, because we had a fleet, we took over command and leadership from the Spartans. They had no more right than we to give orders, except in as far as they were temporarily the stronger. We were appointed leaders of those who were formerly subject to the King, and it was our view that if we had the power with which to defend ourselves, we were least likely to come under the Peloponnesians. In strict truth we have done nothing unjust in subjecting the Ionians and islanders, whom the Syracusans accuse us of enslaving when they were kin. [82.4] After all, they attacked their mother city as part of the Persian invasion, and did not dare risk their own fortunes by revolting as we risked our fortunes by abandoning our city; rather they were willing to endure slavery and wanted to impose the same on us. [83.1] In return for that, we are worthy of the empire we have, both because we provided the Greeks with the largest fleet and unhesitating enthusiasm, and because they did us harm in providing ready help for the Persians, and also because we are keen to strengthen ourselves against the Peloponnesians. [83.2] We do not make fine claims about being the only people who defeated the Persians, and so the only people with a claim to rule, or about having faced danger for the freedom of these, rather than for the freedom of all, including ourselves. No one is begrudged seeing to their own safety. And now, present here for our own security, we see that exactly the same things are in your interest. [83.3] We can demonstrate this from the Syracusans' slanderous accusations against us and your fearful suspicions, for we know that those who are full of fear and suspicion in the short term enjoy a charming speech, but when it comes to action they do what is in their own interests. [83.4] We have said that we hold the empire there because of fear and that it is because of fear that we have come here, to secure our position with the help of our friends, not to bring slavery but rather to prevent it.'

Thucydides 6.82.3-83.4

The Athenian speech to the same assembly at Kamarina.

Replacement of tribute by 5% tax

162 Because of this [the Sicilian expedition] and because of the great harm the Spartans were doing to Attica from the fort at Dekeleia and the other great expenses that were falling on them, the Athenians were financially crippled. It was about this time that they introduced a 5 per cent tax on seaborne trade instead of tribute, judging that this way they would increase their income. For the expenses were not as they had once been but much greater because the war was greater, but the income was being destroyed.

Thucydides 7.28.4

Although normal re-assessment of tribute will have occurred in autumn 414, Athenian income seems unlikely to have been in decline until 413, and autumn 413 is the most likely date for this change. Given that tribute seems to have been running at about 900 talents a year, if the Athenians did indeed calculate that a 5 per cent tax would be more lucrative, then they must have estimated that the value of goods moving about the Empire exceeded 18,000 talents (108,000,000 drachmas.).

163 CHORUS. [There is no place in the choros for a man who] betrays a fort or ships, or exports prohibited items from Aigina when an accursed collector of the 5 per cent tax like Thorykion, and sends rowlock-linings, linen and pitch to Epidauros, or...

Aristophanes *Frogs* (405) 362-3

The issue here is how contemporary with *Frogs* Thorykion's crime was. Other indications suggest that tribute was brought back instead of the 5% tax in around 410 (see **181**).

Revolts of allies after Sicilian disaster
First moves from Euboia, Lesbos, Khios and Erythrai

164 [5.1] While both [Athenians and Peloponnesians] were so engaged and getting equipped as if they were just beginning a war, during this winter [413/2] first the Euboians sent an embassy to Agis about revolting from the Athenians. Agis listened to what they said and sent for Alkamenes son of Sthenelaïdas and Melanthos from Sparta for dispatch as commanders to Euboia. They came with

300 *neodamodeis* [freed helots] and made ready to cross. [5.2] Meanwhile the Lesbians came, also wanting to revolt, and Boiotians joined them and persuaded Agis that he should delay over Euboia and get ready for the revolt of Lesbos, giving the Lesbians Alkamenes, who was about to sail to Euboia, as a garrison commander. The Boiotians promised 10 ships and Agis 10....

[5.4] Agis made these arrangements with the Lesbians, but the Khians and Erythraians, who were also ready to revolt, did not turn to Agis but went to Sparta. And an ambassador from Tissaphernes, who was the commander of the coast appointed by King Dareios son of Artaxerxes, was present in Sparta with them at the same time. [5.5] Tissaphernes called in the Peloponnesians and promised that he would provide maintenance. He had recently been appointed by the King and owed the tributes from his province which because of the Athenians he had been unable to exact from the Greek cities. He thought that if he did the Athenians harm, he would be more likely to get in the tribute, secure an alliance between the Spartans and the King, and bring in, alive or dead, Amorges, bastard son of Pissouthnes, who had revolted in Karia, as the King had ordered him.

Thucydides 8.5.1-2, 4-5

The question of what the arrears of tribute owed to the King are is a vexed one. Are they owed by cities within the Athenian empire, or just by places outside the empire involved in Amorges' revolt, which the Athenians had supported? If the former, then this is evidence that some cities within the Empire chose to pay two ways in order to keep their options secure. See also note to **36**.

Khios revolts; Athens reacts

165 [7] During the following summer [412], because the Khians were urging them to send ships and were afraid that the Athenians might perceive what was happening (all the Khian embassies had been secret), the Spartans sent three Spartiates to Corinth to get them to carry all the ships, both those that Agis was preparing for Lesbos and the others, over the Isthmos as quickly as possible from the other sea to the sea facing Athens and sail to Khios. The total of allied ships here was 39.

[9.1] The Spartans urged setting sail, but the Corinthians were not keen to do so before they had celebrated the Isthmian Games which were happening then. Agis was willing that they should not break the Isthmian truce and that the expedition be treated as his private expedition, [9.2] but the Corinthians were not prepared to agree, and a delay occurred. The Athenians were becoming more aware of the situation on Khios and sent Aristokrates, one of the Generals, and asked them about it. The Khians denied plotting and the Athenians ordered them to send ships with them for the allied fleet as a pledge. The Khians sent 7 ships. [9.3] The reason why they sent the ships was that most Khians did not know what was going on. The few who were in the plot did not want to face a hostile people yet, before they had strengthened their position, and they did not expect the Peloponnesians to come yet because they were wasting time.

[10.1] Meanwhile the Isthmian Games took place, and the Athenians, who had been notified, sent representatives who got clearer information about what was happening on Khios.

Thucydides 8.7, 8.9.-10.1

This episode shows in a familiar way the impossibility of keeping political decisions secret for long in ancient Greece.

166 [14.1] Khalkideus [the Spartan commander] arrested all they fell in with in order to give no warning of their approach. They first attacked Korykos on the mainland, released their captives there and themselves joined up with their Khian collaborators, who urged them to sail against the city without warning, and suddenly arrived at Khios. [14.2] The people of Khios were amazed and shocked. The few arranged for a council meeting to be held at which Khalkideus and Alkibiades said that many other ships were on their way (they did not reveal that the ships at Speiraion were being besieged). The Khians, and also the Erythraians, decided to revolt from the Athenians. [14.3] After this they sailed to Klazomenai with three ships and secured the revolt of Klazomenai. The people of Klazomenai immediately crossed to the mainland and fortified Polikhna, in case they might need it, as a place of retreat for themselves from the little island on which they lived. All those who revolted were busy with fortifications and preparations for war. [15.1] A message quickly reached Athens from Khios. The Athenians realised that the danger that faced them was manifest and great, and that the other allies would not want to keep quiet once the largest city had changed allegiance. Shocked, they immediately removed the penalties on anyone proposing or putting to the vote a proposal to use the 1,000 talents which throughout the war they had managed not to touch, and decided to use it to man no small number of ships...

Thucydides 8.14-15.1

When the war with Athens moved to Ionia and became a naval war, Spartan military leadership fell completely into the hands of annual magistrates rather than the Kings. But Spartiates had no naval training and little training in leadership, and not only was the quality of the commanders extremely variable, but, as in the following extract, non-Spartiates too had to be recruited.

167 [22.1] After this, during the same summer [412], the Khians continued to display the enthusiasm that they had shown at the beginning. Without Peloponnesian aid they committed a substantial force to making cities revolt and wanted as many men as possible to share their danger. They made an expedition against Lesbos with 13 ships, in accordance with the Spartan plan to attack Lesbos second, and then go to the Hellespont. The infantry force of the Peloponnesians who were present and of their local allies went towards Klazomenai and Kyme under the command of the Spartiate Eualas, with Deiniadas, a *perioikos*, commanding the ships. [22.2] The ships sailed to Methymna, first secured its revolt and left four ships there; the rest went on to Mytilene and made it revolt.

Thucydides 8.22

168 [24.2] [The Athenian generals] Leon and Diomedon ... using Lesbos as a base made war on the Khians from the ships. They had marines pressed into service from the hoplite register. [24.3] They landed at Kardamyle and at Boliskos where they defeated those Khians who came to the rescue, killing most of them and laying waste the land about. They were victorious in a second battle at Phanai and a third at Leukonion. After this the Khians no longer came out to attack them and they ravaged a land that was well equipped and had never suffered from the time of the Persian Wars until then. [24.4] After the Spartans, the Khians were, to my knowledge, the most fortunate and most moderate of people. The greater the city became, the more securely they ordered themselves. [24.5] Not even in the case of this revolt, though they may seem to have chosen to act in a slightly risky way, did they dare to make a move before they knew they had many allies who would share in the risk and perceived that even the Athenians would not claim that after the Sicilian disaster their affairs were anything other than in a bad way.

Thucydides 8.24.2-5

169 [38.2] The Athenians from Lesbos had already crossed to Khios with an army, had control of land and sea, and fortified Delphinion, a place not far from the town of Khios and naturally defended by land and with harbours. [38.3] The Khians had been beaten in many previous battles, and they were in very poor shape physically. Those with Tydeus son of Ion had already been executed by Pedaritos for sympathy with Athens, and oligarchy having been imposed on the rest of the people by force they kept quiet but were suspicious of one another. For that reason they did not think of themselves as in a position to fight battles, nor did they think the mercenaries with Pedaritos were.

Thucydides 8.38.2-3

The name of the executed Athenian sympathiser here should be noted. That his father bore the name of the legendary Athenian after whom Ionia was named may imply that Athenian sympathies were a family tradition. It is likely that the father was indeed the Ion of Khios (491-c.422) who lived for a time in Athens, and wrote tragedies for the Athenian stage. See F. Jacoby *Classical Quarterly* 41 (1947) 1ff.

Rhodes revolts

170 [44.1] The Spartans decided to sail to Rhodes as a result of appeals from the most powerful men there. They expected to bring over an island that was strong in both infantry and sailors, and thought that they would be able to maintain the navy themselves on the basis of the allies they already had, without asking Tissaphernes for money. [44.2] So, during this same winter [412/11], they sailed from Knidos and attacked Kameiros on Rhodes first with 94 ships. Most of the people, who did not know what was being arranged, were frightened and fled, particularly since the city had no wall. The Spartans then called these people together, along with the inhabitants of the two other cities, Lindos and Ialysos, and persuaded all the Rhodians to revolt from the Athenians.

Thucydides 8.44.1-2

It is not clear how important the fact that Rhodes was a Dorian island was to the success of Spartan persuasion here.

Samos resists a move to revolt

171 About this time [summer 412] there was a political uprising against those in power on Samos by the people, assisted by the Athenians who were present in three ships. The Samian people killed those who were most powerful, some 200 in all, and punished 400 more with exile, taking over their land and houses for themselves. After this the Athenians voted them independence, on the grounds that they were firm supporters, and they both ran the city in other respects and denied the landowners (*geomoroi*) permission in future to marry either their sons or their daughters to members of the people.

Thucydides 8.21

This episode offers support to the idea that even in cities that had been punished for earlier revolts, the people remained keen to stay under Athenian rule.

172 The Council and People decided, when the tribe Akamantis held the prytany [—]
to praise the people of Samos because [they liberated themselves, ending the existing oligarchic regime, and threw out] those Samians who had invited the
Peloponnesians in to Samos and [to Ionia. As to the property of those exiled, let
them rent out] [5] the field of Kleomedes from Klamadon [—] let the Samians pay
the income produced from it [to the Athenians, bringing it to Athens annually at the
time of the City Dionysia. If] the people of Samos [condemn any Samian] to exile
or death or confiscation of property, [the decision is to be valid — It is also to be
possible for the People] of Athens [to condemn] them to exile, death and [confisca-
tion of property, if it needs to.] Let the Samians send to Athens [all the prisoners
they have taken] and hand them over [10] [—] in the city within thirty days.

[Lacuna]

[—] [15] the Athenians and the Samians. But concerning[—] since he is a man
good [to the People of Athens and of Samos, now and formerly. And to ensure
that] neither Athenians nor Samians are harmed [and the war is not broken off,
the Generals are to set up everywhere whatever garrison] the people of Samos
[and the Generals] think [best - -]

Inscriptiones Graecae i³ 96 (*SEG* 41.7)

This decree plausibly belongs to 412/11, but it is not clear whether it is the decree that Thucydides alludes
to. It reveals an Athenian belief that the Samian oligarchs had been in negotiation with the Peloponnesians,
which is not mentioned by Thucydides.

Euboia revolts after an Athenian naval defeat

173 [95.5] Although so ill prepared, the Athenians put to sea and fought a sea battle
outside the harbour of Eretria. Despite everything, they resisted for a short time
before turning in flight and being pursued to land. [95.6] Those of them who fled
to Eretria itself, thinking it was friendly, could not have fared worse, for they
were murdered by them. Those who fled to the fort at Eretria, which the Athenians
themselves held, survived, as did the ships that got away to Khalkis. [95.7] The
Peloponnesians captured 22 Athenian ships, killed some of the crews and
captured others alive, and set up a trophy. Not much later they brought about the
revolt of the whole of Euboia except for Oreos [=Hestiaia], which the Athenians
themselves held, and settled other Euboian affairs.

Thucydides 8.95.5-7

174 Gods. The Council decided that Hegelokhos from Taras be *proxenos* and benefactor, himself and his children, and that free maintenance be given to him and
his sons whenever they visit, and tax exemption and front seats at contests, since
he helped to free the city from the Athenians

ML82

A decree passed by an oligarchic Eretria in the wake of the events of 411 (for Tarantine help then, see
Thucydides 8.91.2). For Athenian proxeny grants see below **235-8**.

Was freedom more important than constitution?

175 Phrynikhos said that he was confident that the promise to the allied cities that
they could have oligarchic government, because Athens would no longer be a
democracy, would not make them return to allegiance to Athens, if they had
revolted, nor be firmer allies if still loyal: what they wanted was not to be subjects
having an oligarchy or a democracy, but to be free with whatever constitution
they happened to have.

Thucydides 8.48.5

Phrynikhos, who will soon himself join the oligarchic cause, is here made to voice reservations as to whether changing to oligarchy will have any advantages for Athens.

The case of Thasos

176 [64.2] [The Athenian Dieitrephes] arrived in Thasos and put an end to democracy there. [64.3] In the second month after Dieitrephes had departed [July 411] the Thasians fortified their city, reckoning that they had no further need of the 'aristocracy' that the Athenians brought, when every day they were expecting the arrival of the Spartans with freedom. [64.4] There were Thasians who had been exiled by the Athenians who were with the Peloponnesians, and they were working with all their strength with their friends in the city to bring a fleet and make Thasos revolt. It all worked out just as they wanted: they set the city to rights without risk and suppressed the people who would oppose them. [64.5] So on Thasos the opposite happened to the aims of those of the Athenians who set up the oligarchy, and so also in my view in many other of the subject allies. For the cities which took up 'moderate' government and freedom of political determination went all out for freedom, setting no value on good government from the Athenians that was still subject government.

Thucydides 8.64.2-5

177 Thrasyboulos went to the area of Thrace with 30 ships. There he got control of the other places which had changed to the Spartan side, and also Thasos, which was in a bad way because of war, internal strife, and hunger.

Xenophon Hellenika 1.4.9

Xenophon may run together here Thrasyboulos' activities over the period 410-407. Thasos was probably recovered in 407. On the chronological difficulties in Xenophon's account of the Ionian War see P. Krentz, *Xenophon: Hellenika I.-II.30* (Warminster, 1989) 11-14.

178 While these events [the battle of Notion] were taking place, Thrasyboulos the Athenian General sailed with fifteen ships to Thasos and defeated the forces of the city in battle, killing some 200 of them. He besieged them and forced them to take back exiles with pro-Athenian sympathies, accept a garrison and become Athenian allies.

Diodoros 13.72.1

Diodoros includes this incident in his account of events in 408.

Athens rewards her supporters at Neapolis

179 Gods. About the people of Neopolis by Thasos.

The Council and People decided, in the prytany of the tribe Leontis, [5] when Sibyrtiades was Secretary and Khairimenes was President, in the archonship of Glaukippos [410/09], on the proposal of [....]thos, to praise the people of Neopolis by Thasos, first because although they were settlers from Thasos [and were] besieged by them and by the Peloponnesians, they were [unwilling] to revolt [from the Athenians] and turned in good service [10] [to the army and] People [of Athens and her allies].
       [Lacuna]

[Lines 21-7 are too fragmentary to be restored but mention a sum of more than 4 talents, apparently a loan from Neopolis for the war effort]

... from the harbour of Neopolis. The [Generals] on [Thasos have recorded sums] as taken by [themselves each] year [30] [until complete] payment is made, and they are to do this as long as [their war against] Thasos lasts.

Whatever the people of Neopolis give now [— they gave] voluntarily and willingly [to the *Hellenotamiai*] 5 talents 4,800 drachmas and are keen to do whatever good [they can], as they themselves have promised, both [in word and deed to [35] the city] of Athens, and in return for their good services [they are to be given by the Athenians what they ask for], since they are good men, and to have [access] to the Council and People [first, after any sacred business, because of] their good services to the Athenians.

The [ambassadors are to hand over to the] Secretary of the Council [the records] [40] of these transactions that the people of Neopolis gave, [those already given and the rest] separately, and [the Secretary] of the Council, having inscribed this decree on a stone stele, is to set it up [on the Akropolis at the expense of the] people of Neopolis. And [having written it up] in Neopolis [they are to set it up] [45] in the temple of the Parthenos on a [stone] stele. [And summon] the embassy to hospitality at the Prytaneion [tomorrow].

To Oinobios of Dekeleia, General: 3 talents 638 drachmas 4 obols.

Axiokhos proposed, to praise the Neopolitans from [Thrace because they are men good] to the army and city of the Athenians, and because [they campaigned against Thasos and helped] [50] the Athenians to besiege it, and because they took part in the sea battle [and were victorious, and joined in the land battles the whole] while, and because they do good service to the Athenians in other ways, and in return for this the Athenians' [gifts to them are to be valid] as decreed by the People. In order that [they be not harmed in any way] by a private individual or by a city community, whatever [generals] are in office shall [all] look to their needs, along with the Athenian magistrates in office at any time [—] [55] protecting the Neopolitans and their city and being keen to do whatever [—] and now they shall acquire from the Athenians whatever seems good [—].

Concerning the first-fruits to the Parthenos which have customarily been given to the goddess, the People [are to discuss the matter in the Assembly].

The Secretary of the Council is to correct the former decree, and [change the writing on it] and instead of settlers [from Thasos] write that they fought the war [with the Athenians].

[60] [—] praise the good things they now do and say for Athens and that they are keen to do every good service to the army and the city for the future as before. And summon them to hospitality tomorrow.

[- said, otherwise as proposed by the Council, but [the first-fruits] to be offered to the Parthenos [as before —] the people pray for.

ML 89 (*SEG* 39.11)

The passages underlined here were cut out when Axiokhos' decree was inscribed and replaced by the words Axiokhos suggested.

Athens reasserts control at the Hellespont

180 [21] [In 410] The people of Perinthos received Alkibiades' army into the city; the people of Selymbria did not, but they did give him money. [22] From there [Selymbria] [the Athenians] went to Khrysopolis in Kalkhedonia and fortified it.

They established a tax office there and collected the ten per cent tax (*dekate*) from ships from the Black Sea. They left thirty ships and two generals, Eumakhos and Theramenes, to guard the place, looking after the territory and the shipping sailing out of the Black Sea and doing any harm they could to the enemy. The other Generals went on to the Hellespont.

Xenophon *Hellenika* 1.1.21-2

The 10% tax referred to here may be identical with that mentioned in the Kallias decrees of the late 430s (ML 58.7).

181 [9] [In 408] The Athenians exchanged oaths with Pharnabazos that, until the ambassadors returned from the King, the Kalkhedonians would contribute their accustomed tribute to the Athenians and would pay the money they owed, and the Athenians would not make war on the Kalkhedonians. [10] Alkibiades was not present for the oaths but was at Selymbria. He captured that city and then came to Byzantion with the whole army from the Khersonesos and soldiers from Thrace and more than three hundred cavalry.

Xenophon *Hellenika* 1.3.9-10

Reference to tribute here suggests that the Athenians have gone back to tribute from the 5% tax alternative (cf. **162-3**).

Athenian settlement at Selymbria

182 [No complete words in first six lines] ...list [—], [the Athenians are to give back] the hostages whom they hold, and in future are not to take [hostages].

[10] The people of Selymbria are to [set up] the constitution in whatever way they know [to be best —]

[Whatever] the Selymbrian state [or any individual] Selymbrian owed to [—], if the property of anyone has been confiscated [or if anyone] was in debt [to the state] [15] or if anyone has been deprived of civic rights [—] of the Selymbrians is in exile [—] enemies and friends [—] any [Athenian] or allied [property] that was lost in the war, or if someone has a debt [20] or deposit which [the magistrates] exacted, there shall be no exaction except in the case of land and houses. [All] other contracts formerly concluded between private individuals or between a private individual and the state or the state and a private individual, or any other, [25] they are to settle mutually. In the event of dispute, the [case] is to be settled according to contractual agreements (*symbolai*).

The agreement to be written up on a stele and placed in the temple of [—].

The Athenian generals and [trierarchs] and hoplites and any [30] [other Athenian] present and all the Selymbrians took an oath.

[Al]kib[iades] proposed: to act in accordance with the agreement that the Selymbrians made with the Athenians. And the Generals with the Secretary of the Council are to write up the agreements [35] [erasure here] on a stone stele at their own expense along with this decree.

And praise [Apo]llodoros the son of Empedos and release him from being a hostage, and the Secretary of the Council to wipe out tomorrow in the presence of the prytaneis the names of the Selymbrian hostages and of their sureties [40] wherever they are recorded.

And write up [—]omakhos of Selymbria on the same stele as Athenian *proxenos*. And grant proxeny to Apollodoros as to his father.

Summon the ambassadors and Apollodoros to hospitality at the Prytaneion tomorrow.

ML 87 (*SEG* 36.20)

For Athenian ownership of property in the allies see **239-43**.

Loyal Samians rewarded with Athenian citizenship

183 Kephisophon of Paiania was Secretary [403/2]. For the Samians who sided with the Athenian People.

[5] The Council and People decided, when the tribe Kekropis held the prytany, Polymnis of Euonymon was Secretary, Alexias was Archon [405/4], and Nikophon of Athmonon was President. A proposal of Kleisophos and his fellow prytaneis: to praise the Samian ambassadors, both those who came previously and those who have come now, and the council, generals, and other Samians because they are men good and keen to do what good they can, [10] and what they do they seem to do correctly for the Athenians and the Samians. And in return for their good services to the Athenians and because even now they display much concern and introduce good measures, the Council and People decided that the Samians should be Athenian citizens, governing themselves as they themselves want. And in order that this may happen in whatever way is most advantageous for both parties, as they themselves propose, when peace comes, then [15] there will be common deliberations on other matters. They are to use their own laws and be independent, and do everything else according to the oaths and agreements that the Athenians have made with the Samians. As to any complaints that arise with each other, they are to give and receive legal cases in accordance with all the legal treaties. If some necessity happens as a result of the war which relates to the constitution before the war ends, [20] as the ambassadors themselves say, the People are to do whatever seems best to them in the circumstances. As to peace, if peace is made, it is to be on the same conditions for those now living on Samos as for the Athenians. And if it is necessary to fight, they will make the best preparations they can, acting together with the Generals. If the Athenians send an embassy anywhere, those from Samos who are present [25] are to join that embassy, if they wish, and join in counselling any good they can. To grant them the triremes which are at Samos to equip and use as they think best. [The ambassadors], with the Secretary of the Council and the Generals, are to list the names of the trierarchs whose ships these are, and the dockyard superintendents are to expunge completely [any debt] recorded as incurred on the triremes anywhere against their names in the public record, [30] but the equipment they are to [exact as quickly as possible] and compel those who have it to give it back [in good condition] to the public store.

[Kleisophos] and his fellow prytaneis [proposed]: in other respects let it be as the Council proposes, [but the gift should be made to those of the Samians who] have come, as they themselves ask, and [they] should be distributed [straightaway into demes and] ten tribes. [35] And [the Generals should immediately provide] travelling expenses [for the ambassadors], and praise Eumakhos and [all the other Samians who have come with Eumakhos] as men [good to the Athenians. And summon Eum]akhos to supper at the prytaneion [tomorrow]. The Secretary of the Council with the [Generals is to write up what has been decided

The upper part of the stele recording the decree granting citizenship to Samians (**183**), showing the decree relief in which Athena is shown shaking hands with Hera, the patron goddess of Samos. The stele is 56 cm. wide, and the height of the letters (from line 5 onwards) is 6 mm.

on a stone stele and] set it up on the Akropolis, and the *Hellenotamiai* [40] [are to give the money. Also to be inscribed on Sa]mos in the same way at [their own] expense.

ML 94 (*SEG* 43.2)

Although the decree was passed in 405, this copy was inscribed only in 403-2, possibly because the Thirty destroyed the original. The citizen status of Eumakhos is signalled by his being invited to 'supper' [*deipnon*] rather than 'hospitality' [*xenia*]. In 403-2 these honours were reaffirmed and further honours given to a Samian named Poses, and these measures were inscribed lower on this same stele.

Part II. An Institutional Survey of the Empire

Note F   The Tribute Quota Lists

Introduction: the importance of the Tribute Quota Lists

Literary sources tell us about the fact of tribute, and something about the way in which it was assessed, re-assessed and collected (**14, 18-20, 184-190, 192-4**). They even give us some, not entirely unproblematic, totals of tribute paid (**15, 19, 20, 111**). But from literary sources we would know nothing of what any individual city paid, and indeed we would not know how many cities paid. For knowledge of these two fundamental features of the Athenian Empire we rely upon records put up annually (with one exception) at Athens from 454/3 onwards, which recorded the 1/60th part of the tribute which was dedicated to Athena. (In the discussion below Athena's share has been multiplied by 60 to give the total tribute.)

What were the lists like?

These Tribute Quota Lists were headed by a prescript which indicated both their date and their number in the sequence, and were written up when the money was handed over to the Treasurers of Athena after the accounts of the *Hellenotamiai*, who received the tribute (**190**.20), had been audited by the public accountants (*logistai*) at the end of their year of office. Although only fragments of the lists remain, scholars have been able to piece together more than 180 fragments and work out that the first 15 lists were recorded on all four sides of a single massive stone pillar more than 3.5m tall; they call this the 'First Stele'. The more than 70 fragments of the next eight lists (Lists16-23) can be pieced together to show that they were inscribed on a second, smaller, stele. Subsequent lists seem to have been inscribed on separate stelai. Very few fragments have been preserved of any stelai later than that on which the list for 428 was inscribed.

How were the lists arranged?

The earliest lists record cities in no consistent geographical groupings. The practice of geographical grouping is first found in the lists which prescribed what was to be paid. The Athenians normally issued such lists every four years (**184**), in the year when the Great Panathenaia was held. In those years they made a regular re-assessment of all tribute payments and determined the sum that cities were expected to pay each year until the next re-assessment. Geographical arrangement of these re-assessments may reflect the way in which the Athenians divided up the task of informing the allies of their assessment between a number of heralds, each sent to a different area (cf.**138**.4-6 and also **198** clause 7).

A tendency to geographical grouping is first to be seen in the Tribute Quota Lists themselves in that for 446/5, and when in 443/2 a re-assessment was carried out a year early and tribute payment was clearly reorganised in various ways, the records were systematically arranged by region under the headings 'Ionia', 'Hellespont', 'Thraceward', 'Karia' and 'Islands'. This arrangement continues in subsequent years, except that the Karian district was absorbed into the Ionian from 438/7 onwards.

What is the historical interest of the lists?

Because of their intrinsic limitations (they are only a record of payments) and their fragmentary condition, interpretation of the Tribute Quota Lists is no easy matter, but,

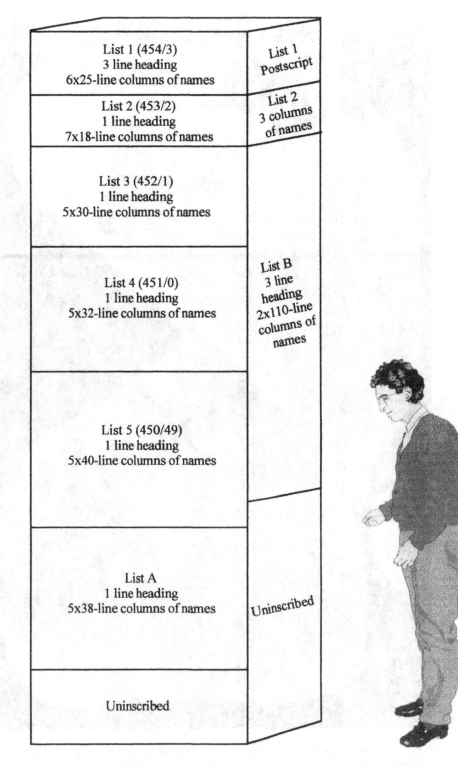

Layout of the earliest Tribute Quota Lists on the First Stele

Part of the Tribute Quota List for 440/39 (*IG* i³ 272) showing the payments made by cities in the Hellespontine and Thraceward regions. The smaller letters (not the headings) are c.10 mm. high.

handled with care, they can offer insights into the nature of the empire, the financial burden imposed by Athens, how tribute quotas changed over time, how the empire was run, and the relations between Athens and individual allies. I take these topics in turn.

1 The nature of the empire

How many cities were in the empire, and what sort of places were they? Before the Peloponnesian War, some 248 cities are known to have paid tribute (though in no single year had more than 190 paid). The highly optimistic 425/4 re-assessment (**138**) seems to have listed up to about 410 cities. (See maps pp.xxv-xxvii). If the sums assessed in 442/1 (when 54 entries are completely preserved and many others can be restored from other years in the same assessment period) are plotted graphically (see pp.90-1), it is immediately obvious that the empire was primarily a collection of small communities: 107 of the 205 cities for which a figure can be hazarded pay 3,000 drachmas or less, and of those 68 pay 1,000 drachmas or less. Only 24 allies pay more than 5 talents (30,000 drachmas), only 6 more than 10 talents. Looked at another way, 86% of the total revenue from the empire came from just 29% of the contributing cities. Thucydides' account is dominated by big cities (including Lesbos, Khios and Samos which in 442/1 were still providing ships, not money), but the empire itself was dominated by small ones.

2 The financial burden of the tribute

How much of a burden was tribute? On whom did it fall? It is much easier to quote the sums paid than to get a feel for what those sums mean. How hard was it for the people of Mylasa in Karia to find 5,200 drachmas? Even if the sums are converted into days' wages (unskilled workers on the Erekhtheion were paid 1/2 drachma a day, skilled 1 drachma a day) or commodity prices (the median price for slaves sold off among the property confiscated from those found guilty of impiety in 415 (cf.**241**) was 157 drachmas), it does not become much clearer what the impact of tribute on Mylasa was to say that it was the equivalent of purchasing 33 slaves.

To get a sense of the burden Athens was imposing, it helps to have some idea of how the tribute assessments were arrived at. Crudely and generally speaking larger cities paid larger amounts. Sometimes the correlation between size of city and amount of tribute is striking; so we know from an inscription that the quorum of judges on Teos was 200 and on Abdera 500, and Teos pays precisely 2/5ths of the tribute of Abdera (6 talents as against 15 talents). But the simple fact that the largest payers (Thasos and Aigina at 30 talents) pay 1,800 times as much as the smallest payers makes it inconceivable that population is the only factor involved. Nor can size of territory have been the basis for difference: it is easy to assess the territories of islands and the tribute of Paros (108,000 drachmas) does not relate to the tribute of Syros (1,000 drachmas) in the same ratio as that of their areas (196 sq. km. to 85 sq. km.).

The identity of the two biggest payers suggests that tribute was related to perceived resources: Thasos had silver and gold mines, and Aigina had been unusually deeply implicated in trade since the sixth century; so both were exceptional in their resources. In the absence of special resources, economic wealth tends to be closely related to population size and area of territory (which are not independent variables) since agricultural productivity depends on access to land and to the labour to farm it. It is not surprising therefore if tribute also is often found to relate to population and to land area. Particularly where several cities belong to a single more or less homogeneous region (e.g. the Troad) the relationships between the tributes of the cities can be used with caution to give an indication of the relationships of their sizes.

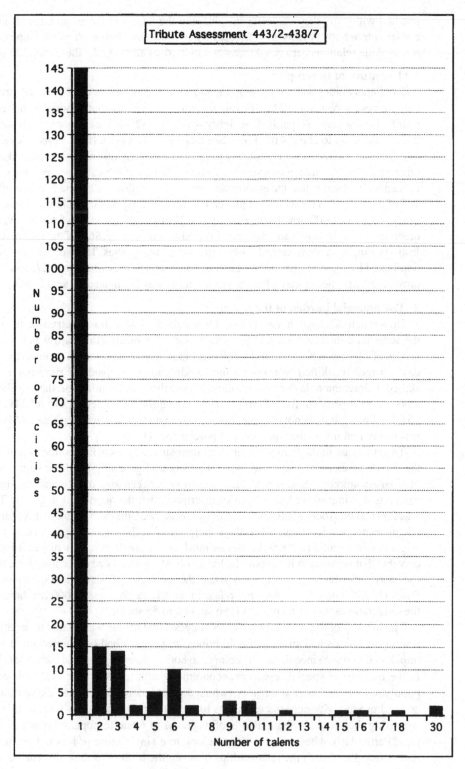

Distribution of Tribute Assessments, 443/2-438/7

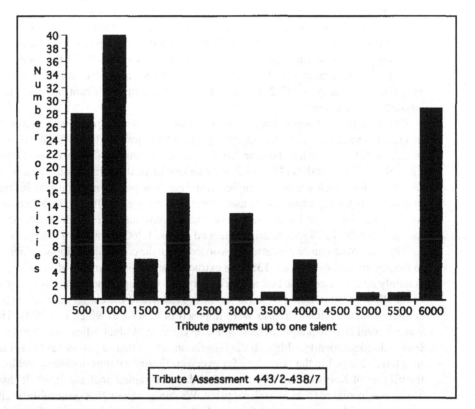

Distribution of Tribute Assessments of up to one talent, 443/2-438/7

One further calculation may help to put the level of tribute payment yet further into perspective. When the Athenians divided up the territory of Lesbos (excluding the territory of Methymna) following its revolt in 427 and gave it to Athenian settlers, Thucydides tells us that those settlers found local men prepared to rent back those lots of land at 200 drachmas per plot per year (**133**). There were 2,700 settlers and 300 lots sacred to Athena (compare note on p.110), and we may assume that the latter were also rented out. In this way the people of Lesbos came to pay out no less than 100 talents a year for the privilege of renting back the land they had once owned. The territory of Lesbos was indeed very large — it is the largest of the Aegean islands — but as far as we know, there were no special resources associated with it (and the uniformity of the rent suggests agricultural use). We cannot tell what Lesbos might have had to pay in tribute (it had been a ship-provider); comparison with other purely agricultural territories suggests that it is unlikely to have been more than Thasos and Aigina's 30 talents. Yet agricultural profits must have been sufficient to enable the people of Lesbos to meet the rent of 100 talents. It is safe to conclude that paying tribute was relatively trivial compared to the profits that could be expected even from agricultural land.

3 How tribute changed over time

The above discussion treats the burden of tribute as something that was constant. Although there were significant changes for individual allies from one four-year assessment period to another, this assumption is generally quite valid down to the outbreak of the Peloponnesian War. The rhythm of assessment periods became upset with extraordinary assessments in 428/7 after only two years, 425/4 after three (there seems to have been no assessment in 426/5, even though it was a Great Panathenaic year), and an ordinary assessment in the Great Panathenaic year of 422/1 (just three years after the 425/4 assessment). And the two extraordinary assessments here, unlike the irregular assessment of 443/2 mentioned above, brought significant increases in the amount of tribute demanded.

Although the condition of the relevant list makes certainty impossible, it appears that in 432/1 not more than 175 cities together paid a total of just less than 400 talents, a total actually slightly less than that demanded of them in mid-century. (To get to his 600 talent figure for 432 Thucydides (**111**, 2.13.3) must include under the term 'tribute' other income from the allies, which was not insignificant, and the same is presumably true of his figure of 460 talents for the initial tribute assessment of Aristeides (**15**)). We do not know the totals of the 430/29 and 428/7 re-assessments or how many cities those assessments included, but the 425/4 re-assessment claimed at least 1,460 talents from *c.*400 cities.

Although Athenians were certainly worried about the cost of the Peloponnesian War in the middle of the 420s (see **135**), the extraordinary re-assessments of the 420s were certainly a serious exercise and not merely a piece of propaganda either for Athenian or for allied consumption. (We have too little evidence of the earlier assessment to be confident about which increases were imposed in 428/7 and which in 425/4). There was no blanket percentage increase for everyone; individual allies were clearly re-assessed independently, although the criteria on which that re-assessment was based may have changed in the same way for everyone. Many tributes double or treble, but the tributes of Karystos and Imbros seem to have remained unchanged, while that of Tenos was increased from two talents to ten. We can be certain that some of those cities (they include Melos, assessed at fifteen talents) never paid, and it may be that nothing like 1,460 talents was ever gathered. The 425/4 decree was put up both on the Akropolis and in the Council Chamber: one of its aims was indeed to make an impression on Athenians, perhaps particularly to persuade them that they could afford to continue the war. Subsequently demands were scaled down. Although so few fragments of Tribute Quota Lists from later years survive that it is difficult to be confident about the overall picture, some cities certainly returned to their pre-war level, and others to a level between the pre-war level and the 425 assessment.

When we add to this the three expeditions of 'money-collecting ships' mentioned by Thucydides (**60, 117, 118**), which may have been sent to raise additional funds rather than collect tribute, it is clear that financially the burdens of empire on the allies increased significantly in the Arkhidamian War. This is of a piece with Athenian tight-ening up on tribute payment procedures in the Kleonymos decree of 426 (**136**), with raising money from taxes at the Hellespont (**121**), which is something likely to have been instituted earlier but is not certainly attested pre-war, and with adding a new gratu-itous obligation to use Athenian coins, weights and measures (**198**). It does not follow, of course, that all harsh treatment of and burdensome demands on the allies should be dated to the 420s, let alone that they should be attributed to the malign influence of Kleon (see note to **138**).

4 How the empire was run

If the Athenian allies had behaved as the Athenians expected them to, the Tribute Quota Lists would consist of sets of four identical lists, with every ally paying its allot-

Tribute assessment for selected cities in the Athenian Empire

This table shows the changing tribute of a range of cities within the empire. It does not attempt to show the record of what the cities in fact paid, whether they paid late, and so on, but rather it shows for each assessment period how much they were assessed to pay. Figures under 100 are of talents; figures over 100 are of drachmas. Where no figure is shown, no figure is preserved for any year in the assessment period for that city. Square brackets are used where the figure depends upon a restoration.

Place	454-50	450-46	446-43	443-38	438-34	434-30	430-28	428-5	425-1	421-18	418-14
IONIA											
Priene	1	1		1							
Ephesos	7.5	7.5	6	6		7.5					
Kolophon	3		1.5	1.5		[3]		500		500	500
Teos	6	6	6	6		6					
Klazomenai	1.5	1.5	1.5	1.5				6			14
Kyme	12	9	9	9		9					
HELLESPONT											
Tenedos	4.5	4.5	4.5	2.88	[2.88]	2.88	2.88				
Sigeion		1000	[1000]	1000	[1000]	1000	1000				
Abydos	[4.38]		4.05	4		6	6				
Lampsakos	12	12		12		12		>13.8			
Sestos				500	1000		1000				
Kyzikos		4320		9	[9]	9	9		20		
Daskyleion	500	500				500	500				
Astakos	1.5	1000	1000								
Kalkhedon	7.5	9	9	9		6	6				
Selymbria		6		5	900	900	9				
THRACEWARD											
Skiathos			1000	1000	1000	1000					
Methone											
Poteidaia			6	6	6	15					
Aphytis		3	1	1	3	3		5			
Skione	6		6	3	15	4	9				
Mende	8	15	5	9	8	8	8				
Torone		7.91	6	6	6	6	12				
Akanthos			3	3	3	3	3				
Olophyxos	2000	1500	2000	2000	2000	2000	2000				
Spartolos	2	2	2	2	2	3.08					
Olynthos	2.66	2	[2]	2	2						
Neapolis by Antisara		1000	1000	1000	1000	1000	1000	1000			
Thasos	3		30	[30]	[30]	30	30		60		
Abdera	15	15	15	[15]	15	15	10				
Samothrace	6	6	6	6	6	6	2		15		
Ainos	12	12	10	10	4				20		
KARIA											
Iasos	2	1	[1]	1		1				3	3
Astypalaia	2	2		1.5		2					
Halikarnassos	1.66	2	1.66	1.66		1.66					
Mylasa		1	5200	5200							
Knidos		5		3				2			
Karpathos			1000	1000		1000					1500
Lindos	8.45	10	6	6		10				15	15
Ialysos		10		6		6		10	6		
Kameiros	9	9		6		6			[10]		
Kaunos	3000	[3000]		3000					10		
Phaselis	6	3	[3]	3		6					6
ISLANDS											
Karystos	12→7.5	5		5		[5]			5		5
Eretria		[6]		[3]	[3]	3			15		
Khalkis				[3]	[3]	3			10		
Aigina	30		[30]	30							
Keos		4	4	4		3			10		6
Siphnos		3	3	3		3			9		
Naxos		6.66	[6.66]	6.66		6.66			15		9
Paros		16.2		18					30		18
Tenos		3		2		2			10		
Andros	12	6	6	6		6			15		7
Imbros		3300		1					1	1	

ted tribute as demanded in each four-year assessment period. Variations from this ideal pattern do a good deal both to indicate the way the empire was run and to indicate the histories of individual allies' relations with Athens. Variations take two basic forms: special rubrics or headings; and unexpected appearances and disappearances of cities' names on the lists.

From 440/39 to 431/0 payments appear that are labelled *'epiphora'* ('additional contribution'). These payments are additional to payment of the basic Tribute Quota and comprise a small fraction (between 2/60 and 10/60) of that quota. They appear to be penalties imposed for late payment, presumably in accordance with some lost decree of the late 440s tightening up on tribute payment.

The Peloponnesian War brought some new rubrics, which seem to show the Athenians using some tribute payments to meet pressing demands. In 430/29 and 429/8 some cities in the Hellespont/Bosporos area are recorded as 'These cities furnished pay out of their Hellespontine tribute' or 'These cities presented a voucher for tribute', and these seem to correspond with Athens establishing garrisons in the area (Thucydides 2.24.1). The rubric 'These cities furnished pay for a military force out of their tribute' appears in 430/29, 428/7 and 421/20, and again can, in some cases at least, be linked to military activity recorded by Thucydides. Not only was such direct payment efficient, but it will have reassured the allies that their money was contributing to their own security.

One special rubric can be connected with a known decree, and usefully allows us to see how exceptional that decree was. In 430 the Athenians agreed to allow Methone to pay Athena's share of her tribute assessment alone (**121**.30-31). 'These cities paid Athena's share only' duly appears as a rubric, but it is a rubric only ever applied to a couple of other cities besides Methone.

5 Relations between Athens and individual allies

If these rubrics help to show something of the way the empire was run and changing Athenian priorities, other rubrics, and the unexpected appearances and disappearances of cities, together with changes in the amounts of tribute that they pay, reveal instead the relations both between Athens and the allies in general and between Athens and individual allies.

a) Communities wanting to join Athens

In the 435/4 and 434/3 lists some small Thracian cities appear labelled 'unassessed cities'. One of these is in the company of cities against which in 434/3-432/1 the rubric appears 'Cities which private citizens registered as paying tribute'. In 430/29 and 429/8 some of those cities then appear with the rubric 'On these cities the Council and the Court of 1,500 assessed tribute'. Some of the other Thracian 'unassessed cities' appear among 11 cities which are recorded in 434/3-432/1 as 'Cities themselves assessing their own tribute'. What we seem to have here are cities in which either the community as a whole or some part of the community sees advantage in joining the empire; given Athenian activity in the Thraceward area with the foundation of Amphipolis, some may simply have decided to jump before they were pushed. Not all liked what they got: one 'unassessed city' appears in one list only; others in these categories disappear from the lists soon after the start of the Peloponnesian War.

b) Absenteeism and disaffection

Given the fragmentary nature of what survives, being sure that a particular city is absent from a list is possible only once the lists are geographically organised. In the case of the earliest lists, it is possible to be confident that absenteeism occurs on a wide scale without being certain which cities were absent. This is important since who is missing from which lists matters for questions relating to the changeover from providing ships to paying tribute and for questions of disaffection among the allies.

c) Evidence for revolt in 451/0

The case for disaffection among allies at the end of the 450s is strong. 45 names are known to be lost from the surviving fragments of the list for 451/0, but there are some 69 cities (excluding abnormal entries) who pay in one or more of the lists for 453-451 but do not appear in the 451/0 list: some 24 cities that had paid previously must not have paid in 451/0, and although perhaps as many as 16 of these may be places whose later record is patchy, there still seems to be a core of allies who generally pay with regularity but are exceptionally absent in 451/0. This is by contrast with 452/1 where 50 names can be calculated to be lost, and these gaps can be filled almost completely with the 47 cities recorded in either or both of 454/3 and 453/2. It is possible to conclude with some confidence that from 454/3 to 452/1 practically all the allies paid in a regular way, but that in 451/0 a significant number of those allies chose not to pay. While individual cities may have had different circumstances preventing them paying, the core of allies absent in 451/0 must have been in revolt. But this is not the worst of it.

d) Evidence for prolonged revolt in the late 450s

In addition to the absence in 451/0 of cities previously listed, there are some 23 cities which appear for the first time ever on the list for 450/49 (it is statistically very unlikely indeed that more than one of these 23 can have been on all four previous lists and yet had its name survive on none). Of these 23, 10 are significant contributors, who pay a talent or more, and the large majority are cities that must have been in the empire before 450. Either they have been consistently absent previously because they were still providing ships, or because they were disaffected, and effectively in revolt, continuously during the late 450s, perhaps from the time of the failure of the Egyptian expedition (**39**, Thuc. 1.109-110).

Looking at what happens to individual cities helps to suggest how we should interpret this disaffection in general. The sending of Athenian settlers to Naxos (**68, 70, 230-31**), should be connected with the fact that, when Naxos is listed in 449 for the first time, it pays a surprisingly small amount (6 talents 4,000 drachmas) for a large island: it is reasonable to conclude that the tribute is small because of the settlement, and that the settlers were sent because Naxos was previously in revolt. The tribute of Karystos, like Naxos a place with a history of resistance to Athens (**29**), goes from 12 talents in 453 to 7 talents 3,000 drachmas in 450 and then 5 talents in 449 and subsequently; this suggests that the Athenian settlers were sent there in 450. Likewise, too, Andros first appears in the 450 list with a tribute of 12 talents but subsequently pays only 6 talents; literary sources tell of Athenian settlers being sent to Andros (**231**), and this change in tribute suggests that they also were sent out in 450/49.

These Athenian settlers are the first we hear of who were sent to allied territories. Athens seems to have invented a new policy in response to new trouble from major allies. Disaffection, rather than a change from ships to money, is clearly at issue in these cases, and that strongly suggests (despite **33**) that disaffection also explains the other absences. There was a major imperial crisis in the late 450s, even though Thucydides and our literary sources give little hint of it. This crisis preceded, rather than followed, coming to terms with Persia, and it is more likely to be a product of Athenian failure (in Egypt) than of Athenian success (in Cyprus).

This case can be further strengthened by a different sort of anomaly. From time to time lists preserve payments made by a sub-set of a community which normally pays as a unit (see also note to **216**). Why this occurs is not always clear: we have no idea why separate contributions from 'Phokaians from [.]e[.]ko' and 'Phokaians' were recorded on successive lines of the 453-2 list (for a similar problem with regard to Miletos see **218**). But in other cases we can work out what the background is. The list for 451/0 includes a payment of 2 talents 1,500 drachmas from Koresia on Keos, and then, near the end of the list, a (late) payment from Keos as a whole of something between 1 talent 1,200 drachmas and 1 talent 3,000 drachmas. Neither Koresia nor Keos as a whole appears in earlier extant fragments, and subsequently the island always pays a single sum of 4 talents. A story of revolt from which Koresia returns to loyalty in advance of the rest of the island seems called for (in the fourth century there was more trouble for the Athenians from Keos, focused on the city of Ioulis).

e) The problem of the missing list

The most debated of all absences occurs in the early 440s. It is clear that the fifth list on the First Stele dates to 450/49, but there are then only two more lists before the list that dates to 446/5. Those two lists (known as lists A and B) are certainly for consecutive years, either 449/8 and 448/7 or 448/7 and 447/6. One whole year's list is missing, either that for 449/8 or that for 447/6. If tribute was paid by the allies, it is hard to imagine any circumstances in which no share of it would be paid to Athena; and although scholars have speculated that there might have been widespread disaffection in 448 following the Peace of Kallias or in 446 following the defeat at Koroneia, it seems impossible that revolt could have been so complete as to result in no tribute coming in without that leaving more trace in the records for the following years or in the literature. Either no tribute was payable for one year for some special reason, or the Athenians recorded Athena's share on some other stone for one year, even though the First Stele was not full.

f) Late payments: inefficiency or disaffection?

From the earliest of the lists onwards, it is evident that some absences are caused by late payment: a group of 18 contributors have the payment that belonged to 454/3 listed at the start of the list for 453/2. I have already mentioned the late payment by Keos in 451-50. In 450-49 some 20 cities pay in two instalments. Keos pays late again on list A, along with Kythnos and Karystos and with Mende (a big payer, at 15 talents). A further ten cities, mainly from the Hellespont area, make partial payments in that list. List B has cities in substantially the same order as list A, but has a list at the end which appears to have back-payments from the year of list A and supplementary payments. Three entries on list B record payments made elsewhere than in Athens — at Tenedos and Eion. Either Athenian collection procedures were in disarray, or there was widespread disaffection (note Athenian casualties at Byzantion in 447, **67**). It is possible that Kleinias' decree (**190**) was addressed to these problems.

g) Problems in the Khersonesos

These same lists show that the Athenians faced trouble in the Khersonesos, which almost certainly was what led them to send out the settlement mentioned by literary sources (**68-9, 230-31**). In the late 450s several communities of the Khersonesos pay (18 talents) as 'Khersonitai'. In 450/49 Khersonitai pay 18 talents 4,840 drachmas. In list B and in 445/4 and 444/3 the amount Khersonitai pay is lost, but from 443/2 onwards Khersonitai pay just 1 talent. Two other communities in the area, Neapolis-by-Antisara and the Alopekonnesioi each pay more or less the same amount every year from their first surviving appearance in the lists to the outbreak of the Peloponnesian War. A number of other Khersonesos communities, Elaiousioi in Khersonesos, Sestioi, Limnaioi in Khersonesos, and Madytioi, are listed for the first time either on list B, in 446/5, or in 445/4, but even when their tribute is added to that of the Khersonitai it amounts to little more than 2 talents. Neapolis-by-Antisara is the only Khersonesos community certainly to appear on list A. The picture seems to be one of revolt in the area in the early 440s followed by the imposition of an Athenian settlement in 448-7 and a subsequent 'divide and rule' policy by the Athenians, who made the emasculated Khersonesos communities pay in a number of different units.

h) Tribute reductions in 446/5 and the case of Poteidaia

Curiously, when Thucydides makes the most of the danger to Athens of her empire falling apart, with the revolt of Euboia in 446-5 and the Spartan invasion, the tribute lists show little sign of problems. It is true, however, that in the new assessment which came into force in 445 some 30 states have their tribute reduced, and only 3 have it increased (including Thasos which jumps from 3 talents to 30 talents, perhaps because she had finished paying off an indemnity for her revolt 20 years earlier or because she was given mining possessions back). Some new contributors are found, including Poteidaia, whose assessment for the first time can hardly have been welcomed by Corinth (although it is compensated for by a reduction by an equal amount of the tribute from the rest of the Pallene peninsula). A marked increase in Poteidaian tribute from 6 to 15 talents in between 439/8 and 435/4 may have had a political motivation (see **100** (Thuc. 1.56.2)).

For all the difficulties and complexities of interpretation, the Tribute Quota Lists provide a quite invaluable insight into the Athenian empire, its finances, its working and its fortunes. Deductions from information which was always terse and which has become also fragmentary must be made with the utmost care, but our understanding of the empire and its development would be much the poorer were it not for the precious fragments of these inscriptions.

Note G Religious aspects of Athenian imperialism

Payment of a share of tribute to Athena

Because they enable us to trace payments of tribute, it is easy to forget that the surviving Tribute Quota Lists are actually lists which mark the fulfilment of a religious obligation. This is almost certainly not accidental: the Athenians made temporary lists of various financial transactions, usually on whitened boards, but permanent lists inscribed on stone seem to have been made much more frequently when there was a religious aspect than for purely secular purposes. If whitened boards were often sufficient to ensure accountability to men, accountability before the gods demanded inscription on stone.

Much more is at issue here than Athenian attitudes towards accountability: religious obligation rather than petty-mindedness lies behind Athens' insistence that Athena's share is paid even when the rest of the tribute is remitted (**121**). We are ignorant of any religious aspects to the payment of tribute to the League Treasury while it remained on Delos, but the numbering of the Athenian lists allows us to be reasonably confident that the payment of a share ('first-fruits') of the tribute to Athena began only in 454/3, that is, presumably (see **24, 66** and p.36) when the League Treasury was moved to Athens. Delos had long been a religious centre for the Greeks of the Aegean, as important to them as Olympia and Delphi were for the Greeks of the mainland and the west. The Homeric *Hymn to Apollo* celebrated the gathering at Delos in Apollo's honour of 'the long-robed Ionians with their children and modest wives'. Sanctuaries of Delian Apollo and/or Artemis are known in a number of other Aegean islands - Naxos, Paros and Keos in the Cyclades, Amorgos, Khios, Nisyros, Syme and Kalymnos beyond them. It was indeed because Delos was so widely shared a cult centre, as well as because it was out of reach of the Persians, that Delos was chosen as the place for the Treasury in the first place. The diversion of a sacred share of their tribute from the sanctuary at Delos to the Akropolis sanctuary of Athens must have carried a much greater symbolic charge than did the mere geographical movement of the 'bank' from one location to another. It may also have had a material impact on Delos: the temple of Delian Apollo which had been begun, on a scale almost identical to that of the early fifth-century temple of Aphaia on Aigina, after the Persian Wars had to wait until the fourth century for its ceiling, roof, and floor, most probably because the departure of the Treasury starved the cult of funds (see below p. 125).

How religious experiences were shared

Little religious activity in Greece was solitary. Sacrifices and festivals were communal. The citizens, only perhaps one-third of whom lived in or immediately around Athens itself, were united by their shared religious experiences. But they shared these experiences in a variety of ways. One way was that Athenians who lived in villages distant from Athens came into Athens on the occasion of major city festivals and either made their own group sacrifice or took part as a group in the massive sacrifices laid on at state expense. Another was that the villagers held celebrations in their own villages to coincide with and mark the festivals being celebrated on a grander scale in the town of Athens. A third way of sharing cult activity was the duplication of major cults which had their centre outside the town by building sanctuaries for the same cults in the town - or indeed in another village. Thus there was an Eleusinion in Athens as a focus for the worship of the two Eleusinian goddesses, Demeter the giver of grain and her daughter Kore (Persephone), and a sanctuary of Brauronian Artemis on the Akropolis in which duplicate lists of the dedications made at the sanctuary at Brauron on the east coast of Attica were put up.

In a variety of ways the Athenians came to treat their allies like Athenian citizens and to expect them to do things that Athenian citizens did (above p.36-7). How far was this also true in the sphere of religion? It is worth looking in turn at the three ways in which Attica was turned into a single religious community, to see how far similar methods were used to make a single religious community out of the allies.

Allied participation in Athenian festivals

Participation in Athenian festivals certainly came to be expected to some extent. The Athenians commanded the allies to bring their tribute at the Dionysia (**192-4**, and compare **190**.19, 29) and to join in its grand procession, to which Athenian settlements abroad seem also to have contributed a phallos (**232**.12-13). They also demanded their presence at the Great Panathenaia, held once every four years, which was made the occasion for re-assessing tribute levels (see **138**.26-8). On that occasion they were expected to bring with them a cow for sacrifice and a full set of armour. Although the evidence we have is not itself primarily concerned with allied behaviour, it looks as if allies were also expected to bring first-fruits of their grain, and perhaps, if Lampon's amendment ever got anywhere, their olive oil to Eleusis (ML 73 cf. **205**), as Athenian demes and settlements abroad were doing a century later, though by that time no one else seems to have joined them (see *IG* ii^2 1672.263-88).

When allies came to Athens for the Panathenaia, they were faced from the 430s onwards with the glories of the newly built Parthenon. Although the surviving accounts give no support to the idea that the main body of the tribute was used to finance this largest of all classical temples on the Greek mainland and its extravagant gold and ivory cult statue (**195-6**), there can be no doubt that without the profits of empire, which were not restricted to tribute, Athens would not have had the surplus money available to indulge in such a monument. The unprecedented wealth of architectural sculpture on the temple offered multiple images of conflict, but none of them made direct reference to fifth-century battles. Together with the frieze, the position of which obliged any visitor that viewed it in effect to join the procession which it represented, the sculptures of the metopes presented the image of an ideal citizen, facing whatever difficulties and dangers might arise with sensitivity but with unswerving purpose. Any participant in the Panathenaia, Athenian or not, could aspire to that citizen role: nothing about the sculptures depreciated other Greeks, despite the local allusions contained in the frieze and the west pediment. Allies too could see their own reflection here and take pride in these images - provided they were willing to conform.

Allied adoption of Athenian cults?

Did allies also, either on their own initiative or under pressure from Athens, adopt Athenian cults and festivals? Scholarly belief in a cult of 'Athena who rules at Athens' (**220**) exported from Athens to her allies has recently been undermined (see note p.110). Settlements abroad seem in general to have adopted the calendar and festivals of the community primarily responsible for their foundation (Abdera and Teos provide a particularly clear example of this). When Athens founded settlements abroad, the cult arrangements were a central concern, as the decree setting up Brea (**232**) and the tradition that Lampon the religious expert (the same man who moved the amendment to **205**) was sent out to found Thourioi (**82**) attest. Such settlers continued to cultivate links with Athenian religious cults, making group dedications on the Athenian Akropolis, for example (so Pausanias 1.28.2 of the Lemnians). But what evidence there is from the settlements themselves suggests that they also respected existing local cults, although they might organise the cultic activities there along Athenian lines. So it is that the Athenians who were settled on Aigina inventoried the property of the Aiginetan cults of Aphaia and of 'Mnia and Auxesia' (*IG* i^3 1455, 1456). From the late fourth century there is evidence for the Athenian-derived settlers on Lemnos celebrating the cult of the 'Great Gods' or 'Kabeiroi', but doing so as a 'citizen body of the initiated' moving decrees framed entirely in the Athenian manner and with officials listed in the official order of the Athenian tribes.

Athenian adoption of cults from the Empire

If evidence for the Athenians exporting their own cults to allies is scarce, evidence of the Athenians themselves adopting cults from the empire is more abundant. The occasional appearance of such exotic deities as Orthanes, a major cult figure on Imbros, who is always represented in a state of sexual excitement, is one aspect of this. Far more important is the Athenian adoption of the cult of Delian Apollo. One aspect of this was that the Athenians followed the example of several of those Aegean islands mentioned above and built a temple to Apollo Delios at Phaleron, perhaps in the late 430s (**207**); but what will have had much more impact upon the allies is the way in which they took over the cult of Apollo on Delos itself.

Athenian involvement in the cults of Delos

Evidence for Athenian running of cult on Delos is substantial. Thucydides attests three actions on two separate occasions. First (**137**) they purified the island, something which the Athenians of the sixth century had also attempted, and which on this occasion involved removing the graves of the Delian dead and for the future forbidding anyone to give birth or die while on the island. Once Delos was purified the Athenians restored the Delia, which Theseus was held to have founded, as a grand four-yearly festival (**208-9**); in the fourth century it involved sacrificing some 109 oxen (*IG* ii^2 1635.36). But then (**154-5**) they intervened again to expel the Delians from the island.

Inscriptions enable us to see in some detail how Athenian control worked. They show that, in a total perversion of the institution all the Amphiktions (see note to **6**) running the sanctuary in the late fifth century were Athenian (**210**). Archaeology reveals not only the deposition of the contents of the Delian graves on the neighbouring island of Rheneia, but the building, in Pentelic marble and Athenian techniques, of a small temple, whose construction probably belongs to the 420s and 410s. (That temple was in the Doric order, though small temples in classical Athens were constructed in the Ionic order. Is this connected with Athens' courting the Dorian islanders who also looked to Delos as their centre?) Some sort of Athenian intervention in the running of the Delian sanctuary certainly goes back to the 430s, when surviving accounts date themselves by the Athenian as well as Delian archon (see **210**), but of the intensification of Athenian interest and activity in the 420s there can be no doubt.

Delos was the most important cult centre within the Athenian Empire, and the closest parallel to Athenian activities there comes not from elsewhere among the allies but from the borders of Attica. Athens certainly much developed the cult of Amphiaraos in the territory of Oropos, control of which she disputed with Thebes, and it is possible that she introduced the cult there as a rival to Amphiaraos' cult at Thebes. Rivalry certainly plays a part in Athenian religious activities, as she tries to ensure that it is Athens and Delos rather than Olympia and Delphi to which the allies send their religious embassies. Athens seems to have courted the Delphic Amphiktiony in the years of her 'land empire' in the middle of the fifth century - part of the text of an alliance survives (*IG* i^{3}9) - but in the last third of the century Olympia and Delphi seem rather to have been foci for resistance to Athens. It is at Olympia in 428 that the Mytileneans appeal for Peloponnesian support for their revolt (see **126** note), and Athens seems to have been more than once reprimanded by the Delphic oracle (see **152, 205**); a further piece of epigraphic evidence (Fornara 137) may show Andros seeking a special relationship with Delphi, but the date is quite uncertain.

Cult and politics

Cult activity lay at the very centre of Athenian life, and as Athenian life acquired an imperial dimension, so too did her cult interests. Piety and politics were necessarily intimately involved with one another. Just as in recent years there has been increasing opposition to the notion that Athens' relations with Eleusis and other cult places in Attica were a matter of 'take-over', so too in the Empire we should rather be surprised if there were no Athenian interest in the prosperity of such central sanctuaries as that on Delos than shocked to find the Athenians taking control there. Where Athenian imperialism shows through most clearly, however, is in her unwillingness to let allied piety have political consequences: allied participation in the Dionysia, at the Great Panathenaia, at Delos or at Eleusis was never accompanied by the extension of political rights - rather the reverse (see **48-9**).

2.1 TRIBUTE
Assessment
For Aristeides' initial assessment see **15, 18-20**.

Re-assessment
Frequency of re-assessment
184 There is much that I omit here, but I have described all the most important things, except the assessment of the tribute. This generally happens at four-yearly intervals.

[Xenophon] *Constitution of the Athenians* 3.5

On the years in which re-assessment actually took place see above p.93.

For the extraordinary re-assessment of 425 see **138**.

Involvement of Alkibiades with a re-assessment?
185 So Alkibiades first persuaded you to assess afresh the tribute assessment that Aristeides had made for the cities with scrupulous justice, and when he was elected with nine others to do this he practically doubled the tribute of each of the allies.

[Andokides] *Against Alkibiades* 4.11

This speech contains many dubious assertions (see above **158**). If this one is true, it would surely have to be before the 425 assessment (therefore, given Alkibiades' age, that of 428). Using 10 men as assessors contrasts with the large court responsible in **138**.

Role of Council in assessment procedures
See **138**.17-20, 58-9; **190**.

Appeal against assessment
The case of the Samothracians
186 'The island which we inhabit can be seen from afar to be high and rough. Little of it is of any use or can be worked, much is unworked and the total area is small.'

Antiphon *On the tribute of the Samothracians* frg.50

For court cases in connection with tribute payment, compare **138**.12-15, **78**.26-7, **190**.61-3 and see p.38.

187 Collectors (*Eklogeis*): Those who collect and exact what is owing to the public treasury. Antiphon in his speech *On the tribute of the Samothracians* [frg. 52] says: 'We [Samothracians]chose the men who were apparently most wealthy to be Collectors'. Lysias in his speech *Against Aresander* [frg. 9] says 'Now we register all our property with the Collectors of tribute'.

Harpokration *Lexicon* s.v. *Eklogeis*

For Collectors of tribute compare **136**.

188 Separate assessment (*apotaxis*): This refers to the separate assessment of those who previously had been assessed with one another to pay a stated tribute. Antiphon uses the word in his *On the tribute of the Samothracians* [frg.55].

Harpokration *Lexicon* s.v. *Apotaxis*

189 Joint contributors (*synteleis*): Those who share an expense or share a tax. The act is called 'joint contribution' (*synteleia*), as one can find in Antiphon's *On the tribute of the Samothracians* [frg.56]

Harpokration *Lexicon* s.v. *Synteleis*

Collection of tribute

The Kleinias Decree

190 Gods. The Council and People decided, in the prytany of the tribe Oineis, when Spoudias was Secretary and [—]on [5] was President, on the proposal of Kleinias: that the Council and the magistrates in the cities and the Inspectors (*episkopoi*) should look after the collection of tribute every year [10] and bring it to Athens.

They are to make identification tokens for the cities to prevent those who bring the tribute from committing offences: the city is to write on [15] a tablet the amount of the tribute which it is sending and then seal it with the identification token before it sends it to Athens. Those who bring the tribute are to give the tablet to the Council to read whenever they hand over the tribute.

The prytaneis are to hold a meeting of the Assembly after the Dionysia, at which the [20] Hellenotamiai are to list for the Athenians separately the cities which have paid all their tribute and the cities that have defaulted.

The Athenians are to elect four men and [send] them to the cities with a record of the [tribute that has been paid] to ask for [25] the remaining tribute from defaulters. Two are to sail on a swift trireme [to the Island region and to Ionia, and two to the Hellespont and] the Thraceward region. [The prytaneis are to introduce this matter to the] Council and the [People immediately after the Dionysia and [30] are to keep them up to date on this matter until it is completed].

If any Athenian [or ally commits an offence over] the tribute which [the cities have written on the tablet and] must [send to Athens] with their tribute-carriers, any [Athenian] [35] or ally [shall be free to indict him before the prytaneis, and the prytaneis] are to bring [any indictment that anyone] makes to the Council [or else suffer a fine of 1,000 drachmas] each at their scrutiny. [Whatever penalty the Council] condemns [an offender to] shall only become valid when [immediately] confirmed [by the Heliaia]. When a [guilty verdict] is declared, [40] the prytaneis [are to make] a decision as to what the offender should [pay or] suffer.

If anyone commits an offence over the bringing of the cow or [the full set of armour], indictment and [punishment] are to follow the same procedure.

The [*Hellenotamiai* are to write up and [45] display] on a whitened board the tribute [assessment] and [the cities that have paid all of it and] to list [—]

[10 lines missing]

the incoming Council [is to discuss those who bring in the tribute.] All of those bringing tribute [to Athens who] are written up [on the noticeboard] as owing money [60] [—] it is to display to the People [— If] any city [argues about the handing over of the tribute], asserting that it did [hand it over —] the common meeting of the [city —] the cities and the [65] [—], it shall not be possible to indict

The two largest fragments surviving from the stele recording Kleinias' decree (**190**). The uninscribed rectangle at the top right may once have had a painted image on it. The letters are 12 mm. high.

[— or] the man who brings the indictment is to owe a fine [—] the indictment [is to be brought to the Polemarch in the month of Game]lion. But if anyone argues [—] prosecutions, let the Council [70] consider the matter and [—] those [responsible for introducing cases] are to bring [to the Heliaia those who owe] tribute to the Athenians [in order, according to the record] of the denunciation. [—] the new tribute and last year's tribute [—] the Council is to consider the matter first and bring [—] at the meeting on the next day [—] arrangements for the choice [—].

ML 46 (*SEG* 42.8)

Kleinias is not a common name, and the Kleinias most politically active during the fifth century is Kleinias the father of Alkibiades, killed at Koroneia in 446 (above Thuc. 1.113.2 **64**). But some scholars prefer to date this decree close to the Kleonymos decree (**136**) rather than in the early 440s. For tribute problems in those years to which this decree could be a response see p.96.

For changes in tribute collection procedures in 426 (the Kleonymos Decree) see **136**.

For 'ships to collect money' sent out by Athens during the Arkhidamian war (which may not have been primarily to collect tribute) see **60, 117-8,144.**

On arrears and supplementary payments see p.96.

Receipt of tribute
Role of *Hellenotamiai*: **15, 190**.20

The role of the Council
191 The Council deals with much business to do with war, much to do with finance, much to do with law-making, much to do with the day-to-day running of the city, and much with allied matters; it also receives the tribute and looks after the ship-sheds and temples.

[Xenophon] *Constitution of the Athenians* 3.2

Brought in at City Dionysia
Affecting the audience at the dramatic festival
192 DIKAIOPOLIS. Anyway Kleon can't abuse me now for speaking badly of the city in the presence of foreigners. We are on our own here and this contest is at the Lenaia - the foreigners haven't come yet. I mean, neither tribute nor allies have come from the cities [of the empire].

Aristophanes *Akharnians* (425) 502-6

193 The arrangement was that the cities brought tribute to Athens at the Dionysia, as Eupolis says in his *Cities* (*Poleis* fr.254).

Scholiast to Aristophanes *Akharnians* 504

Ceremonial procession of surplus tribute?
194 They worked out in the finest detail how to get men most to hate them, and so voted to carry the surplus left after expenditure talent by talent into the theatre at the Dionysia when the theatre was full. And as well as doing this, they led in the sons of those who had died in the war, displaying to the allies the value of their property that was brought in by hirelings and to the other Greeks the number of orphans and the misfortunes that they incurred through their greed.

Isokrates 8 (*On the Peace*) 82

For replacement of tribute by a tax in *c*.413 and its restoration *c*.410 see **162-3, 181**.

Use of Athena's share of the tribute
For Parthenon
195 From the *Hellenotamiai* [to whom] Strombikhos of Kholleidai [was Secretary] [444/3]: [37,]675 dr. 5 obols.

B43.36-8

196 From the *Hellenotamiai* to whom Protonikos of Kerameis was Secretary [434-3], a mina per talent of allied tribute [total not preserved].

ML 60.11-13

These two entries, **195** from the Parthenon accounts and **196** from the Propylaia accounts, indicate that Athena's share of the tribute was used to fund the Akropolis building works. There is no evidence that the other 59/60ths of the tribute was ever used for these works (despite the implications of **66**). The sum restored in **195** would correspond to a total tribute of 376 talents, 4550 drachmas.

For an occasion when the *Hellenotamiai* might be expected to meet expenses but do not, see **90**.

For work on Athenian water-supply

197 [The expenditure on the water-supply is to be met from the money] that is paid towards the Athenian tribute [whenever the goddess] takes her accustomed share [of it].

Inscriptiones Graecae i³ 49.14-16

This comes at the end of a very fragmentary decree that seems to date to the 430s.

For Athenian finances during the Arkhidamian War see p.92.

2.2 OTHER IMPOSITIONS IMPOSED ON ALL ALLIES

Coins, weights and measures:
The Athenian Standards Decree

198 [— magistrates] in the cities or magistrates [—]

[2] The *Hellenotamiai* [—] are to register. If they do not register correctly the obligation of any of the cities, [let anyone who wants to immediately] bring [those who have offended] before the Heliaia of the [Thesmothetai according to the law]. The Thesmothetai are to ensure [hearings for those who have brought the accusation] within five [days] in each case.

[3] If [anyone else apart from] the magistrates in the cities fails to act in accordance with the decree, either a citizen or a foreigner, he is to lose his civic rights, and his property is to be confiscated and [a tenth] given to the goddess.

[4] If there are no Athenian magistrates, the magistrates [of each city are to put into effect the provisions] of the decree. If they fail to act in accordance with [the decree—].

[5] [Those who have received] the silver [in] the mint [are to strike not] less than half and [—] the cities [— three (or five)] drachmas in the mina. They are to exchange [the other half within ? months] or be liable [—]

[6] [They are to strike the] surplus of the money [exacted and hand it over] either to the Generals or [—]. Whenever it is handed over, [—] to Athena and to Hephaistos [—, and if anyone] proposes or puts to the vote a proposal on [these matters, to the effect that it should be permitted] to use or lend [this money, let him immediately be brought before] the Eleven, and let the [Eleven] administer the death penalty. [But if] he appeals, [he is to be led before the court].

[7] The [People] are to choose heralds [and send them to announce what has been decreed], one to go to the Islands, [one to Ionia, one to the] Hellespont, one to the Thraceward region. [The Generals are to prescribe the route for each of these and] send them out. [If they fail to do so], they are to face a fine of ten thousand drachmas [each] at their scrutiny.

[8] The magistrates in the cities are to write up this decree on a stone stele and [place it] in the agora of [each] city, and the Overseers [*epistatai*] are to place a copy [in front of] the mint. [The Athenians are to see to] this, if the cities themselves are not willing.

[9] The herald who goes is to ask them to do all that the Athenians order.

[10] The Secretary of the [Council] is to add the following to the Council Oath [for the future]: If anyone strikes silver coinage in the cities and does not use Athenian coins or weights or measures, [but foreign coins] and measures and weights, [I will administer punishments and penalties according to the former] decree that Klearkhos [proposed].

[11] [Anyone may hand over] the foreign silver [that he has and exchange it on the same basis] whenever he wants. The city [will give in exchange native (= Athenian) coin]. Each individual is to bring his own coins [to Athens] himself [and deposit them at the] mint.

[12] The Overseers are to write up [all that is handed over by each person] and set up [a stone stele in front of the mint] for anyone who wants to to see. [They are to write up the total of] foreign coin, separating [the silver and the gold, and the total of native] silver [—].

Inscriptiones Graecae i³ 1453; cf.ML45 (*SEG* 43.3)

This text is made up from fragments found in the territory of various allies (Aphytis, Kos, Hamaxitos, Odessa, Siphnos, Smyrna, Syme): hence its numbering by clause rather than by line.

Both the Kos and the Hamaxitos fragments are in the Attic alphabet, perhaps because these allies refused to inscribe the decree themselves (see clause 8). The Kos fragment includes a three-bar sigma, once thought to indicate a date in the 440s, but confidence in dating on letter forms in general and on three-bar sigmas in particular has recently been dented (see p.8).

That one fragment comes from Hamaxitos in the Troad, which seems not to have been part of the empire until the 420s, strengthens the case for a date in the 420s or 410s, closer to the date of Aristophanes' parody of the decree in *Birds* (see next passage). Some 60% of Athenian allies never minted coins at all either before or during the period of the Athenian empire, and 80% of tribute-payers were not coining by the 440s. Detailed die studies of a number of cities in the Empire (including Samos, Kos, Khios, and Akanthos) make it clear that those cities at least did not cease minting silver coins in the 440s, but allow for the possibility that there was a break in the later 420s.

Figueira has recently argued that the decree may not have banned the minting and use of local silver but simply have insisted that allies should also treat Athenian coins as valid, as part of a move to ensure that tribute was paid in Athenian coin. However, a) since Greek cities did not normally refuse genuine coins, whatever the minting authority, this decree would seem otiose; b) Figueira's argument against restoring 'foreign coins' in clause 10 is weak, since it does not take into account that this is part of the oath of the Athenian Council, and his alternative restoration of the clause seems epigraphically implausible.

Since the decree only affects silver coins, and Kyzikene staters made of electrum, an alloy of gold and silver, continued to be an important currency throughout the fifth century, this measure does not bring a single currency. In any case, the economic advantages of a single currency were rather less in a world where coins were worth their face value than in the modern world of token coinage, and uniformity of weights and measures would similarly bring little gain to merchants long used to converting from one unit to another. Athens may have made some gain from the 3% or 5% minting fee, and in the atmosphere of the 425 Tribute Reassessment (**138**), that may have been part of the motivation. Striking one's own coinage was not seen by Greek cities as an essential part of sovereignty, but there can be little doubt that this more or less gratuitous demand (compare **97-8**) above all emphasised to allies their subject status (see further pp.36-7).

199 DECREE-SELLER (reading). If a citizen of Cloudcuckooland wrongs an Athenian...

PEISETAIROS. What, another horrible little scroll?

DECREE-SELLER. I am a Decree-seller, and I have come here to you to sell you new laws.

PEISETAIROS. Like what?

DECREE-SELLER. [1040] The people of Cloudcuckooland are to use these measures and weights and decrees just like the Olophyxians.

PEISETAIROS. You'll soon be using what the Ototyxians [i.e. those who cry out 'Ototoi' because beaten] use.

DECREE-SELLER. What's wrong with you?

PEISETAIROS. Won't you take those laws away? [1045] I'll show you some nasty laws right now. [Hits him.]

DECREE-SELLER. I indict Peisetairos for gross violence, case to be held in the month Mounykhion.

PEISETAIROS [turning away from Decree-seller and seeing Inspector]. Is this really you? Are you still hanging about here?

INSPECTOR [reading]. [1050] If anyone drives out the officials and does not accept them in accordance with the stele...

PEISETAIROS. What an unlucky man I am, you are still hanging about!

INSPECTOR. I will bring about your destruction and indict you for 10,000 drachmas.

PEISETAIROS [aiming a kick?]. I'll do for your two voting urns...

DECREE-SELLER. [1055] Do you remember when you defecated over the stele one evening?

PEISETAIROS. Yuck! Arrest him someone!

Aristophanes Birds (414) 1035-55

This continues **224**. There is much scholarly dispute over who says what lines after 1045. Figueira's recent claim that this must refer to some 'unknown Athenian monetary legislation' and not to the coinage decree, and that it therefore shows the 'extent of the legislation and diplomacy that has been lost from sight', allows too little scope for comic licence.

For Athenian control of grain supply from Black Sea see **121-3**.

Obligations to refer cases to Athenian courts

Removal of capital cases to Athens

200 [1.16] The people of Athens also seem to be badly advised in the following, that they compel the allies to sail to Athens for court cases. But they argue that the people of Athens get many advantages from this: first, that they get pay throughout the year from the court fees; second, that it enables them to administer the allied cities while staying at home, without sailing off on ships, and that they use the courts to protect some members of the people and condemn those who oppose democracy, and if all the allies dealt with cases at home, then because they are fed up with the Athenians, they would condemn precisely those who are the friends of the people of Athens. [1.17] In addition to this the people of Athens benefit in the following ways from hearing allied court cases at Athens. First, it increases the city's income from the one per cent tax at the Peiraieus. [1.18] Second, anyone who has rooms to let does better out of them. Third, anyone who has a carriage or a slave to hire does better out of them. Fourth, heralds do better because of allies' visits. In addition to all those reasons, if the allies did not come for court cases, they would honour only those Athenians who sailed out to visit them — Generals, trierarchs, and ambassadors; but as it is, every single ally has been forced to suck up to the people of Athens, in the knowledge that the man who comes to Athens as prosecutor or defendant is involved in a case not before some select officials but before the People, as the rule is at Athens; he has to plead in the courts and take the hand of anyone who comes into the court in supplication. It is this in particular that makes the allies slaves of the Athenian people.

[Xenophon] *Constitution of the Athenians* 1.16-18

See **106** (Thuc.1.77.1).

201 But as it was, they bought the man and then privately on their own killed their informer, when he wasn't himself guilty of murder, without a vote by the city. They should have put him in chains and kept him under guard, or released him on security from my friends, or handed him over to your officials and had a vote taken about him. But as it was, they condemned the man to death and killed him, when it isn't even possible for the city to punish a man with the death penalty without Athenian say-so.

Antiphon 5 (*On the murder of Herodes* [*c.*420]) 47

Euxitheos of Mytilene, in defending himself on the charge of murdering an Athenian named Herodes, claims that those who accuse him did away with the slave who had laid information against him. It is not clear whether Athens did in fact extend her jurisdiction over capital cases to those involving slaves.

Allies afraid of Athenian accusations against them

202 HERMES. [The speakers in the Assembly] used to shake down the wealthy and prosperous among the allies, laying accusations that they were Brasidean sympathisers. And then you tore at them like hounds - the city, sitting there pale and frightened, gobbled up with pleasure whatever slanders anyone told it. The foreigners, seeing the blows that were being struck, bunged up the mouths of those who made these accusations with gold, making them rich, while you were never going to notice that Greece was on its way to desolation. And the man who did this was the tanner [i.e. Kleon].

Aristophanes *Peace* (421) 639-48

The claim about Kleon here is consistent with the claims made about him (i.e. the character Paphlagon), and his use of accusations of conspiracy, in Aristophanes *Knights* of 424.

Summoning to Athenian court a hated feature of Athenian rule

203 PROSECUTOR. No, no, no. I am the Island Summoner (*kleter*) and bringer of troublesome prosecutions...

PEISETAIROS. What a wonderful job!

PROSECUTOR. ... and probing busybody. When the summons arrives, I need to put wings on and go chasing round the cities [of the empire].

Aristophanes *Birds* [414] 1422-5

Athens had no real equivalent to our system of public prosecution, and bringing criminal as well as civil cases to court depended upon the injured parties or other private individuals making prosecutions. In the case of the allies, however, it seems that there may have been a state mechanism for ensuring that those allied cases which were supposed to be referred to Athens were indeed so referred.

Trial in Athens a hated memory

204 [63] [Those hostile to Athens] try to go through the worst of the deeds done during our naval empire, to say bad things about the court cases and trials that the allies had to experience here and the imposition of tribute, and to dwell on the sufferings of the people of Melos and Skione and Torone. They think that by making those accusations they can muddy the reputation the city won by the benefits which I have previously outlined.

[66] So if they mention the court cases which the allies had to fight here, there is no one who is not bright enough to find the riposte that the Spartans have executed more Greeks without trial than we made stand in court and face trial before us in the whole history of the city.

Isokrates 12 (Panathenaic Oration) 63, 66

Isokrates makes similar allegations, in less detail, in 4 (*Panegyric Oration*) 113, delivered some forty years earlier. Compare Athenian fears in 404 that they will be treated as they themselves had treated the people of Melos, Hestiaia, Skione, Torone, Aigina, 'and many other Greeks' (Xenophon *Hellenika* 2.2.3).

See also **78**. 70ff (Khalkis).

Cases involving Athenians
See **235**.10-13, **237**.15-17, and perhaps **199**.1046

For the imposition of judicial procedure on Erythrai see **216A**.30-37, **216B** 26-33, on Miletos see **218**.76ff., on Hestiaia see **76**, on Khalkis see **78**.5-10, 71-76, on other Euboean cities see **76**.

On judicial agreements with particular cities (*symbolai*) see below **234**.

Religious obligations

For obligations at the Panathenaia see **190**.41-4 and cf.**216A**.3

For attendance at the Dionysia see **193**.

First-fruits for Demeter and Persephone at Eleusis
205 Timoteles of Akharnai was Secretary. The Council and the People decided, in the prytany of Kekropis when Timoteles was Secretary and Kykneas was President: the commissioners proposed the following:

That the Athenians should give first-fruits of the harvest to the two goddesses according to the ancestral practice and the [5] oracle from Delphi at the rate of not less than a hekteus per hundred medimnoi of barley [=1/600] and not less than half a hekteus per hundred medimnoi of wheat [=1/1200].

[12] [The sacred officials] are to deposit [in the newly built granary] the grain that they receive from the demarkhs [locally elected magistrates who were in charge of each of the demes of Attica], and the allies are to contribute first-fruits in the same way. The cities are to [15] choose collectors of grain in whatever way it seems best to them that the grain be collected. When it has been collected they are to send it to Athens.

[30] The Council is to have it announced to all the other Greek cities, whichever ones it seems possible to get an announcement to, explaining the conditions on which the Athenians and the allies give first-fruits, and not ordering them but instructing them, if they wish, to give first-fruits according to ancestral practice and the oracle from Delphi.

[43] To write on the dedications [made from the proceeds of the sale of the grain] that these dedications were made from the first-fruits of the grain, and the names of the Greeks who gave first-fruits. To those who do this may [45] much good come and good and plentiful harvests, as long as they do wrong neither to the Athenians nor to the city of the Athenians, nor to the two goddesses.

ML 73. 1-6, 12-16, 30-34, 43-6 (*SEG* 42.17)

This is a rather puzzling decree, partly because the occasion for moving the decree is unclear, and the precise date of its passing is uncertain: Lampon, who moved an amendment, is mentioned in religious contexts from 443 to 414; the frequent omission of the aspirate points to the 420s or later but is not decisive. Money appears in Eleusinian accounts for 422-1 to 419-8 'from the first-fruits granary', suggesting that the provisions of this decree were in place by then, but some scholars prefer a date later in the 410s. If the practice of offering first-fruits to Eleusis was really ancestral, why were these regulations needed? The passage following line 30 may imply that the Delphic oracle had said 'No' to an Athenian request to order other Greeks to give first-fruits, in which case it may be that we have here the rather emasculated remnants of an Athenian attempt to have all Greek states honour the Eleusinian goddesses. But it is clear that Athenian allies are expected to follow Athenian practice.

206 In memory of the ancient benefaction [the invention of agriculture] most cities send us first-fruits of grain annually, and the Delphic oracle has often commanded the rest to pay us part of their harvest and behave in the ancestral way towards our city.

Isokrates 4 (*Panegyrikos*) 31

That Athens obliged allies to come and take part in cults in Athens is clear, but did she also export cults to the allies? Boundary markers have been found in subject states that record, partly in the Attic alphabet and partly in local alphabets, sacred land (*temene*) of 'Athena' (on Aigina, Khalkis and Kos), 'Athena who rules at Athens' (Samos, Khalkis, Kos), 'Apollo and Poseidon' (Aigina), 'the Eponymous Heroes at Athens' (Samos) and 'Ion at Athens' (Samos) (*IG* i^3 1481-99, 1502, *SEG* 42.84 and 43.5). Does this mark the introduction of cults (whether by Athens or by allies fawning on Athens)? or just the confiscation of land and its dedication to an Athenian deity (as in **133** Thuc.3.50.2, in **77** and in *IG* i^{3}386.147, 394B.7,10, 418)? The former view, championed by J. Barron in *JHS* 84 (1964) 35-48 and *JHS* 103 (1983) 1-12, has been prevalent, but the latter, argued for by B. Smarczyk *Untersuchungen zur Religionspolitik und politischen Propaganda Athens im Delisch-Attischen Seebund* (Munich, 1990) 58-153 and R. Parker *Athenian Religion: a history* (Oxford, 1996) 144-5 is probably to be preferred.

2.3 ATHENIAN INTERFERENCE WITH INDIVIDUAL ALLIES

Religious interference

Athens and Delian Apollo

See above **137**, **152**, **154-5** and p.100.

207 Gods. The Council and the People decided, [in the prytany of] Antiokhis, [when —] was Secretary and Stratos was President, on the proposal of Lysikles: [to sacrifice to Delian Apollo, and] when the ships' captains [who moor at Phaleron] contribute a drachma each per voyage, in order to [keep the money from the drachmas] safe for the god, the [Sellers (*poletai*)] are to hand over [the tax of the drachma in the fifth] prytany, whenever they [pay the tax of the] firstfruits. [And to give for the building], publicly up to 500 [drachmas, privately as they can. And make the temple] as fine as possible, and [let] the present architect [be summoned before the Council and People, and let him prepare —
[Lacuna]
[to sacrifice to Apollo] in the civic centre [at Phaleron] on the seventh [of the month — if anyone behaves] irregularly with regard to the portion, [he is to be fined a mina]. The Delians [are to contribute to the building] of the temple [if they wish to. It shall not be permitted to use this money for] any other temple than the [temple of Delian Apollo.] The Secretary of the Council [is to write up this decree on a stone stele and set it up in the temple. The [Sellers (*poletai*)] are to put it out to tender.

Inscriptiones Graecae i^3 130

A date in the 430s or 420s seems suggested by the letter forms.

Athenian participation in the revived Delian festival

208 These leaders of the sacred embassy chosen for the first quadrennial festival made the dedication to Apollo: — of Plotheia, -es from Oion, -khos of Kydathenaion, — of Melite, -eon of Eleusis, —

Inscriptiones Graecae i³ 1468

This inscription is written on a base found on Delos and records the Athenian sacred embassy to the first celebration of the refounded Delia. See above **137**.

209 [3.4] Nikias' outstanding competitive displays at Delos, which were worthy of the god, are a matter of record. It had been the case that at whatever moment the choruses which the cities sent to sing to the god used to arrive, the crowd met them at the ship and ordered them to sing, with no prior ceremony but as they disembarked hurriedly and in confusion and while they were putting on garlands and their festal clothes. [3.5] But when Nikias led the sacred embassy, he disembarked on Rheneia with the chorus and the sacrificial animals and the rest of the equipment, and then bridged the strait between Rheneia and Delos, which is not large, overnight with a bridge which had been made to size in Athens and was fittingly decorated with gilding and coloured fabrics and garlands and curtains. At daybreak he led the procession for the god and the chorus, adorned at great expense and singing, across the bridge. [3.6] After the sacrifice and the contest and the feasts, he set up the famous bronze palm-tree as a dedication to the god, and buying a piece of land for 10,000 drachmas, he dedicated it to the god and stipulated that its revenues should provide a banquet for the Delians when they sacrificed, on which occasion they should ask the gods for many blessings on Nikias. He had this written up on a stele which he left on Delos, as it were to guard his gift. The palm-tree was broken down by the winds and fell against the colossal statue [of Apollo] set up by the Naxians and knocked it down.

Plutarch *Nikias* 3.4-6

This anecdote must relate to one of the first three celebrations of the Delia, but we do not know which. Reference to previous disorganisation would seem to rule out 426/5, and the third celebration in 418/7 is perhaps the most likely.

Athenians control Delian Amphiktiony

210 Gods. This is what the following Athenian Amphiktions did: Theodotos son of Neoikos, Apsephion son of Apsithyllos, Demokritos son of Phanias, Olympiodoros son of Telesias. In the archonship of Glaukippos at Athens [410/09] and in the archonship of Apemantos on Delos, we received money from the Amphiktions Theangelos of Phegaia and his fellow magistrates and from the Delian temple officials Phillis and his fellow magistrates in the sanctuary and the Artemision, to the total of 20 talents 2866 drachmas... [Further fragmentary details of rentals and other financial transactions follow]

Inscriptiones Graecae i³ 1460

The scale of the moneys handled by the Amphiktions here is in accordance with what is known of other sanctuary finances, and once more helps to put into perspective the sums demanded by Athens in tribute.

Political interference
General
The connection between foreign policy and internal politics

211 Such was the savage progress of the revolution. It seemed worse because it was the first. Later practically the whole of Greece was in convulsion: everywhere there was opposition between the democratic leaders who sought to bring in Athens and the oligarchs who sought to bring in the Spartans. In peace men had no excuse to summon them in and were not prepared to do so, but in a state of war when alliances were on offer which enabled the opposition to be harmed and yourself to make gains, occasions were readily at hand for those who wanted revolution.

Thucydides 3.82.1

Thucydides makes this comment at the beginning of his account of civil strife on Corcyra in 427. For opposition to Athens beginning from a small section within a city cf. **128**, **145**, **165** (Thuc.8.9.3), **213** and p.38.

The logic of Athenian interference

212 [1.14] As to allies and their [the Athenians'] sailing out and bringing vexatious litigation against the upper classes whom they hate — the point is that they know that the ruler is bound to be hated by the ruled, and if the rich and respectable prevail in the cities [of the Empire], then the power of the Athenian people will be short-lived, so they remove the rights of the upper classes and confiscate their property, exile them and execute them, and they promote the poor. Respectable men at Athens protect respectable men in allied cities, aware that it is a good thing for them always to protect the best men in the cities.

[1.15] Someone might suggest that Athenian strength is based on the allies being able to pay money. But those favouring the interests of the people think that there is more benefit in every individual Athenian having the allies' property [through confiscation], and the allies having enough to live and work on but not enough to enable them to plot.

[Xenophon] Constitution of the Athenians 1.14-15

Athenian experiments with supporting oligarchy

213 [3.10] The Athenians seem to me not to have thought this out correctly either: in cities where there is civil strife they side with the worse element. They do this deliberately, since if they chose the better element, they would side with those who were not in sympathy with them. There is not a single city in which the better element favours the people; it is the worst element in each city that favours the people, since like favours like. So the Athenians do choose what suits them. [3.11] On all the occasions when they tried to side with the best, things turned out badly; in only a short time the people in Boiotia were enslaved. And when they sided with the best of the Milesians, in a short time they revolted and massacred the people. So too when they favoured the Spartans instead of the Messenians, in a short time the Spartans had made the Messenians subject and were fighting the Athenians in war.

[Xenophon] Constitution of the Athenians 3.10-11

214 The Athenians everywhere destroyed oligarchies, the Spartans democracies.

Aristotle Politics 1307b22

As well as the oligarchies mentioned in **213**, all of which date to before the mid-440s, the Tribute Quota Lists include payments from a number of non-democratic dynasts in Karia – Sambaktys, Tymnes of Termera, Pigres of Syangela - men who may also have paid to Persia at the same time to keep their options open.

Athenian use of 'friends' in the cities

215 Again, to give another example, the Athenians took over many Greek cities that
they did not themselves found and which had been hard hit by the Persians but
were still inhabited, and they nevertheless kept control of them for seventy years
because they had friends in each of the cities.

Plato Seventh Letter (c.352) 332b-c

Specific cases:
Erythrai

216A [The Council and People decided —] when [—] was President [— that the people
of Erythrai] should bring corn to the Great Panathenaia worth [not less than] three
minas and distribute it to those Erythraians present. [—] [5] the sacred officials
[—] if [they] bring [—] worth less than three minas according to what has been
laid down, [—] buy corn [—] the people [—] anyone who wants to of the
Erythraians.

There is to be a council of 120 men selected by lot [—] [10] on the council
and [not of foreign birth] to serve on the council aged not less than thirty. [Those
rejected] to be prosecuted. No one to serve twice within four years. The
[Inspectors] and Garrison Commander are to draw lots and set up the current
council; in the future the council and the Garrison Commander [15] to do this not
less than 30 days before the term of office expires. Councillors are to take an oath
by Zeus and Apollo and Demeter, calling down destruction on themselves if they
break their oath.[-] and destruction on their children [-] over sacred victims [—
] And the Council shall burn not less than [-] or else be fined 1,000 drachmas [20]
[—] The People is to burn not less [-] .

The council is to swear as follows: I will give the best and most just counsel
I can for the People of Erythrai and of Athens and of the allies, and I will not
revolt from the People of Athens nor from the allies of the Athenians, neither I
myself nor will I be persuaded by another to do so [25] [—] neither I myself nor
will I be persuaded by another to do so. [—] I will not receive any of the exiles,
nor [—] I will be persuaded by [another] of those who flee to the Persians without
the agreement of the Council of the Athenians and the People, and I will not drive
out any of those who have stayed without the agreement of the Council of the
Athenians and the People. If any Erythraian murders [30] another Erythraian, let
him die if condemned [—] if condemned let him be exiled from the whole
Athenian alliance and let his money be confiscated and belong to the Erythraians.
If anyone [—] the tyrants [—] the Erythraians and [—] let him die [—] his children [35] [—] his children [—] the Erythraians and [—] the Athenians [—] after
depositing the money [—] children [—] be [-]ed in this way [—] the Athenian
People [——] [40] [——] of the allies [—] ten archers from the garrison [——]
[45] Council [—] from each tribe [—] Garrison Commander [—] Athenian [—]
the members of the garrison [—]

Inscriptiones Graecae i³ 14 (Engelmann and Merkelbach Die Inschriften von
Erythrai und Klazomenai I (1972) 4; SEG 36.5; cf. ML 40)

216B The first 35 lines, preserved on three separate fragments, are very fragmentary. Lines 10 and 12
involve money; line 19 mentions Inspectors (*episkopoi*), line 21 a Garrison Commander, line 23 an
archer and line 24 a garrison. In lines 26-7 the Garrison Commander appears to acquire judicial
responsibilities and the lines that follow deal with judicial procedure. From line 36 a fourth fragment
can be more completely restored:

[they are to swear an oath] in front of [the council at Erythrai and the Garrison Commander, calling down] destruction [on themselves and their children if they swear falsely. The people are to swear] the following: I will not revolt [from the Athenian people nor from the allies] of the Athenians, neither myself [nor will I persuade another, and I] will obey the Athenians' [decision. This oath and the oath of the council are to be written up] on a stone stele [on the Akropolis], and on the akropolis at Erythrai [the Garrison Commander is to write up] the same.

Inscriptiones Graecae i³ 15 (Engelmann and Merkelbach *Die Inschriften von Erythrai und Klazomenai* I (1972) 5)

216A and 216B were once considered to belong to the same stele, and it is not impossible that this is the case. Certainly both appear to be of much the same date and to involve at least closely parallel situations.

Erythrai first appears in the Tribute Quota Lists in 449 when she pays not only for herself but for other cities of her peninsula. In 453 and 452 one of those cities, Boutheia, appears paying 2 talents, whereas, when she is later listed alone, she pays only 1,000 drachmas. It seems likely that Erythrai was in revolt in 453 and that Boutheia had taken on paying for the rest of the peninsular cities. This inscription, found at Athens and known only from an eighteenth-century copy, may record the settlement imposed after that revolt. The problem of the disaffected in Erythrai seeking help from Persia (216A line 27) is one for which there is also fourth-century evidence.

217 [Column A] ... neither allotment [—] nor honours. If he breaks this rule, let him owe ten staters, and anyone who wishes to can prosecute, with half the fine going to the man who secures a conviction and half to the city. But if the prosecutor gives up his suit let him owe what he would have got had he won, and let prosecution on this matter be according to the same rules. Judgement to be given by nine men from each of the [three] tribes whose property is worth not less than 30 staters, having sworn the same oath to the council to judge according to the laws and decrees. Not less than 61 men are to fill the court. They are to give judgement having made and deposited a pledge according to the law. The prytaneis are to bring in the cases and record them and write up the names of those owing fines, or else themselves to owe a fine [—].

[Column B] ... [— the decree] on a stone stele and stand it at the circle of Zeus Horaios during the second prytany. There shall be prosecution against whoever himself is living contrary to the law, having been born of a freedman or a foreigner. Against anyone whose father or older ancestor held public office or received a position by lot [—].

[Column C] But if he is from a bastard, let him be inspected and let there be enslavement. If any of the true [citizens] does not come when the prytaneis make the announcement, let him owe half a stater. Let it belong to the prytaneis, unless some necessity prevented him coming.

B116 (Engelmann and Merkelbach
Die Inschriften von Erythrai und Klazomenai I (1972) 2)

Found at Erythrai and also relating to constitutional arrangements at Erythrai in the middle of the fifth century, this inscription may represent the situation either before or after Athenian interference; if before, it shows how detailed the constitutional arrangements of a small city might be and how widely diffused such practices as rewarding prosecutors were; if after, then it indicates the degree of variation from home Athenian practices that Athens was prepared to tolerate.

Miletos

218 [Regulations] for the Milesians. The Council and [People decided], in the prytany [of Kekropis, — was Secretary and Onet[or] President, [in the archonship of Euthynos (450/49)]: the commissioners [drew up these regulations]:

The customary [rites are to be performed for the gods].

[The People] are straightaway [to choose] 5 men [from [5] their whole number, over thirty years] of age, [with no possibility of refusal of office] or substitutes. These are to hold office and [—].

[Of the fragmentary lines that follow, 10-22 include provisions about troops and the rest seem to concern judicial arrangements, including the administration of an oath (11.73-4), and]:

[76] [If any] Milesian or member of the garrison [disobeys the magistrates] they are to be able [to fine him up to —. If anyone] deserves a greater fine [he is to be summoned to] Athens [and brought to court there and] whatever he seems to deserve is to be imposed.

[A few further fragmentary lines follow]

B30 (SEG 37.4)

The date of this decree derives from the preservation of the archon's name in line 63, but since there was another archon of the same name in 426, the placing of this decree in 450 is not certain. It is not entirely clear in what circumstances the decree was passed. Recent discoveries have shown that the Milesians paid tribute regularly from 453-451 although they are absent from the list for 450 (cf. above p.95) and seem to have paid late in 449. In 453 and perhaps 452 there are also payments from a Milesian 'splinter group', called in 453 'Milesians from Leros and Teichiussa'. The existence of such a group implies political tension in Miletos and a group in exile keen to demonstrate their determinedly pro-Athenian stance. Miletos then appears to be absent from the list for 446, and from 442 onwards pays half the sum recorded as her tribute in 449. The presence of a garrison in this inscription implies that there has been trouble, and the absence of Miletos from the 450 list may support that. Whether this inscription implies a democratic or oligarchic system at Miletos is not clear, and it is possible that what [Xenophon] says about Miletos (**213**) can be fitted into the epigraphic data to tell a story of oligarchy being supported, despite revolt, in 450/49 only to have to be replaced following a further revolt in the middle of the 440s.

Kolophon

219 [Lines 1-36 are too fragmentary to yield any continuous sense]

[37] The Secretary of the Council [is to write up this decree and the oath on a stone stele on the Akropolis at the expense] of the Kolophonians. [And at Kolophon the] settlers [sent to Kolophon] [40] are to write [these and the oath] up [on a stone stele —].

I will speak and counsel [as well and excellently as I can] about the [Athenian] People [—] [45] and I will not revolt [from the Athenian People either] by word or deed, [neither I myself nor will I be persuaded to do so by anyone else], and I will love the [Athenian People and I will not] desert and [I will not subvert] democracy [at Kolophon — neither] myself nor will I [be persuaded] to do so [by anyone else - [50] —]

[—] by Zeus and Apollo [and Demeter, and if] I transgress [these conditions may I be destroyed, myself and] my family [to all time; but if I keep my oath, may] [55] many good things [come] to me.

ML 47 (SEG 42.9)

The date of this inscription is uncertain, but it seems closely related to the inscriptions concerning Erythrai, Miletos, and Khalkis (**216, 218, 78**) whose dates are more or less secure. Kolophon is a regular tribute-payer in 454-450 but absent from the lists for the next four years. When she reappears in 445, she pays only half the tribute she had previously paid ($1\frac{1}{2}$ T not 3T). For later events at Kolophon see **119-20**.

Karpathos

220 The Council and the People decided, in the prytany of [—], Tei[sias] was
Secretary and Athenodo[ros was President], on the proposal of Ktesias: [5] to
record [—] the [Eteo]karpathian and [his sons] and the [state] of the
Eteokar[pathians] as benefactors [of the Athenians] because they gave [the
cypress wood] for the [temple [10] of Athena] who rules [at Athens; and] to allow
the [state] of the Eteokar[pathians] to be independent [—]

[Lines 13-17 cannot be satisfactorily restored]

The [soldiers who] now occupy it are to depart from [20] the akropolis. If anyone
[— wrongs] either the Eteokarpathian [state or] takes away or [razes] the stele
[— he is to owe] fifty talents [25] [to the state] and a tenth of it [is to belong to
the goddess]. The case is to be tried [before the Thesmo]thetai in A[thens.] [30]
The Ko[ans and the Kni]dians and the Rhodians [and] all [the allies] who [are
capable] around these [regions are to provide] all the [good] they can [to the]
Eteoka[rpathians if they] ask for anything. This [to be written] on a [stone] stele
[35] on the Akropolis, and at Kar[pathos in the] sanctuary of Apoll[o, from which]
the cypress was cut. [Hagesa]rkhos the Lindian, as he requested, is to [deliver]
the cypress to the Athenians.

Inscriptiones Graecae i³ 1454/Tod 110

On the basis of letter forms this seems to date from *c.*445-430. The circumstances in which Karpathos had
acquired a garrison and lost its autonomy are unknown. On the possible use of the timber mentioned here
as a ridge-pole in the Parthenon, see R. Meiggs *Trees and Timber in the Ancient Mediterranean World*
(Oxford, 1982) 200-201.

For 'Athena who rules at Athens' see p.110.

Other Athenian reactions to revolts:

Cases for which there is literary information: Naxos see p.21, Thasos see p.21, Euboia see **64, 70-81**, Samos
see pp.39-40 and **84-91**, Mytilene see **124-34**, cities of Khalkidike and Thraceward region see **145-52**, cities
of Ionia following defeat of Sicilian Expedition see **164-78**.

Athenian imposition of oaths after revolts:

for Erythrai **216**, for Miletos see **218**, for Kolophon see **219**, for Khalkis see **78**, for Eretria see p.45, for
Samos see **91**.

Athenian officials sent to allies
General

For Athenian decrees sending officials to allies see **198** sections 1,3,4 and 8; **190**.6-7. Compare **122**.6, **237**.5.

Serving abroad as part of Athenian education

221 What is more, because of their property overseas and because of the offices they
hold overseas, both the Athenians and their slaves have learnt how to row without
realising it. A person who is frequently sailing often has to take an oar, himself
and his slave, and to learn nautical jargon...

[Xenophon] *Constitution of the Athenians* 1.19

The number of Athenians involved in running the empire

222 From the tribute and the taxes and the allies, more than 20,000 men came to be
supplied with maintenance payments. To explain, there were 6,000 dikasts, 1,600
archers, and in addition to these 1,200 cavalry; the Council consisted of 500 men,
the shipyard garrison 500, and in addition 50 garrison troops on the Akropolis;
there were about 700 magistrates at home and up to the same number abroad. On

top of these, when they later went to war, there were 2,500 hoplites, 20 guard ships, and 2,000 men chosen by lot on the other ships bringing the tribute. There were also the Prytaneion, the orphans, and the prison guards. All of these were maintained at public expense.

[Aristotle] *Constitution of the Athenians* 24.3

Thucydides makes the desire for an everlasting source of public pay one of the motives for the Sicilian Expedition (6.24.3). The general idea here may derive from the next passage, but the precise figures given in the first two sentences are all accurate when they can be checked and only over the crucial number of 700 magistrates abroad is there serious doubt (a scribe's careless repetition of the previous figure is to be suspected). The third sentence, by contrast, is almost entirely puzzling, and scholars have proposed a variety of emendations to the text, none of which has commanded universal support: see Rhodes *Commentary* pp.305-8.

Just how directly radical democracy at Athens depended upon empire has been debated. Pay for dikasts was certainly introduced during the empire and it is probable that pay for the Council (first attested when abolished in 411) and for other magistrates was not introduced until after the Persian Wars. On the other hand Athens both continued to pay these officials in the fourth century and actually introduced pay for attendance at the Assembly in the 390s when she no longer enjoyed income from her allies. Whether public pay actually depended upon income from empire may be less important than that Old Comedy suggests that fifth-century Athenians themselves associated pay for political activity with imperial income.

The number of men the empire supported

223 BDELYKLEON. There are a thousand cities which bring us tribute. If you ordered that each of them maintain twenty men, then there would be twenty thousand ordinary people living off every delicacy...

Aristophanes *Wasps* [422] 707-9

For the number of cities assessed by the Athenians even at their most optimistic, see p.89.

Specific officials

Arkhontes

In Miletos **218**, in Samos **64** (Thuc.1.115.5), in Mytilene **201**, in Neapolis **179**, in Skiathos **238**.

Episkopoi (Inspectors)

See **216A**.13-14; **216B** 19; **190**.7

An Inspector visits Cloudcuckooland

224 INSPECTOR. Where are our *proxenoi*?

PEISETAIROS. Who's this Sardanapallos here?

INSPECTOR. I have been chosen by lot and come here as Inspector to Cloudcuckooland.

PEISETAIROS. Inspector? Who sent you here?

INSPECTOR. A measly document drawn up by Teleas.

PEISETAIROS. What? Then how about your taking your pay for not making trouble and clearing off?

INSPECTOR. Yes, please! I need to stay at home and go to the Assembly. I have some business I'm transacting with Pharnakes.

PEISETAIROS. Take it and go. Here's your pay [Beating him.]

INSPECTOR. What was that?

PEISETAIROS. An Assembly meeting about Pharnakes.

INSPECTOR. Witness everybody! I'm being beaten, I, an Inspector.

PEISETAIROS. Shoo! Take your voting urns. Isn't it dreadful - they are already sending Inspectors to the city before we have even sacrificed to the gods!

Aristophanes *Birds* (414) 1021-34

For the immediately following lines of *Birds* see **199**. Aristophanes seems here to combine ridicule of the luxurious garb and pretensions of ambassadors to Persia with satire on the Athenian propensity to send Inspectors to run the constitutions of allied cities. (For sacrifices when a new city is set up, see **232**).

The overtones of the name

225 Inspector (*episkopos*): Used by Antiphon in his speeches *On the tribute of the Lindians* [frg.30], and *Against Laispodias* [frg.23]. Some men were frequently sent out to the subject cities who inspected their affairs. Theophrastos in the first book of his *Politics* [frg.129] says this: 'As far as the giving of names is concerned, it is much better to claim, as the Spartans do, that one is sending 'Managers' (harmosts) to the cities, not Inspectors or Guards, like the Athenians.'

Harpokration *Lexicon* s.v. *Episkopos*

Harmosts, who were essentially garrison commanders, became one of the most hated features of Spartan rule over the former Athenian allies in the years immediately after the war.

Military interference
Garrisons and Garrison-Commanders

226 And then, when the mass of the people were sovereign over affairs, we garrisoned the akropoleis of the other cities...

Isokrates 7 (*Areopagitikos*) 65

Compare **66** (12.5).

227 CHORUS [of old men]. The remnants are here, alack and alas, of that youth of ours when you and I were together on garrison duty at Byzantion.

Aristophanes *Wasps* (422) 235-7

228 SPEAKER A. And the final city, where is that?

SPEAKER B. Here it is, Kyzikos, full of staters.

SPEAKER A. I was once on garrison duty in that city...

Eupolis *Cities* [?422] frg.233

The electrum staters of Kyzikos were coins widely used (cf. **198** note).

For garrisons at Erythrai see **216A**.14-15, **216B** 21-26, 38-45, at Miletos see **218**.77, on Euboia see **78**.77-9, at Karpathos see **220**.19, at Samos see **64** (Thuc.1.115.5) and **172**.

Athenian settlements in allied territory

Cleruchies and colonies: Our sources use two terms for Athenian settlements abroad: *kleroukhia* and a word traditionally translated 'colony' (*apoikia*). In one inscription (*IG* i³ 237) 'cleruchy' and 'colony' both occur together, suggesting that Athenians did think of them as distinct institutions. One possible distinction is that those who took land in cleruchies retained Athenian citizenship, those who went out to colonies did not, but colonists too do seem to keep the duties, at least, of citizens. It does appear that colonies were new settlements, on virgin territory or completely replacing a previous settlement, whereas *kleroukhoi* seem, often at least, to have lived side by side with the old inhabitants but occupying their land.

For possible evidence to support the view that cleruchies were a self-financing form of Athenian garrison see note to **133**.

In the Charter of the Second Athenian Confederacy (**246**) the Athenians renounce all public (and private) landholding in allied territory.

229 SOCRATES' PUPIL. Geometry

STREPSIADES. What use is that?

SOCRATES' PUPIL. Measuring out land.

STREPSIADES. Land for settlements (*kleroukhiai*)?

Aristophanes *Clouds* (423) 202-3

For settlements abroad in general see **245**.

Extent of Athenian occupation of allied land

230 We had the Khersonesos and Naxos and more than two-thirds of Euboia. As to the other settlements abroad (*apoikiai*), it would take a long time to go through them one by one.

Andokides 3 (*On the Peace* [392/1]) 9

The number of Athenians settled abroad by Perikles

231 [5] In addition Perikles sent 1,000 *kleroukhoi* to the Khersonesos, 500 to Naxos, half that number to Andros, 1,000 to Thrace to live among the Bisaltai, others to Italy, when Sybaris was refounded and given the name Thourioi. [6] He did this to relieve Athens of a mob that was idle and meddlesome because it had nothing to do, and to solve the people's difficulties, and by planting settlers alongside the allies to make them fearful and provide a guard against any revolution.

Plutarch *Perikles* 11.5-6

Compare **68-70**. Settlements of different dates are combined here, and Perikles may not have been responsible for all.

The settlement at Brea

232 [Roughly 35 lines are missing before the inscription begins]

...to which a denunciation or prosecution is made, let it be introduced. But if the denunciator or prosecutor introduces [the case —]

The [founders of the settlement abroad] are to provide [5] [means for sacrificing] to obtain good omens on behalf of the settlement.

They are to choose [ten men], one from each tribe, to divide up the land, and they are to divide up the land.

Demokleides is to be given power to establish the [settlement] in the [best] way he can.

The [10] lands of the gods are to be exempted, as they are now, and no other land is to be consecrated.

They are to bring a cow and a [full set of armour] to the Great Panathenaia and a phallos [to the Dionysia].

If anyone launches an expedition against [the territory] of the settlement, the [cities] are to help [15] as quickly as possible in accordance with the agreements made when [—] was Secretary [concerning the cities] in the Thraceward region.

[This] is to be written [on a stele] and placed on the Akropolis. The settlers [are to provide] the stele at their [own expense].

[20] If anyone puts anything to the vote contrary to the [stele or] any orator

makes a proposal or [tries] to use the courts to modify in some way or rescind what has been decreed, he is to [lose his civic rights] and so are [his] children, and their property is to be confiscated and a [tenth] part given to the [goddess], [25] unless the settlers themselves [—] make this request.

All soldiers enlisted [to go as settlers, are to go as settlers] to Brea within thirty days of their return to Athens. The settlement is to be put into operation within thirty [days]. [30] Aiskhines is to accompany it and give the money.

Phantokles proposed: as to the settlement at Brea, Demokleides' proposal should stand, [35] but the Erekhtheid prytany is to summon Phantokles before the Council at its first sitting. [40] And the settlers to be drawn from the Thetes and Zeugitai.

ML 49 (*SEG* 37.9)

233 Brea: Kratinos [frg.426] mentions the settlement at Brea. It is a city in Thrace to which the Athenians sent a colony.

Hesykhios *Lexicon* s.v.Brea

The Brea settlers may be the 1,000 referred to by Plutarch **231** as sent to live among the Bisaltai, and it has been thought that it may have been the foundation of Brea that caused the tribute of Argilos to be reduced from 10.5 talents (some would amend to 1.5 talents) to 1 talent between 453 and 445. Never heard of again, Brea may have been abandoned when Amphipolis was founded.

For Athenian settlement in Khersonesos see **68-9**, **230-31** (cf.**67**); in Euboia see **68**, **70**, **80**, **230**, **240**; at Khalkis **75**; at Hestiaia/Oreos **64** (Thuc.1.114.3), **159** (Thuc. 7.57.2), **73-5**; at Kolophon (?) **219**.40-41; on Naxos **68**, **70**, **230**, **231**; on Aigina **159** (Thuc. 7.57.2); at Mytilene **133-4**.

Judicial agreements with individual cities

Agreements (*symbolai*) with individual allies
234 The Council and the People decided, in the prytany of Akamantis [.]nasippos was Secretary, [-]des was President, on the proposal of Leon: [5] to inscribe the decree for the people of Phaselis.

Whatever cause of action arises at Athens [for] anyone from Phaselis, the case is to be heard at Athens before [10] [the] Polemarch, just as for Kh[ians, and] in no other court. Cases [in other categories] shall follow the judicial agreements (*symbolai*) according to the judicial agreements with the people of Phaselis. The [15] [—] are to be abolished.

If [any other] magistrate accepts [a case against] any person from Phaselis [—], if he condemns him, [the condemnation] is to be invalid. [20] If anyone transgresses the terms of the decree, he is to be fined 10,000 drachmas sacred to Athena.

[The] Secretary of the Council [25] is to write up this [decree on a stone stele] and place it [on the Akropolis] at the expense of the people of Phaselis.

ML31

The precise date of this agreement is not known, and dates from the 460s to the 420s have been proposed.

For judicial agreements (*symbolai*) with Mytilene see **134**.15, with Selymbria see **182**.25, with Samos see **183**.17-8.

2.4 THE BENEFITS OF EMPIRE FOR INDIVIDUALS

For individual allies
The privileged status of being an Athenian *proxenos*

Athenian protection of *proxenoi*.

235 [He is to be *proxenos* and] benefactor [of the Athenians. And if] Akheloïon [is wronged by anyone, the case] against this man [is to be heard at Athens before the] [5] Polemarch, [and the prosecutor is to pay no court fees] except five drachmas. And if anyone kills [Akheloïon or] any of his children [in any of the cities] that the Athenians [rule, the city is to be fined] [10] five talents, [as in the case of] anyone killing [an Athenian. The prosecution is to be held at Athens] in the [same way as when an Athenian] is killed.

Inscriptiones Graecae i³ 19

Dated on letter forms to *c*.450, this inscription, like the next two, seems to attest early use of the curt formula 'cities which the Athenians rule' at a time when the Athenians seem to have been more diplomatic in decrees which were directly addressed to the cities of the empire.

236 The [Council and the] People decided, [in the prytany of] Leontis, when ...ostratos [was President and Aristok]rates was Secretary, on the proposal of [5] [—]khos: that the [Secretary of the] Council should record on the Akropolis [on a stele and in] [10] the Council Chamber A[—] and [his] brothers [who are Del]phians and [their father as *proxenoi*] of the Athenians, [because they do whatever] good [they can] in word and deed, and if anyone [kills] any of them in [any city that the] [15] Athenians [rule], he is [to be punished according to the decree relating to *proxenoi*].

Inscriptiones Graecae i³ 27 (*SEG* 37.5)

On letter forms a date of *c*.450 is suggested. If those honoured are correctly restored as from Delphi, this decree would show that from an early date the Athenians felt that even their friends outside the empire might be victimised by hostile groups in the cities of the empire.

237 ...allow to do wrong, neither [at Athens nor] in any city that the Athenians rule. At Athens, the prytaneis and Council are to look after this; [5] in the other cities, whichever Athenians hold office abroad are to do all they can to see that they are not wronged.

The Council [10] and People decided, in the prytany of Antiokhis, when Kharoiades was Secretary and Hegesandros was President, on the proposal of Khairestratos, that if anyone kills Leonidas in the cities [15] which Athenians rule, the punishment should be as if someone kills an Athenian. And to praise all the good things that Leonidas does for the Athenians. [20] The Secretary of the Council is to write up the decrees about Leonidas at Leonidas' expense on two stelai, set one up on the Akropolis and [25] the other in the temple of Apollo at Halikarnassos. Let Leonidas select a man to collect the stele and set it up.

Inscriptiones Graecae i³ 156

On the basis of letter forms this inscription seems to date between 440 and 425.

Athenian support needed to be phrased in precisely the right way

238 Gods. The Council and People decided, in the prytany of Antiokhis, when Eukleides was Secretary and Hierokles [5] was President, in the archonship of Euktemon [408/7], on the proposal of Dieitrephes: since Oiniades of

Palaiskiathos is a man good to the city of the Athenians and keen to do [10] all the good he can, and does good to any Athenian who arrives at Skiathos, he should be praised and recorded as *proxenos* and benefactor of the Athenians [15] together with his offspring. Whatever Council is in office and the Generals and the officer (*arkhon*) in office on Skiathos are to protect him against harm. [20] The Secretary of the Council is to write up this decree on a stone stele and set it up on the Akropolis. He is to be summoned to [25] hospitality at the Prytaneion tomorrow.

Antikhares proposed: otherwise as proposed by the Council, but to change the resolution so that instead of 'of Skiathos' is written [30] 'Oiniades of Palai[skiathos'].

ML 90

See also **62, 125, 182**. And compare Eretrian proxeny grant, **174**.

For individual Athenians
Land-holding by Athenians among allies on the Attic Stelai

239 [217] [Property] of Oionias of the deme of Atene, proceeds of sale of unharvested crops in the plain of Le[l]a[nton].

[375-8] [Property] of Oionias son of O[ionokhares of the deme of Atene:] at Lelanton [—] and in Diros [and in — and] in Gera[istos]: 81 1/3 talents.
Inscriptiones Graecae i³ 422.217-8, 375-8

240 ...overseas properties [—-]. [Property of Nikid]es son of P[hoinikides of the deme of Meli]te, land in Diros between Roos [= Euripos?] and Kanethos and a house complete with door. In the rows of trees in the land is also [—-]
Inscriptiones Graecae i³ 424.15-23

241 [43] [Property] of [Adeiman]tos son of Le[uk]olophides of the deme of Ska[mbonidai]: a man [i.e. slave] Aristomakhos; a field at I[—] on Thasos and a house. Included are [9] storage jars in good condition, [20] broken ones, [with] lids. [—] jars of wine [with a capacity of] 590 amphoras and 3 choes [= 7,083 choes].

[144] Land at Tha[sos], at Khytrinoi: 90 dr. 3 ob.
[161] at Eretria
Inscriptiones Graecae i³ 426.43-51, 144-6, 161-2

242 [In list of Axiokhos' property] House in field [—] at Abydos: 310 dr.
Inscriptiones Graecae i³ 427.77-8

243 On the 25th of Gamelion [mid to late January] property of [A]deimantos son of Leukoloph[ides of the deme of Skambonidai:] unharvested crops were brought in from the land which is at Ophryneion: 50 dr.
Inscriptiones Graecae i³ 430 11-13

These five items all come from the Attic Stelai, the inscribed record of the confiscation of the property of those found guilty of profaning the Eleusinian Mysteries and/or mutilating the Herms in 415. They indicate both the spread of Athenian land-holding (Diros, Geraistos, and Lelanton, as well as Eretria, are in Euboia; Ophryneion is in the Troad) and the size of the properties held: Oionias' Euboian properties are sold for a sum far above the known value of any estate owned by an Athenian in Attica itself.

2.5 FOURTH-CENTURY RETROSPECTIVES ON THE ATHENIAN EMPIRE

What the Athenians wanted to hear

244 [55] With great labour, brilliant battles, and glorious perils our ancestors made Greece free and their own homeland the greatest. They ruled the sea for seventy years and kept their allies free from civil strife, [56] not letting the mass of the people become the slaves of the few, but imposing equality on all. They did not make their allies weak but established them as strong and displayed so great a power themselves that the Great King ceased to desire others' territory and rather gave up some of his own and came to fear for the rest: [57] no Persian ships sailed from Asia at that time, no tyrant was set up in Greece, and no Greek city was enslaved to the barbarian. All that is a measure of the great fear that the virtue of our ancestors inspired in all men. It is right that as a consequence they became champions of the Greeks and leaders of cities.

Lysias 2 (*Funeral Oration* [392?]).55-7

What the political pamphleteer wanted them to believe

245 [103] All men agree, I think, that those under whom they most flourished will come to seem the best champions of the Greeks. And under our leadership we shall find that private households gained most prosperity and cities became greatest. [104] We did not begrudge cities growth or introduce strife to them by insisting on constitutional change to ensure civil strife in which both parties would court us for help. No, we considered concord among our allies to be good for us and administered all the cities with the same laws, taking thought for them as an ally rather than a master, and overseeing all matters. [105] We left the allies free at an individual level, helped the mass of the people, and fought against narrow régimes. Our view was that it was a bad thing for the many to be subject to the few, or for the poor to be driven out of magistracies by the propertied, when in other respects they were no worse, or that among men with a common fatherland some should act as tyrants while others were like foreign residents, citizens by nature but deprived of citizenship by law. [106] These and more being our arguments against oligarchy, we gave to our allies and to others the same constitution as we had ourselves. There is no need for me to praise that constitution at greater length, especially since its merits can be swiftly established. Under this constitution they lived for seventy years innocent of tyranny, free from the barbarians, without civil strife, and in peace with all men.

[107] Sensible men should be thankful for all of this instead of abusing us for the land settlements (*kleroukhiai*) that we established in deserted cities so as to guard their territories. We did not send them out through greed, as the following shows: although we had the smallest territory per person, and the greatest empire, including double the number of triremes of everyone else together, [108] and those able to face double their number, although Euboia lay there just off the coast of Attica, well placed for a naval empire, in other respects too the most attractive of islands and easier for us to control than Attica itself, and although we were also well aware that among both Greeks and barbarians those get the greatest reputation who uproot their neighbours and have themselves an affluent and lazy life, nevertheless none of these considerations excited us to doing any wrong to the inhabitants of the island. [109] On the contrary, we are the only people who

have obtained massive power who turned a blind eye to the fact that we ourselves lived more impoverished lives than those who had reason to be our slaves. If we had wanted to indulge ourselves, we would never have conceived a desire for the land of the people of Skione, which we openly handed over to the Plataians, who had taken refuge with us, and neglected so great a territory as Euboia which would have made us all more prosperous.

Isokrates 4 (*Panegyric Oration* [380]) 103-9

What the Athenians had to admit to their allies

246 [15] If any Greek or barbarian who lives on the [mainland] or islander who is [not] subject to the King wants to be an ally of the Athenians and their allies, he may do so, [20] being [free] and independent and under whatever constitution he chooses.

No [garrison] will be imposed and no magistrate, nor will allies pay tribute: all new members are to enjoy the same conditions as the Khians, the Thebans [25] and the other allies.

For those who make an alliance with the Athenians and their allies the people of Athens gives up all landed property that the Athenian state or an Athenian privately holds in the [territory of those who make] [30] the alliance and it gives a pledge [to them about this].

If stelai exist at Athens that are unfavourable to any of the cities [making] the alliance with the Athenians, whatever Council is in office [35] has power to repeal them.

From the archonship of Nausinikos [378/7] on, neither an Athenian privately nor the Athenian state may obtain property in the lands of the allies, neither a house nor land, neither by purchase [40] nor as security, nor in any other way. If anyone does buy or acquire property, or obtains it as security in any way, any of the allies who wishes may make a denunciation before the Common Meeting of the allies. Those at the Common Meeting [45] are to sell the property in question and give half the proceeds to the man making the denunciation and keep the rest for the common use of the allies.

Tod 123.15-46

The promises which the Athenians give here in order to attract allies to their new confederacy give an indication of the features of the empire about which the Greeks retained strong feelings a quarter of a century after the end of the Peloponnesian War.

Note H Archaeology and the Athenian Empire

A book which collects only literary and epigraphic texts cannot pretend that it collects all the relevant evidence, and it is appropriate finally to survey the main type of evidence which this book has neglected: the evidence of archaeology.

The limitations of the archaeological evidence

Potentially, archaeology can recover evidence extending over the whole range of material life, from settlement patterns and funerary practices to sanctuary dedications, monumental architecture and 'high art'. In fact, only for Athens itself can we range over all these areas; archaeologists have paid far less attention, to Athens' allies, and where they have paid attention that attention has often been relatively narrowly focused. Only for part of one island, Keos, has a systematic and intensive archaeological survey been published, which gives some information on fifth-century settlement patterns outside the towns, and nowhere among the allies has there been any extensive cemetery excavation. Discussion of the impact of the Athenian empire upon the material culture of Athens and her allies has therefore to be restricted to monumental buildings and the sculptures that, in Athens at least, went with them.

Monumental building outside Athens

Apart from Athens itself, only one place in the Athenian empire shows extensive monumental building in the period 479-404, and that is Delos. As well as the temple of Apollo, abandoned at frieze height in the middle of the century and only completed in the late fourth century, and the small temple built by the Athenians in 423-17 (see above p.100), the following buildings were also erected: the Prytaneion (*c.*500-450) was finished (*GD* no. 22), a court wall and stoa to the Archagesion were built *c.*480-70 (*GD* no. 74), the so-called Thesmophorion (perhaps the Hestiatorion of the Keans) (480-50) (*GD* no. 48), no fewer than four treasury buildings (*GD* nos. 17-20), and Stage II of the Propylaia (*GD* no. 5). In addition, late in the century, both the North Building (Graphe) (*GD* no. 35) and the temple of Artemis Lochia (*GD* no. 108) were begun.

The absence of monumental building elsewhere has sometimes been interpreted as evidence that paying tribute to Athens impoverished the allies. In particular, the contrast in Ionia between the building of enormous temples at Ephesos, at the Heraion at Samos and at Didyma, the sanctuary linked to Miletos, in the sixth century and the almost complete absence of construction in the fifth century has been linked to the claim that cities on the Ionian seaboard continued to pay money to Persia as well as to Athens (see **164**).

Monumental buildings did demand wealth, but wealth alone was not sufficient to generate building. The absence of fifth-century monumental building is by no means limited to the Athenian Empire. There is very little building in many fifth-century Greek cities and sanctuaries, suggesting that after the busy building programmes of the sixth century most cities had come to feel adequately adorned with temples. At Delphi, for instance, apart from monuments directly generated by the victory over the Persians, the only major constructions in these years are a 'clubhouse' built by the Knidians (allies of Athens) and a Treasury built by Brasidas and the Akanthians to house spoils taken from the Athenians (compare **145-7**). Argos rebuilt the temple of Hera, but only after it was burnt down in the 420s, and there are no major constructions at Corinth. Indeed apart from the temple of Zeus at Olympia, said to have been built from the spoils of a local war, it is only small Arkadian cities like Alipheira, Asea and Phigaleia, building the temple at Bassai, that show fifth-century temples.

If we move our sights from large temples, there is in fact some evidence of constructions in the cities of the Athenian Empire. The best known of all archaeologically is
Thasos, and there, although the amount of building is indeed less in the years of the
Athenian Empire than in the period 520-480, there are signs of fifth-century activity
in most parts of the town with additions to the Artemision, a new sanctuary of Soteira
and a theatre. At Samos, where the Heraion has been well investigated and there has
been some excavation in the town, there is building in both places, including small
temples. A late fifth- or early fourth-century temple and theatre complex is also known
from Tholós on Rhodes.

There is a down-turn in building activity after 480 in the cities of the Athenian
empire, but that down-turn does not distinguish the cities of Ionia from those of the
rest of the empire or the cities of the empire from cities on the Greek mainland. Failure
to build cannot be taken to be a sign of impoverishment - we know independently that
the spoils of the Persian Wars significantly enriched the Greek cities that had fought
against Persia, and there is direct literary testimony to the wealth of some of the cities
of the Athenian empire (compare **168** and **14**).

Motivations for building

Greek cities other than Athens built little during the years 479-404. This is to be
explained in terms of the way those cities interacted with each other. There can be no
doubt that the monumental temples constructed at Samos, Ephesos and Didyma, cities
very close to one another, in the sixth century were partly a product of inter-city rivalry,
with each city competing to be the focus of attention for all Greeks in the area. Temple
construction on the neighbouring islands of Naxos and Paros in the sixth century is to
be similarly explained. The Athenian Empire did change that. Not only was the field
of competition vastly extended, but Athens established a position within that field that
could not be challenged. The treasuries built at Delos between 480 and 450 suggest
that some Delian League allies, at least, initially saw the League as itself an arena for
competition, and the sanctuary at Delos was a place where they could display their
piety and their investment in the common good. Once the League Treasury was moved
to Athens, however, the futility of such competitive displays must have been apparent.
All the various ways described in Note G in which Athens turned herself into a religious centre for the allies undermined allied pride and independence and emphasised
that Athens was the measure against which allies had to, but could not, match themselves.

Monumental building at Athens and in Attica

It is not hard to see why even the largest of allied cities felt unable to compete with
Athens. During these years Athens built on the Akropolis three marble temples (the
massive Parthenon, which was the largest temple on the Greek mainland, the ornate
Erekhtheion, and the tiny temple of Athena Nike), decorating them all with sculpture,
and a monumental marble gateway building (the Propylaia); she built a further marble
temple (the Hephaisteion) and a number of stoas, including the Painted Stoa and the
Stoa of Zeus, in and around the Agora; and she ringed Attica with yet more marble
temples and other monumental sanctuary buildings (clockwise from Rhamnous in the
north-east: the temple of Nemesis at Rhamnous, the temple of Artemis at Loutsa, an
architecturally innovative stoa at the sanctuary of Artemis at Brauron, a temple of
Demeter at Thorikos, a temple of Poseidon at Sounion, a temple of Apollo at
Vouliagmeni, a temple of Apollo Delios at Phaleron, the Telesterion (Hall of Initiation)

at Eleusis, and, at the centre of the clock, the temple of Athena at Pallene). This building programme may not have been funded directly from tribute (see **195-6**), but Athens could hardly have undertaken it had she been obliged to meet all military expenditure from her own resources without the aid of tribute and of the other substantial income that she derived from the empire.

More interesting is the issue of why the allies did not compete with each other or attempt as they had in the sixth century to establish local hierarchies. The inability of the allies, even following the Sicilian disaster, to gang up effectively together against Athens is one indication that local rivalries, and suspicions, remained strong, and the unwillingness of the city of Neapolis (**179**) to admit to having been founded by Thasos is another. Why then did these cities not continue to try to outshine each other by their building programmes - as the tiny cities of Arkadia clearly did? If we accept the literary evidence that Athenian allies were not impoverished, we must look for an answer to this question in terms of changed ambitions. Allies did not focus on local rivalries because they were too much focused on Athens: serving and pleasing Athens was the central issue; competing with other subjects of Athens was an irrelevance. Whether or not this implies that allies were happy with Athens, it certainly implies that resistance to Athens was too restricted to succeed in changing an agenda that was not just political but also cultural.

Athenian attitudes: the evidence of sculpture

If archaeology suggests in this way that Athens dominated the thoughts of her allies, does it also suggest that the allies dominated Athenian thoughts? To answer this question it is necessary to consider the sculptures with which many new temple buildings, in Attica as well as in Athens, were adorned. Those sculptures were certainly dominated by conflict: the Parthenon metopes showed battles with Amazons, Centaurs, Giants and Trojans, and the west pediment showed Athena struggling with Poseidon; all four sides of the frieze of the temple of Athena Nike showed battles; and similar conflicts are to be found on the Hephaisteion and at Sounion. But what political reference should be seen in these scenes of conflict? The likelihood that the battle of Marathon was shown on the frieze of Athena Nike, as it was in the Painted Stoa, has led scholars to see all these scenes of conflict as images of the Persian Wars. Such a reading is hard to sustain, however, particularly in the face of the scenes of the sack of Troy on the north metopes of the Parthenon: for it is the Trojans who are in the besieged city whose patron is Athena, as Athenians were besieged by Persians on the Akropolis in 480, and it is the Greek invaders who parallel the Persians. As in tragedy, so also in sculpture, we should see generalised exploration of the nature and effects of war, on both victor and vanquished, rather than jubilant commemoration of military successes.

If any of the architectural sculpture of fifth-century Athens reveals Athenian attitudes towards the allies, it is perhaps the Parthenon frieze. The young cavalrymen of the frieze are notoriously similar in their facial features. Whatever their clothing, however docile or wild the horse with which they have to cope, these young men remain virtually impassive. They offer an image of what it is to be a democratic citizen, and it is an image as of peas in a pod. The Centaurs of the south metopes are allowed an extremely wide range of facial expressions, but the young men of the Parthenon frieze, the model participants in a procession which viewers peering up at sections of the frieze between the outer columns of the temple find themselves joining, are all of a type. The empire offered Athens the chance to embrace a heterogeneous section of the Greek world; in the Parthenon frieze such heterogeneity is rejected. Athenians set themselves apart in these sculptures as, by the Periklean citizenship laws (**48-9**), they set themselves apart in real life.

Archaeology is the study of material remains, but that does not necessarily mean that it is the best source of information about material conditions. In the case of the Athenian empire, I have tried to show that it is a better guide to the thought-world of the allies and of the Athenians than it is to their prosperity.

BIBLIOGRAPHY

This bibliography is weighted towards publications since the appearance of Meiggs' *Athenian Empire* in 1972. Works that are listed in 'I General' are not generally listed subsequently under specific topics. For further bibliography see *Cambridge Ancient History* 2nd edition Vol.5 (Cambridge, 1992) 535-9. For all passages of Thucydides reference should be made to the commentaries by Gomme et al., Hornblower, and Rhodes.

I General

Works devoted to the Athenian Empire:
M.F. McGregor, *The Athenians and their Empire* (University of British Columbia Press, Vancouver, 1987).
H.B. Mattingly, *The Athenian Empire Restored: epigraphic and historical studies* (Michigan, 1996).
R. Meiggs, *The Athenian Empire* (Oxford, 1972).
P.J. Rhodes, *The Athenian Empire. Greece and Rome New Surveys in the Classics* no.17 (revised ed. Oxford, 1994).

Chapters in general works covering fifth-century Greece:
P.J. Rhodes, 'The Delian League', and D.M. Lewis 'The Thirty Years' Peace' in *Cambridge Ancient History* ed. 2 vol. 5.*The Fifth Century* (Cambridge, 1992).
J.K. Davies, *Democracy and Classical Greece* ed. 2 (Fontana, 1993) chs. 5 and 7.
S. Hornblower, *The Greek World, 479-323 B.C.* (revised edition Routledge, 1991) esp. chs. 2 and 3.

Source books:
C.W. Fornara *From Archaic Times to the Peloponnesian War. Translated Documents of Greece and Rome Vol.1* (Cambridge, 1983)
M. Crawford and D. Whitehead, *Archaic and Classical Greece* (Cambridge, 1983).

II Particular (related to the material in this book, in the order of occurrence)

Note A. When did Athenian Imperialism begin?
R. Osborne, *Greece in the Making 1200-479 B.C.* (London, 1996).
P.A. Brunt, 'Athenian Settlements Abroad in the Fifth Century B.C.' in E. Badian ed. *Ancient Society and Institutions: Studies presented to Victor Ehrenberg* (Oxford, 1966) 71-92, reprinted in P.A. Brunt *Studies in Greek History and Thought* (Oxford, 1993) 112-36.
I. Morris, *Burial and Ancient Society: The Rise of the Greek City State* (Cambridge, 1987).
P. Garnsey, *Famine and food supply in the Graeco-Roman world* (Cambridge, 1988).
P. Siewert, *Die Trittyen Attikas und die Heeresreform des Kleisthenes* (Munich, 1982).
C. Conophagos, *Le Laurium Antique* (Athens, 1980).

O. Murray, 'The Ionian Revolt' *Cambridge Ancient History* 2nd edition, Vol.4 (Cambridge, 1988) 461-90.

Note B. Handling Thucydides on the Athenian Empire

On Thucydides in general see:

A.W. Gomme (with A. Andrewes and K.J. Dover) *A Historical Commentary on Thucydides* 5 vols. (Oxford, 1945-1981). There is important general material in the introduction to vol. 1 and the appendices to vol. 5.

S. Hornblower, *A Commentary on Thucydides* (2 vols. so far, covering 1.1-5.24) (Oxford, 1991, 1996) (with important introduction to vol. 2)

P.J. Rhodes, *Thucydides History Book II* (Warminster, 1988).

P.J. Rhodes, *Thucydides History Book III* (Warminster, 1994).

P.J. Rhodes, *Thucydides History Book IV* (Warminster, 1999).

S. Hornblower, *Thucydides* (Duckworth, 1987).

W.R. Connor, *Thucydides* (Princeton, 1984).

L. Kallet-Marx, *Money, Expense and Naval Power in Thucydides' History 1-5.24* (Berkeley, 1993).

On the issues particularly discussed here see:

A. Andrewes, 'Indications of Incompleteness' in A. Andrewes, K.J. Dover and A.W. Gomme *A Historical Commentary on Thucydides* vol. 5 (1981) 361-83, discussing the Pentekontaetia at 380-1.

E. Badian, *From Plataia to Poteidaia: studies in the history and historiography of the Pentekontaetia* (Baltimore, 1993).

W.R. Connor, *Thucydides* (Princeton, 1984) 42-7.

G.L. Huxley, 'Thucydides on the Growth of Athenian Power' *Proceedings of the Royal Irish Academy* 83 (1983) 191ff.

P.J. Rhodes, 'Thucydides on Pausanias and Themistocles' *Historia* 19 (1970) 387ff.

G.E.M. de Ste Croix, *The Origins of the Peloponnesian War* (London, 1972)

P.K. Walker 'Purpose and method of the Pentekontaetia in Thucydides, Book I' *Classical Quarterly* 7 (1957) 27-39.

H.D. Westlake, 'Thucydides and the Pentecontaetia', *Classical Quarterly* 5 (1955) 53-67 reprinted as H.D. Westlake, *Essays on the Greek Historians and Greek History* (Manchester 1969) ch.2, and modified in H.D. Westlake, *Studies in Thucydides and Greek History* (Bristol, 1989) 1ff.

Note C. Using Literary Sources other than Thucydides

Comedy:

P.A. Cartledge, *Aristophanes and his Theatre of the Absurd* (London, 1990).

N. Dunbar, *Aristophanes* Birds (Oxford, 1995).

W.G.G. Forrest, 'Aristophanes and the Athenian Empire' in B.M. Levick ed. *The Ancient Historian and his Materials* (1975) 17ff.

S.D. Goldhill, *The Poet's Voice: Essays on Poetics and Greek Literature* (Cambridge, 1991) ch.3.

S. Halliwell, 'Comic satire and freedom of speech in classical Athens' *Journal of Hellenic Studies* 111 (1991) 48-70.

M. Heath, *Political Comedy in Aristophanes* (Göttingen, 1987).

D.M. MacDowell, *Aristophanes and Athens: an Introduction to the Plays* (Oxford, 1995).

G.E.M. de Ste Croix, *The Origins of the Peloponnesian War* (London, 1972) Appendix xxix (abridged version in E. Segal ed. *Oxford Readings in Aristophanes* (Oxford, 1996) 42-64.

A.H. Sommerstein, *Aristophanes* Birds (Warminster, 1987).

Orators:

K.J. Dover, *Greek Popular Morality in the Time of Plato and Aristotle* (Oxford, 1974) 8-14.

S.C. Todd, 'The use and abuse of the Attic Orators' *Greece and Rome* 37 (1990) 159-77.

Later historians:

S. Hornblower, 'The story of Greek historiography' in S. Hornblower ed. *Greek Historiography* (Oxford, 1994) 7-54 at 29-54.

The Aristotelian *Constitution of the Athenians*

P.J. Rhodes, *A commentary on the Aristotelian* Athenaion Politeia (revised edition Oxford 1993).

Plutarch

F.J. Frost, *Plutarch's* Themistokles. *A historical commentary* (Princeton, 1980).

A. Podlecki, *Plutarch:* Perikles. *A Companion to the Translation of I. Scott-Kilvert* (Bristol, 1988).

P. Stadter, *A Commentary on Plutarch's* Perikles (Chapel Hill, 1989).

Note D. Chronology

M. Chambers, R. Gallucci, P. Spanos, 'Athens' Alliance with Egesta in the year of Antiphon' *ZPE* 83 (1990) 38-63, with subsequent discussion in *ZPE* 91 (1991) 137-46 and *ZPE* 98 (1993) 171-4.

A.W. Gomme, *A Historical Commentary on Thucydides* vol. 1 (Oxford, 1945) 1-8; vol. 3 (Oxford, 1956) 699-715.

H. Mattingly, 'Epigraphy and the Athenian Empire' *Historia* 41 (1992) 129-38, reprinted in H.B. Mattingly, *The Athenian Empire Restored: epigraphic and historical studies* (Michigan, 1996).

R. Meiggs, 'The Dating of Fifth-Century Attic Inscriptions' *Journal of Hellenic Studies* 86 (1966) 86-97.

A. Samuel, *Greek and Roman Chronology: Calendars and Years in Classical Antiquity* (Munich, 1972).

The formation of the Delian League (1-17)

P.A. Brunt, 'The Hellenic League against Persia' *Historia* 2 (1953-4) 135-63 reprinted in P.A. Brunt *Studies in Greek History and Thought* (Oxford, 1992) 47-83.

A. French, 'Athenian Ambitions and the Delian alliance' *Phoenix* 33 (1979) 134-41.

N.G.L. Hammond, 'The origins and the nature of the Athenian alliance of 478/7 B.C.' *Journal of Hellenic Studies* 87 (1967) 41-61, reprinted in N.G.L. Hammond *Studies in Greek History* (Oxford, 1973) 311-45.

A.H. Jackson, 'The Original Purpose of the Delian League' *Historia* 18 (1969) 12-16.

L. Kallet-Marx, *Money, Expense and Naval Power in Thucydides' History 1-5.24* (Berkeley, 1993) 40-60.

H. Rawlings, 'Thucydides on the Purpose of the Delian League' *Phoenix* 31 (1977) 1-8.
W.K. Pritchett, *The Greek State at War* Vol.1 (Berkeley, 1971) 61-8.
N. Robertson, 'The True Nature of the Delian League, 478-461 B.C.' *American Journal of Ancient History* 5 (1980) 64-96, 110-133.
R. Sealey, 'The Origin of the Delian League' in E. Badian ed. *Ancient Society and Institutions: Studies presented to Victor Ehrenberg* (Oxford, 1966) 233-55.
H.D. Westlake, 'Thucydides on Pausanias and Themistokles - a Written Source?' *Classical Quarterly* 27 (1977) 95-110 reprinted in H.D. Westlake, *Studies in Thucydides and Greek History* (Bristol, 1989) 1ff.

Aristeides' Assessment (18-24)
See below under Note F. The Tribute Quota Lists.

The *Hellenotamiai* (25-7)
A. G. Woodhead, 'The institution of the *Hellenotamiai*' *Journal of Hellenic Studies* 79 (1959) 149-52.

Further hostility between Athens and Sparta (28)
A. Andrewes, 'The government of classical Sparta' in E. Badian ed. *Ancient Society and Institutions: Studies presented to Victor Ehrenberg* (Oxford, 1966).
D.M. Lewis, *Sparta and Persia* (Leiden, 1977).
G.E.M. de Ste Croix, *The Origins of the Peloponnesian War* (London, 1972).

The first 15 years (29-38)
E. Badian, *From Plataia to Poteidaia: studies in the history and historiography of the Pentekontaetia* (Baltimore, 1993) ch.2.
W.G. Forrest, 'Themistocles and Argos' *Classical Quarterly* 10 (1960) 221ff.
R. Meiggs, 'The growth of Athenian Imperialism' *JHS* 63 (1943) 21ff.
M.P. Milton, 'The Date of Thucydides' Synchronism of the Siege of Naxos with Themistokles' flight' *Historia* 28 (1979) 257ff.
N. Robertson, 'The True Nature of the Delian League, 478-461 B.C.' *American Journal of Ancient History* 5 (1980) 64ff.
R.K. Unz, 'The Chronology of the Pentekontaetia' *Classical Quarterly* 36 (1986) 68-85.

War at home and abroad: from 465 to 450 (39-47)
P. Deane, *Thucydides' Dates 465-431 B.C.* (Don Mills, Ontario,1972).
A.J. Holladay, 'The Hellenic Disaster in Egypt' *Journal of Hellenic Studies* 109 (1989) 176-82.

Perikles' Citizenship Law (48-9)
A. Boegehold, '"Pericles"' Citizenship Law of 451/0 B.C.' in A. Boegehold and A. Scafuro edd. *Athenian Identity and Civic Ideology* (Baltimore, 1994).
R. Osborne, 'Law, the democratic citizen and the representation of women in classical Athens' *Past and Present* 155 (1997) 1-33.
C. Patterson, *Perikles' Citizenship Law of 451-50 B.C.* (New Hampshire, 1981).

Peace with Persia? (50-63)
A. Andrewes, 'Thucydides and the Persians' *Historia* 10 (1961) 1-18.

E. Badian, *From Plataia to Poteidaia: studies in the history and historiography of the Pentekontaetia* (Baltimore, 1993) ch.1.

A. Bosworth, 'Plutarch, Callisthenes and the Peace of Callias' *Journal of Hellenic Studies* 110 (1990) 1-13.

S.K. Eddy, 'The Cold War between Athens and Persia c.448-412 B.C.' *Classical Philology* 68 (1973) 241-58.

A.J. Holladay, 'The détente of Kallias' *Historia* 35 (1986) 503-7.

D.M. Lewis, *Sparta and Persia* (Leiden, 1977).

M.C. Miller, *Athens and Persia in the Fifth Century B.C.: a study in cultural receptivity* (Cambridge, 1997) ch.1.

O. Murray, 'HO ARCHAIOS DASMOS' *Historia* 15 (1966) 142ff.

M.W. Stolper, 'The death of Artaxerxes I' *Arch. Mitt. aus Iran* 16 (1983) 223-36.

W.E. Thompson, 'The Peace of Callias in the Fourth Century' *Historia* 30 (1981) 164-77.

J. Walsh, 'The Authenticity and the Dates of the Peace of Callias and the Congress Decree' *Chiron* 11 (1981) 31-63.

Note E. Inscriptions and the Character of the Athenian Empire

D. Bradeen, 'The popularity of the Athenian Empire' *Historia* 9 (1960) 257-69.

G. Cawkwell, *Thucydides and the Peloponnesian War* (Routledge, 1997) ch.6.

M.I. Finley, 'The Athenian Empire: a balance sheet' in P. Garnsey and C.R. Whittaker edd. *Imperialism in the Ancient World* (Cambridge, 1978). 103-26, reprinted in B.D. Shaw and R.P. Saller edd. *Economy and Society in Ancient Greece* (London, 1981/Harmondsworth 1983) 41-61.

H. Mattingly, 'Epigraphy and the Athenian Empire', *Historia* 41 (1992) 129-38.

R. Meiggs, 'The Dating of Fifth-Century Attic Inscriptions' *Journal of Hellenic Studies* 86 (1966) 86-97.

F.G.B. Millar, 'Inscriptions' in M.H. Crawford ed. *Sources for Ancient History* (Cambridge, 1983) ch.2.

W.K. Pritchett, 'The transfer of the Delian Treasury' *Historia* 18 (1969) 17-21.

J. de Romilly, 'Thucydides and the Cities of the Athenian Empire' *Bulletin of the Institute of Classical Studies* 13 (1966) 1-12.

G.E.M. de Ste Croix, 'The Character of the Athenian Empire' *Historia* 3 (1954-5) 1-41.

R. Thomas, 'Literacy and the city-state in archaic and classical Greece' in A.K. Bowman and G.D. Woolf edd. *Literacy and Power in the Ancient World* (Cambridge, 1994) 33-50, esp. 43-5.

The Empire from *c.*450 to the outbreak of the Peloponnesian War (64-102)

Congress Decree and Parthenon debate (**65-6**)

A. Andrewes, 'The opposition to Perikles' *Journal of Hellenic Studies* 98 (1978) 1-8.

J. S. Boersma, *Athenian Building Policy* (Groningen, 1970).

A. Giovannini, 'Le Parthénon, le Trésor d'Athéna et le tribut des alliés' *Historia* 39 (1990) 129-48.

G.T. Griffith, 'A note on Plutarch *Pericles* 17' *Historia* 27 (1978) 218-9.

L. Kallet-Marx, 'Did Tribute Fund the Parthenon?' *Classical Antiquity* 8 (1989) 252-66.

B. Macdonald, 'The Authenticity of the Congress Decree' *Historia* 31 (1982) 120ff.

J. Walsh, 'The Authenticity and the Dates of the Peace of Callias and the Congress Decree' *Chiron* 11 (1981) 31-63.

Euboia and the crisis of the mid-40s **(67-81)**
J. Balcer, *The Athenian Regulations for Chalcis: Studies in Athenian Imperial Law* Historia Einzelschriften 33 (1978).
R. Meiggs, 'The Crisis of Athenian Imperialism' *Harvard Studies in Classical Philology* 67 (1963) 1-36 (with exchanges in *ZPE* 21 (1976) 251ff., 24 (1976) 231f., 25 (1977) 277ff., 30 (1978) 94, and 35 (1979) 287ff.)
On Athenian settlements abroad see below on **229-33**.

Samian revolt **(84-91)**
A.P. Bridges, 'The Athenian Treaty with Samos, ML56' *Journal of Hellenic Studies* 100 (1980) 185-8.
C.W. Fornara, 'On the Chronology of the Samian War' *Journal of Hellenic Studies* 99 (1979) 7-19.
T.J. Quinn, *Athens and Samos, Lesbos and Chios, 478-404 B.C.* (Manchester, 1981).
G. Shipley, *A History of Samos 800-188 B.C.* (Oxford, 1987).

Poteidaia, Megarian Decree and run-up to war **(97-102)**
B.R. Macdonald, 'The Megarian Decree' *Historia* 32 (1983) 385-410.
P.J. Rhodes, 'Thucydides on the causes of the Peloponnesian War' *Hermes* 115 (1987) 154-65.
G.E.M. de Ste Croix, *The Origins of the Peloponnesian War* (London, 1972).

Athens and her empire during the Arkhidamian War (115-55)
(for affairs involving Persians see above 'Peace with Persia?')
A. Andrewes, 'The Mytilene Debate' *Phoenix* 16 (1962) 64ff.
J.G. Griffith, 'A note on the First Eisphora at Athens' *American Journal of Ancient History* 2 (1977) 3ff.
S. Hornblower, 'The Religious Dimension to the Peloponnesian War, or, What Thucydides Does Not Tell Us' *Harvard Studies in Classical Philology* 94 (1992) 169-197, esp. 194-6.
L. Kallet-Marx, *Money, Expense and Naval Power in Thucydides' History 1-5.24* (Berkeley, 1993).
A.G. Keen, 'Athenian Campaigns in Karia and Lykia during the Peloponnesian War' *Journal of Hellenic Studies* 113 (1993) 152-7.
C. Macleod, 'Reason and necessity: Thucydides iii.9-14, 37-48' *Journal of Hellenic Studies* 98 (1978) 64-78, reprinted in *Collected Essays* (Oxford, 1983) ch.10.
H. Mattingly, 'The Methone Decrees' *Classical Quarterly* 11 (1961) 154-65.
H.D. Westlake, 'The Commons at Mytilene' *Historia* 25 (1976) 429-40.

From the Peace of Nikias to the end of the Empire (156-83).
A. Andrewes, 'The Melian Dialogue and Pericles' Last Speech' *Proceedings of the Cambridge Philological Society* 6 (1960) 1-10.
J. Barron, 'Chios in the Athenian Empire' in J. Boardman and C.E. Vaphopoulou Richardson edd., *Chios. A Conference at the Homereion in Chios 1984* (Oxford, 1986) 89-108.

A. Bosworth, 'The Humanitarian Aspect of the Melian Dialogue' *Journal of Hellenic Studies* 113 (1993) 30-44.

C. Macleod, 'Form and Meaning in the Melian Dialogue' *Historia* 23 (1974) 385-400, reprinted in *Collected Essays* (Oxford, 1983) 52-67.

T.J. Quinn, *Athens and Samos, Lesbos and Chios, 478-404 B.C.* (Manchester, 1981).

G. Shipley, *A History of Samos 800-188 B.C.* (Oxford, 1987).

Note F. The Tribute Quota Lists

D.J. Blackman, 'The Athenian Navy and Allied Naval Contributions in the Pentekontaetia' *Greek, Roman and Byzantine Studies* 10 (1969) 179-216.

A.J. Graham, 'Abdera and Teos' *Journal of Hellenic Studies* 112 (1992) 44-73 (esp. 59-61).

F.A. Lepper, 'Some Rubrics in the Athenian Quota-Lists' *Journal of Hellenic Studies* 82 (1962) 25-55.

D.M. Lewis, 'The Athenian Tribute-Quota Lists, 453-450 B.C.' *Annual of the British School at Athens* 89 (1994) 285-301.

B.D. Meritt, H.T. Wade-Gery and M.F. McGregor, *The Athenian Tribute Lists* 4 vols. (Princeton, 1939-53) (texts in vols. 1 and (revised) 2; commentary in vol.3, indexes in vol.4).

L. Nixon and S. Price, 'The Size and Resources of Greek Cities' in O. Murray and S. Price edd. *The Greek City from Homer to Alexander* (Oxford, 1990) 137-70.

Note G. Religious aspects of Athenian imperialism

J.K. Davies, 'Accounts and Accountability in Classical Athens' in R. Osborne and S. Hornblower edd., *Ritual, Finance, Politics: Athenian Democratic Accounts presented to David Lewis* (Oxford, 1994) 201-212.

B. Fehr, 'Zur religionspolitischen Funktion der Athena Parthenos im Rahmen des Delisch-Attischen Seebundes' *Hephaistos* 1 (1979) 79ff.

S. Hornblower, 'The Religious Dimension to the Peloponnesian War, or, What Thucydides does not tell us' *Harvard Studies in Classical Philology* 94 (1992) 169-97.

D.M. Lewis, 'Apollo Delios' *Annual of the British School at Athens* 65 (1960) reprinted in D.M. Lewis, *Selected Papers on Greek and Near Eastern History* ed. P.J. Rhodes (Cambridge, 1997) 150-57.

I. Malkin, *Religion and Colonisation in Ancient Greece* (Leiden, 1987).

R. Osborne, *Demos: the discovery of classical Attika* (Cambridge, 1985) ch.8.

R. Parker, 'Festivals of the Attic Demes' *Boreas* 15 (1987) 137-47.

R. Parker, 'Athenian Religion Abroad' in R. Osborne and S. Hornblower edd., *Ritual, Finance, Politics: Athenian Democratic Accounts presented to David Lewis* (Oxford, 1994) 339-46.

R. Parker, *Athenian Religion: a history* (Oxford, 1996) ch.8.

H.A. Shapiro, 'Athena, Apollo, and the Religious Propaganda of the Athenian Empire' *Boreas* 24 (1996) 101-113.

C. Sourvinou-Inwood, 'What is *polis* religion?' in O. Murray and S. Price edd., *The Greek City from Homer to Alexander* (Oxford, 1990) 295-322.

B. Smarczyk, *Untersuchungen zur Religionspolitik und politischen Propaganda Athens im Delisch-Attischen Seebund* (Munich, 1990).

D. Whitehead, *The Demes of Attica 508/7 - ca. 250 B.C.* (Princeton, 1986) ch.7.

Tribute (184-97) (additional to bibliography listed for Note F)

Role of Council in assessment procedures (**186-9**)
P.J. Rhodes, *The Athenian Boule* (Oxford, 1972).

Tribute brought in at City Dionysia (**192-4**)
S.D. Goldhill, 'The Great Dionysia and Civic Ideology' *Journal of Hellenic Studies* 107 (1987) 58-76 at 60-62, reprinted in J.J. Winkler and F.I. Zeitlin edd., *Nothing to do with Dionysos? Athenian Drama in its Social Context* (Princeton, 1990) 97-129 at 101-3.

Use of Athena's share of the tribute (**195-7**)
See Giovannini and Kallet-Marx cited under 'Congress Decree and Parthenon Debate'.

Other obligations imposed on all allies (198-206)

Coins, weights and measures (**198-9**)
T. Figueira, *The Power of Money: Coinage and Politics in the Athenian Empire* (Philadelphia, 1998).
D.M. Lewis, 'The Athenian Coinage Decree' in I. Carradice ed. *Coinage and Administration in the Athenian and Persian Empires* (Oxford, 1987) 53-63 reprinted in D.M. Lewis, *Selected Papers on Greek and Near Eastern History* ed. P.J. Rhodes (Cambridge, 1997) 116-30.
T.R. Martin, 'Coins, Mints and the *Polis*' in M.H. Hansen ed. *Sources for the Ancient Greek City-State* (Copenhagen, 1995) 257-91.
H. Mattingly, 'New light on the Athenian Standards Decree (*ATL* II, D 14)' *Klio* 75 (1993) 99-102, reprinted in H.B. Mattingly, *The Athenian Empire Restored: epigraphic and historical studies* (Michigan, 1996).
M. Vickers, 'Fifth-century chronology and the Coinage Decree' *Journal of Hellenic Studies* 116 (1996) 171-4.

Obligations to refer cases to Athenian courts (**200-4**)
J. Balcer, *The Athenian Regulations for Chalcis: Studies in Athenian Imperial Law* Historia Einzelschriften 33 (1978).

Religious obligations (**205-6**). See above Note G.

Athenian interference with individual allies (207-34)

Religious interference (**207-210**). See above Note G.

Political interference: general (**211-5**)
S. Hornblower, *Mausolus* (Oxford, 1981) chs. 1 and 5.
D.M. Lewis, 'Democratic Institutions and their diffusion' in D.M. Lewis, *Selected Papers on Greek and Near Eastern History* ed. P.J. Rhodes (Cambridge, 1997) 51-9. and see above under Note E.

Political interference: specific cases (**216-20**)
M. Piérart, 'Athènes et Milet' *Museum Helveticum* 40 (1983) 1-18 and 42 (1985) 276-99.
N. Robertson, 'Government and Society at Miletus, 525-442 B.C.' *Phoenix* 41 (1987) 356-98.

Athenian officials sent to allies (**221-8**)
J. Balcer, 'Athenian magistrates in the Athenian Empire' *Historia* 25 (1976) 257ff.
H. Leppin, 'Die ἄρχοντες ἐν ταῖς πόλεσι des Delisch-Attisches Seebundes' *Historia* 41 (1992) 257-71.

Athenian settlements in allied territory (**229-33**)
P.A. Brunt, 'Athenian Settlements Abroad in the Fifth Century B.C.' in E. Badian ed., *Ancient Society and Institutions: Studies presented to Victor Ehrenberg* (Oxford, 1966) 71-92, reprinted in P.A. Brunt, *Studies in Greek History and Thought* (Oxford, 1993) 112-36.
P. Gauthier, 'À propos des clérouquies athéniennes du Ve siècle' in M.I. Finley ed., *Problèmes de la terre en Grèce ancienne* (Paris, 1973) 163-78.
J. Vartsos, 'The Foundation of Brea' *Ancient Macedonia* 2 (1977) 13ff.

Judicial agreements with individual cities (**234**)
C.W. Fornara, 'The Phaselis Decree' *Classical Quarterly* 29 (1979) 49-52.
G.E.M. de Ste Croix, 'Notes on jurisdiction in the Athenian Empire' *Classical Quarterly* 11 (1961) 94-112, 268-80.

The benefits of empire for individuals (235-43)

For individual allies (**235-8**)
M. Walbank, *Athenian Proxenies of the Fifth Century B.C.* (Toronto, 1978).

For individual Athenians (**239-43**)
D.M. Lewis, 'After the Profanation of the Mysteries' in E. Badian ed., *Ancient Society and Institutions: Studies presented to Victor Ehrenberg* (Oxford, 1966) 177-91.

Note H. Archaeology and the Athenian Empire
J.M. Cook, 'The problem of classical Ionia' *Proceedings of the Cambridge Philological Society* 7 (1961) 9-18.
P. Bruneau and J. Ducat, *Guide de Délos* (ed.3) (Paris, 1983).
G. Shipley, *A History of Samos 800-188 B.C.* (Oxford, 1987).
J.S. Boersma, *Athenian Building Policy from 561/0 to 405/4 B.C.* (Groningen, 1970).
Y. Grandjean, *Recherches sur l'habitat Thasien à l'époque grecque* Études Thasiennes XII (Paris, 1988).
J.-F. Bommelaer, *Guide de Delphes. Le Site* (Paris, 1991).
R. Osborne, 'Framing the Centaur: Reading fifth-century architectural sculpture' in S. Goldhill and R. Osborne edd., *Art and Text in Ancient Greek Culture* (Cambridge, 1994) 52-84.
R. Osborne, 'Democracy and Imperialism in the Panathenaic Procession: The Parthenon Frieze in its Context' in W. Coulson et al. edd., *The Archaeology of Athens and Attica under the Democracy* (Oxford, 1994) 143-50.
R. Osborne, *Archaic and Classical Greek Art* (Oxford, 1998).

INDEX OF PROPER NAMES

All references are to page numbers.

INDEX OF GREEK TERMS

INDEX OF SUBJECTS (see also Glossary)

Printed in the United States
by Baker & Taylor Publisher Services